Fact and Theory in Economics:

The Testament of an Institutionalist

Publication of this book has been made
possible by a grant from the Hull Memorial
Publication Fund of Cornell University

FACT AND THEORY
IN ECONOMICS:

The Testament of an Institutionalist

·

Collected Papers of
MORRIS A. COPELAND

Robert Julius Thorne Professor of Economics
Cornell University

·

Edited and with an Introduction by

CHANDLER MORSE

Professor of Economics
Cornell University

GREENWOOD PRESS, PUBLISHERS
WESTPORT, CONNECTICUT

Library of Congress Cataloging in Publication Data

Copeland, Morris Albert, 1895–
    Fact and theory in economics: the testament of an
institutionalist.

    Reprint of the ed. published by Cornell University
Press, Ithaca, N.Y.
    Bibliography: p.
    1. Institutional economics. I. Title.
[HB99.5.C66 1973]   330.15'5   73-8564
ISBN 0-8371-6965-8

First published in 1958
by Cornell University Press, Ithaca, New York

Reissued in 1973 by Greenwood Press
by arrangement with the original publisher,
Cornell University Press

Reprinted in 1973 by Greenwood Press,
a division of Williamhouse-Regency Inc.

Library of Congress Catalogue Card Number 73-8564

ISBN 0-8371-6965-8

Printed in the United States of America

Introduction:
The Meaning of the
Institutionalist Approach

INSTITUTIONAL economics has meant different things to different men. Veblen and Commons, for example, saw the world through glasses of similar coloration but different resolving powers, as the initial essay in the present collection brings out. Mitchell's view of the world and that of J. M. Clark, to mention two men whose names appear frequently in the following pages, emphasized still other aspects. Yet all these men shared a sense of the shortcomings of traditional economics and a belief in the applicability of natural science methods to social science problems. Probably no member of the group that proudly accepted the institutional label has represented more fully the varied directions of interest, or expounded more systematically the common philosophy, than Morris Copeland.

The essays presented here have been selected from a much larger total with a view to demonstrating the meaning of the institutionalist approach in concept and practice. Taken all together, the essays in the first group, "Objectivity in Economics," outline the institutionalist philosophy and catalogue its main criticisms of neoclassical economics. The two groups that follow reflect the institutionalist emphasis on the need for precision in economic statistics and procedures of verification ("Toward Better Measurement and Testing") and for a continuing refinement of the tools of economic analysis ("Social Accounting Concepts"), though each is only a sampling of what might have been included. A group of theoretical essays brings to a conclusion this expression of belief in the need for a blend of economic fact and theory that has given this volume its title.

The essence of institutionalism has frequently been misunderstood by outsiders. Those who would like a brief, succinct statement of its meaning will find it in "Economic Theory and the Natural Science Point of View" (1931). An institutionalist evaluation of developments in economics during the twenty important years that followed this statement will be found in "Institutional Economics and Model Analysis" (1951). A reading of these essays, both of which are included here, will correct the frequent misconception that the institutionalists denigrated theory. They did disapprove of some kinds of theory, but their aim was a positive one, to push theory into closer contact with life and reality, both by broadening its scope— "from a natural science view hypotheses concerning industrial government or the organization of our railroad system are economic theories as truly as hypotheses concerning variations in price, production and distribution" [1]—and by insisting that economic theory, like other scientific theories, should pass the test of empirical verifiability. "The issue," says the author of these essays, "seems to be precisely that posed by Mitchell in his presidential address [to the American Economic Association] over a quarter of a century ago":

Shall we aim to make economics an empirical, scientific study of the way our economy and other similar economies operate? Empirical model analysts [a product of the post-Keynesian thirties] and institutionalists say yes. The main alternative to so doing—the alternative I think most nonempirical model analysts advocate—is to make it an exercise in deductive reasoning—in reasoning the relevance of which to our present economy must necessarily be a moot point.[2]

[1] Page 52 below.
[2] Page 63.

What, precisely, are the criteria of relevance? It goes without saying that any theory must meet the test of logical consistency, of accurate deductive reasoning, and that it must also, in some essential respect and degree, be abstract. But these necessary conditions are not sufficient. Others must be met as well. First among these is the reality test.

Scientific theories should not be . . . so abstract as to be incapable of factual disproof. They should be useful in enabling one to say *a priori* what he expects to find under certain specific conditions, within the limits of accuracy of the generalization, and they should be such as to be invalidated if he does not find *empirically* what he expected to find *a priori*.[3]

This criterion, it may be noted, constitutes no insistence on concreteness, on a "lack of abstractness," as it is sometimes mistakenly thought to do. Abstraction is the essence of science. It is the *sine qua non* of the ability to generalize. Complete descriptions (if such can be imagined) are descriptions of unique events. Only by concentrating on the common features of events that permit them to be classed together, and ignoring those features that distinguish some members of a given class from other members, is it possible to arrive at general propositions. This is sometimes referred to as concentrating on the essentials. It is the essentials that must be concrete. That is why the abstract concepts that we construct to represent concrete essentials should be defined "operationally." Quantitative concepts in particular ought to be so defined that their content consists of the results of observations (especially those of measurement) made in carefully specified and "publicly" available ways. If available data, such as economic time series, do not fit the relevant concepts as so defined, the investigator has an obligation to attempt to bring the two together. To this end he may either devise new and appropriate methods of observation and measurement or he may redefine the concepts to fit the data. These principles have become automatic for the physical sciences but have made their way more slowly in economics. Insistence that they are fundamental to all descriptive science was a major tenet of the institutional approach.

[3] Page 38 below.

This explains the strong institutional interest in economic statistics. Statistics are more than figures. They are also meanings. The meanings of economic statistics, particularly, have a habit of nonconformity to the concepts of the theories they may be used to test. Even worse, perhaps, they may quietly change character. Administrative convenience or necessity may lead to altered practice by the collector. Subtle mutations of the processes that give rise to the statistics may change their import. The investigator must therefore be alert to the inadequacies of raw data; he must also be both industrious and ingenious in devising methods to remove or neutralize these deficiencies. The theorist, on his part, must be aware of the potential impossibility of forcing data to conform to the concepts he wishes to employ.[4] Whether by developing new techniques of measurement to fit theoretical concepts (as in the case of social accounting, to which institutionalists made important contributions before the impetus given by Keynes) [5] or by bringing the concepts of pure theory more into accord with the realities of the world to be analyzed or described (as in the theory of monopolistic competition),[6] the major test of relevance is that fact and theory should be brought into a mutually compatible relationship.

Appropriateness of this criterion for economics (and the other social sciences) has received only tardy recognition, and the extent of its relevance to problems of human behavior has at times been questioned.[7] A major, perhaps basically the only, reason for these doubts is that the social sciences are "normative as well as descriptive." The normative character sometimes in-

[4] See the second group of essays in this volume, especially "The Equation of Exchange: An Empirical Analysis."

[5] See the third group of essays, also "Statistics and Objective Economics" in the first group and the book, *The Keynesian Reformation.*

[6] See "Monopolistic Competition," especially part A; also "A Social Appraisal of Differential Pricing" and "Communities of Economic Interest and the Price System," all in the fourth group.

[7] See, for example, F. H. Knight, "The Limitations of Scientific Method in Economics," in *The Trend of Economics* (New York, 1924); reprinted in *The Ethics of Competition* (1935). See also his "Fact and Metaphysics in Economic Psychology," *American Economic Review,* June 1925. Compare Copeland, "Professor Knight on Psychology," *Quarterly Journal of Economics,* November 1925.

heres in the choice of concepts. In social accounting, for example,

there are certain ultimate items which do not cancel out. These include ultimate equities in tangible assets, consumer benefits, labor sacrifice, foregone immediate consumption. The selection of these as ultimate involves passing judgment on our economic system. It is equivalent to asserting that the interests of the consumer, laborer, and ultimate property holder are the ends of economic organization, and that business profits are a means thereto, and not conversely.[8]

Alternatively, a model may specify the consequences that would follow if certain normative (e.g., "rational") rules of behavior were generally obeyed, or if certain contrary-to-fact conditions existed. But there is a danger here, for "it is very important to accurate thinking that we should not confuse a statement of what is with a statement of what ought to be." [9] A case of such confusion mentioned by Copeland may be cited:

For purposes of appraisal it seems well to consider the consumer as ultimate and the business enterprise as intermediate. But when the neo-classicist makes consumers' choice ultimate in his description, or explanation of actual price determination, he flies in the face of the facts. He has confused description with appraisal here. Consumers' choices are effects as well as causes of business policy or it would not pay to advertise.[10]

Nonconfusion of normative models and descriptive theories is a criterion no one, presumably, would question. It is essential to objectivity. But it is often supposed that objective theory must be purely descriptive and devoid of normative content— that objectivity implies neutrality. This is not the case. Objectivity resides in procedures, neutrality (or its absence) in results. Operational definitions, standardized public methods of observation, accurate reporting, and sound logic are minimal requirements for objectivity. If, in addition, value judgments are embodied in concepts and premises, objectivity requires

[8] Page 39–40 below.
[9] Page 39.
[10] Page 40.

that this be made explicit. Otherwise the ultimate validity of implicit value judgments will seem to be demonstrated by supposedly neutral reasoning processes, as when neoclassical models seemed to lend support to the judgment that *laissez faire* was a valid policy goal regardless of the institutionally determined inequalities of income, status, and opportunity in the inherited environment. When Robbins says: "Economics is neutral as between ends. Economics cannot pronounce on the validity of ultimate judgments of value," [11] he should only mean (although apparently he does not) that value judgments cannot be derived as logical conclusions by deductive reasoning from value-free premises. With this one must agree.

Whether the premises are in fact value-free is another question. For the concepts of social science (unlike those of the physical sciences), and the *ceteris paribus* assumptions that are an inescapable component of every economic proposition, can seldom if ever be value-free. Therefore the value implications carry through to the conclusions, not as pronouncements on the "validity of ultimate judgments of value" but as consequences the implications of which are no more neutral than their premises. Economic growth, for example, may be viewed as the increase in total output (as defined), as the increase in output per capita, and in other ways. Such definitions can be objective, but they cannot be neutral. Their value implications must therefore be specified. Institutionalists have criticized traditional economics for its failure to recognize, admit, and specify the value-laden character of its reputedly neutral premises. They have rejected the view, as voiced by the elder Keynes, that "it is both possible and desirable to discuss economic uniformities independently of economic ideals; . . . to recognize as fundamental a positive *science of political economy* which is concerned purely with what is." [12] Their view was that any such delimitation of the scope of economic science, if indeed it were possible at all, would leave the field of inquiry so narrow as to

[11] Lionel Robbins, *An Essay on the Nature and Significance of Economic Science* (New York, 1932), p. 131.

[12] John Neville Keynes, *The Scope and Method of Political Economy* (New York, 1891), p. 36. Compare section 3, "Science and Welfare," in "Communities of Economic Interest," pp. 215–219 below.

be irrelevant to nearly everything. Moreover, by frankly recognizing the legitimate presence of value judgments in the
premises, the danger of pretending to a false neutrality in the
conclusions would be reduced.

This effort to extend the relevant scope of economics has
reached in still another direction. Economics, it has been
emphasized, is a social science, and as such "it presumably deals
with certain aspects of our social system not sharply marked
off from the aspects with which other social sciences deal." [13]
But "the neo-classical theory of economics offers, on the whole,
somewhat scanty contacts with other social sciences. . . . There
are no sharp lines between economics, political science, and
sociology; and the historical approach is common to all of
them." [14] Had the lines been drawn less sharply, it is possible,
by way of example, that more attention would have been paid
to the character of the psychological premises of neoclassical
models,[15] with the resulting avoidance of some confusion between prescription and description. It is also possible that
greater attention to the legal foundations of the enterprise
system and to the interplay between political and economic
power would have weakened the neoclassical presumption that
relative bargaining power could properly be treated as a given
datum with which economists need have no concern.

In short, it has been a basic belief of the institutionalists that
narrow specialization promotes a kind of social myopia that
makes it difficult to apprehend in their totality the implications
of the determining environment of economic behavior. This
has largely been responsible, as institutionalists see it, for the
mistaken efforts to draw a sharp line between a "positive
science" of economics and a concern for "economic ideals."
And the state of mind reflected in these efforts is believed to
have been responsible for many an improper policy conclusion
based on the inappropriately narrow premises of "pure theory."
One of the virtues of the following collection of essays is that
it reveals a breadth of interest that illustrates the institutional-

[13] Page 38–39 below.
[14] Page 52.
[15] See "Psychology and the Natural Science Point of View" in the first group.

ist precept. Even the casual reader of these pages may learn
that the alternative to narrow specialization is not a shallow
superficiality—a lesson that today's teachers of doctoral can-
didates in economics might well ponder.

Recognition of the essentially historical character of the
social sciences is still another aspect of the effort to extend
economic horizons. As a

biological science [that] . . . studies group relationships among living organisms of the genus *homo sapiens* . . . [economic] generalizations must somehow make peace with the general theory of biological evolution. They can only be true of and relevant to some
definitely specified periods of social evolution.[16]

Insufficient apprehension of this fact may lead, and has often
led, to an unjustified presumption that what is true of one society or at one period (usually "ours") is or ought to be true
of another. This, in one sense, is a special case of confusion
between description and prescription, a type of confusion that
happily seems to be disappearing from the newer literature of
economics as a corollary of the rapidly expanding study of
so-called underdeveloped countries.

In a deeper sense, the inability of economics to escape the
confines of history goes to the heart of an important distinction—that between a basic science like theoretical physics, the
aim of which is to explain types of events and processes that, so
far as is known, could occur anywhere any time and those like
the social (= behavioral) sciences, the aim of which is to explain
types of phenomena where the possibilities of occurrence are
limited to historically particularized times and places. The
point is perhaps less obvious than this statement of it makes it
seem. Basic science is, above all, concerned with elemental
building blocks and elemental processes, and with the all-
pervasive continuities of space, time, and energy that link these
universals to observed particularities in all their complexity.
These observed particularities, which are the stuff and sub-
stance of what we call history, provide boundary conditions

[16] Page 39 below.

for basic science, but they are not its chief concern. They are, on the other hand, the central focus of the less basic sciences, which seek to understand why, amid so much complexity, there still should be patterned sequences of particularities, and which contemplate their meaning for mankind. For these more anthropocentric sciences the universal laws of nature set boundaries within which the elements of understanding must be found, but with these universals these sciences have no direct concern. There is thus a division of labor, but not, as those who prefer to believe in the separation of mind and matter maintain, an unbridgeable gulf that divides the one kind of inquiry from the other.

This distinction between a concern for universals (the exogenous determinants of history) and a concern for particulars (the endogenous variables) is sometimes thought to be the same as the distinction between abstraction and concreteness. This is a mistake. The fact that economics is concerned, among other things, with the processes of capitalism in no sense restricts it to nonabstract description. One could insist, to be sure, that economists should stay on a higher level of abstraction, such as processes of economic systems in general, and this, in effect, is what the devotees of pure-theory-and-nothing-else do insist on. But this is a distinction of degree, not of kind. The distinction of kind is between the behavioral and other sciences, for human behavior generates its own canons, which cumulate as culture and institutions. That is why the behaviorally focused sciences must be particular as to time and place in their descriptive theorizing (though not in their models of "if-then" reality). These sciences can seek and hope to find laws of a high level of generality and therefore of abstraction, but they cannot, by definition of their inquiry, hope to find many universal laws. Rightly or wrongly, institutionalists have felt that the peculiar prestige attached to attaining a high degree of abstraction—perhaps because confused with universality—has seriously limited the empirical scope and usefulness of economic theory. Their view is that the level at which to theorize should be determined pragmatically, not according to a set of a priori principles concern-

ing the nature and limits of "pure" science. A level of generality
that is highly significant for human welfare can, after all, be
achieved far short of Universality, as the contents of this volume
firmly attest.

CHANDLER MORSE

Cornell University
July 1958

Acknowledgments

GRATEFUL acknowledgment is made to the following periodicals and publishers for their kind permission to include in this book the following materials originally published by them:

The Academy of Political Science
  "The Distribution of Wealth and Income" (March 25, 1938)

American Economic Review
  "The Economics of Advertising" (March 1925)
  "Economic Theory and the Natural Science Point of View" (March 1931)
  "The Capital Budget and the War Effort" (March 1943)
  "How Achieve Full and Stable Employment" (March 1944)
  "Business Stabilization by Agreement" (June 1944)
  "Institutional Economics and Model Analysis" (May 1951)

The American Statistician
  "Authority and Reason as Instruments of Coordination in the United States" (June 1948)

Appleton-Century-Crofts, Inc.
  "Communities of Economic Interest and the Price System," in *Trend of Economics,* ed. by R. G. Tugwell (copyright 1924 by F. S. Crofts & Co., Inc.)

Delhi School of Economics and Ranjit Printers and Publishers
  The Keynesian Reformation (1952)

Harvard University Press (*Quarterly Journal of Economics*)
  "Money, Trade, and Prices—A Test of Causal Primacy" (August 1929)
  "Commons's Institutionalism in Relation to Problems of Social Evolution and Economic Planning" (February 1936)

"Competing Products and Monopolistic Competition" (November 1940)

Indian Statistical Institute and International Statistical Institute
  "The Income and Product Circuit and the Money Circuit in India and the United States" (*Bulletin of the International Statistical Institute,* Volume XXXIII, Part III, 1952)

Journal of Marketing
  "A Social Appraisal of Differential Pricing" (April 1942)

Journal of Political Economy
  "Some Problems in the Theory of National Income" (February 1932)
  "The Theory of Monopolistic Competition" (review of Chamberlin, August 1934)

Journal of the American Statistical Association
  "Special Purpose Indexes for the Equation of Exchange for the United States, 1919–1927" (June 1929)
  "National Wealth and Income—An Interpretation" (June 1935)
  "Statistics and Objective Economics" (September 1955)

National Bureau of Economic Research
  "Concepts of National Income," in *Studies in Income and Wealth,* Volume I (1937)

Psychological Review
  "Desire, Choice, and Purpose from a Natural-Evolutionary Standpoint" (July 1926)
  "Psychology and the Natural-Science Point of View" (November 1930)

These articles are reproduced in their entirety, with only minor editorial changes, unless otherwise noted.

Contents

Social Accounting Concepts

Theory

OBJECTIVITY IN ECONOMICS

· I ·

Social Evolution and
Economic Planning*
(1936)

COMMONS'S *Institutional Economics* [1] represents a type of economic theoretical inquiry which is rare in this country, and which is unfortunately becoming rarer. Whether or not one shares Commons's *Weltanschauung,* one cannot but respect and admire the breadth of his intellectual interest and background, and the keenness of his philosophical insight. Altho pursuing a scholarly career that has frequently combined scholarship with active participation in public affairs, Commons none the less appears at home not only in the various branches of economics other than labor problems but also in philosophy and psychology, history and political science. And he treads this vast territory of knowledge with sureness of foot, if with a grand unconcern for accuracy in non-essential details.

Commons's inquiry is broader than his title "Institutional Economics" would lead one to expect, yet narrower within the field of economics than one would expect without the qualifying phrase "Its Place in Political Economy." He presents in this one

---

* Substantially condensed from "Commons's Institutionalism in Relation to Problems of Social Evolution and Economic Planning."

[1] John R. Commons, *Institutional Economics, Its Place in Political Economy,* New York, The Macmillan Company, 1934, pp. 921.

volume his philosophy of history, his conceptions of the logic of social science and of public policy, his theory of sovereignty, and even a suggestion that his is a volitional ontology. Amidst these presentations are interspersed discussions of a variety of topics more familiar to the mere economist. If there remain a number of the staple doctrines of neoclassical and Austrian economic theory on which his position is not made clear, it would be unbecoming to complain when an author has done so much that he has not done more. Moreover, the intellectual fare that he offers us is admirably seasoned both with nicely turned phrases and with shrewd observations on human relations.

Commons recognizes that his conception of institutional economics differs from that of certain others who have employed this expression. Discussions of the evolution of economic institutions may serve to illustrate the divergence of these two types of institutional economics. But it should be recognized that this divergence in economic thinking is a necessary part of a fundamental philosophical difference which makes it difficult for Commons to understand Veblen and hazardous for one in the Veblenian tradition to attempt the comments on Commons's institutionalism which follow. Consequently these comments are offered in due humility. Unfortunately the philosophical difference that underlies these two varieties of institutionalism is itself difficult to name, for both claim to be pragmatic.

Commons's brand of institutionalism is well revealed in his conceptions of social evolution and economic planning. In dealing with the evolution of customs, institutions, and going concerns we must, he tells us, avoid false analogies to "organism." The appropriate concept for understanding this evolutionary process is "artificial selection," not the "natural selection" of the Origin of Species. "What happens among all these variabilities is a choice of customs by those having power to choose and enforce; and the evolution of customs is like that artificial selection which, in the course of centuries, changes the wolf into the dog" (p. 710). Social evolution involves "futurity"; for Commons it is not mere "blindly cumulative causation," but rather adaptation by choice. Artificial selection means "Purpose, Futurity, Planning, injected into and greatly controlling the struggle for

life" (p. 636). As primitive customs become more formalized we
can understand them better. "Not until practices or usages are
converted into precedents by the decision of disputes, do they
become precise enough to be analyzed logically with regard to
the direction of control over individuals" (p. 710). When this
stage is reached we have the pervasive common law method of
making and remaking the working rules of a going concern.[2]
This common law method is extraordinarily flexible, while the
method of codes of rules, he tells us, because of its inflexibility,
may lead to revolutions (p. 223).

The concepts of natural law and natural rights are found to
conflict with the concept of social evolution and with relativity
to time and circumstance. "The theory of free competition developed by economists is not a natural tendency towards equilibrium of forces but is an ideal of public purpose adopted by
the courts, to be attained by restraints upon the natural struggle
for existence" (p. 713). The concept of "natural value" should,
he thinks, be replaced by "reasonable value" or "just price."
Reasonable value emerges from the common law process. "Reasonable value, as formed in the practices of courts, juries, commissions, arbitration arrangements, and so on, is a concept of
collective action in terms of money, arrived at by consensus of
opinion of reasonable men—'reasonable' in that they are men
who conform to the dominant practices of the time. Reasonable
value changes with new combinations of circumstances" (pp.
206–207). Unattainable utopian ideals are ruled out. "Reasonable value and reasonable practices are the highest attainable
idealism of regard for the welfare of others that is found in going concerns under existing circumstances" (p. 741). From all
this it would appear that social *evolution,* because it is artificially selective, *is* social *progress.*

Commons pictures our society now as having to choose piecemeal between "Reasonable capitalism" and communism or
fascism. "Reasonable capitalism" "endeavors to retain, under

[2] Thus the process of social evolution becomes a dialectic of conflict and
synthesis of "working rules." It is not strange that Commons himself finds in his
view of the evolution of modern capitalism "some analogy to Karl Marx's
dialectics" (p. 788).

new conditions, the older principles of equality [of bargaining power] and liberty in all bargaining transactions that determine prices" (p. 891). The alternative, according to Commons, means "economic planning" or rationing of production. "Reasonable capitalism" would involve various changes in present arrangements thru social legislation, taxation, and stabilization of the price level. In considering each of these types of modification Commons's emphasis on futurity leads him to stress the incentive aspect of collective action. In connection with his consideration of unemployment benefit plans as illustrative of social legislation, he urges that such modifications of the present order, according to their nature, may look either toward a more "reasonable capitalism" or toward communism or fascism.

Thus Commons is at once a believer in collective action, who manifests a thorogoing opposition to *laissez faire,* and something of an individualist, "the last Mohican of liberalism." For present-day Americans he is a staunch supporter of the content of the natural rights of free speech and press, free association, and a modernized version of freedom in bargaining transactions, but he is not a believer in the naturalness or universality of those rights. All social evolution involves something of (economic or of) social planning and rationing, but neither rationing nor liberty should be pursued exclusively. What he offers is "a theory of social progress by means of personality controlled, liberated, and expanded by collective action. It is not individualism, it is institutionalized personality" (p. 874).

Commons also strikes a nice balance between conservatism and radicalism. He believes not in setting up codes of law or in revolutions, but in evolution by the common law process of gradually changing working rules thru settling disputes respecting their application. This evolutionary process is pragmatic idealism in that it rejects utopian programs as being impracticable and selects the best *existing* practices for survival.

When one finds that such a view of social evolution and social planning is essentially self-consistent on its own premises, but that he dislikes the premises, there is little to be said other than to point out how his own premises differ and how the conclusions that follow from them differ. No argument is possible where common basic premises are wanting. Consequently what follows is not intended as an argument against Commons's position, but merely as a reaction to it from a basically different viewpoint. For convenience, and because that viewpoint interprets social evolution in terms of natural selection,[3] I shall refer to the viewpoint as "naturalism."

We may note first that the "naturalist" draws a sharp distinction between descriptive judgments and ethical or appraisal judgments, while Commons does not. Stated differently, the "naturalist" regards the statement "This is the best existing practice" as revealing something about its author not revealed by the statement "This is the most frequent existing practice." The former statement illustrates its author's *ethical taste*. Since the goodness of a practice is conceived as consisting in part in the ethical taste of him who thinks it good, ethical tastes become facts about human beings very much like practices. And it becomes the task of the "naturalist" to investigate the social evolution both of practices and of ethical tastes. To some extent, no doubt, it is possible for one who construes social evolution in terms of "artificial selection" to deal with the evolution of tastes. But it would seem that we must consider separately those ethical tastes that constitute the "artificially" selective conditions which practices survive or fail to survive, and that these selective tastes cannot be considered as evolving on a par with the practices selected. Otherwise we shall have the practices acting as selective conditions for the survival of the tastes quite as much as the tastes acting as selective conditions for the survival of the practices, and the selection will cease to be "artificial." If social evolution is to be a process of "artificial selection" some tastes apparently must be held constant for a long enough period to allow the selection to be worked out.

In part, this philosophical issue can be resolved into a matter of degree and a question of fact. If some widely or strategically held ethical tastes change relatively slowly, during the short run in which they may be assumed to remain roughly constant, "artificial selection" by them and "progress" toward their satisfaction

---

[3] Commons clearly recognizes the philosophical divergence between Veblen and himself in these terms, e.g., p. 657.

may take place. But for the longer-run changes of human practices and tastes we shall need to fall back on natural selection.
No doubt the "short run," as a matter of fact, may, in certain
cases, turn out to be long as compared to an individual's life
span. But this will not justify our speaking of "artificial selection" and "progress" as if the direction of change in the whole
course of social evolution were unified. On the contrary, we
should speak of particular "artificial selections" and particular
"advances" toward specific and specified ends. Moreover we
should not identify an "artificial selection" or "advance" that
takes place in a specific historical period with all the social
change of that period. For clearly during that period practices
may survive that do not satisfy the selective ethical tastes which
constitute a particular selection "artificial." A high rate of industrial accidents may survive not because anyone has an ethical
taste for such accidents, but because they are a by-product of
what under given conditions is selected as the most profitable
technique.

From the point of view of "naturalism" Commons's conception of social evolution is not only a conception of artificial selection, it is also an artificially selective conception; it tends to emphasize those phases of social evolution which can be interpreted
in terms of artificial selection, and particularly those where the
process of artificial selection approximates the common law process. And it strongly suggests that practices must become precedents, i.e., must survive thru the common law process of artificial selection [4] before we can analyze them "logically with regard to the direction of control over individuals." For the "naturalist" the fact that a custom, in the process of its coming into
being, has been rationalized, either by a judge or by any other
official, is quite unnecessary to logical analysis of the custom.
And incidentally an economic interpretation of the history of
artificial selection as practiced by our courts might easily be incorporated in the "naturalist's" study of social evolution.

From the above considerations it follows that the "naturalist"
has a place for social and economic planning (artificial selection),
tho that place is a somewhat more modest one than Commons

[4] Cf. pp. 72–73, 704, as well as p. 710.

assigns it, and an increasingly modest one as we delve backward farther into the past. Plans may be one set of factors in social change, but by no means the only one. The extent to which plans can alter existing arrangements is (as Commons so well recognizes) closely limited. The period for which we can plan is also closely limited, or else other social conditions are more likely to alter the plans than the plans are to alter those other social conditions.

Yet to the "naturalist" Commons appears unnecessarily to limit the possibilities of economic planning in another direction thru his principle of pragmatic idealism. According to this principle, each plan must be taken from an existing model, "the best existing practice." How stabilization of the currency thru the money and credit policies of an international central-banking system is pragmatic idealism he does not make clear. But the principle of "best existing practice" does appear to have exercised a restraining influence in his thinking on the Wisconsin Unemployment Compensation Act (cf. p. 860 ff.). The "naturalist" sees no reason why economic planning of the sort involved in framing the original Federal Reserve Act should be limited to the best then-existing practice. Certainly such a limiting principle is not satisfactory if it means encouragement to transplanting bodily a set of practices that works in one situation to a quite different situation. Yet, any use of the principle presumably involves adoption of a practice in a situation at least slightly different from that in which it was previously in operation.

When Commons tells us that the competitive system is not natural in the sense of original, but is something that has evolved slowly, the "naturalist" will heartily agree, tho he may feel that Commons exaggerates the extent to which artificial selection may have been responsible for this development. When Commons draws a sharp *line* between those whose economic planning looks toward the remodeling of the competitive system to fit changed conditions and those whose economic planning looks "towards rationing of Producing Power" (p. 891), when in fact he reserves the term "economic planning" for the second type of planning, the "naturalist" will feel that Commons's *line* will necessarily bisect a continuum. Altho an inveterate opponent of *laissez faire,* Commons yet shares with the classical tradition this artificial dichotomy in types of social organization. It is partly because of this that Commons, as the "naturalist" sees it, has neglected to investigate systematically the infinite variety of possibilities in economic planning, the myriad of forms of competitive and pecuniary organization of economic activity, and the profusion of ways in which "managerial transactions" may be substituted for, or may complement competition and price as regulators of economic activity or in which "managerial transactions" may act *thru competition and price* in regulating economic activity.

There is another possible reason, however, why Commons has done much less in the way of economic theoretical analysis than has been customary for neoclassicists, and why he has done scarcely more than they in the way of statistical investigation. His is a theory of economic planning by selection of the best existing practices. If one's task is only to select the best from a group of houses already built, a somewhat limited investigation of the theory and facts of house construction may suffice.

· II ·

Psychology and the Natural Science Point of View
(1930)

IS psychology a natural science? Can the psychologist deal adequately and satisfactorily with his subject by natural science
methods and on natural science assumptions alone? These and
the correlative questions for the social sciences are the fundamental issues in the anthropological studies today. They underlie the controversy between those who hold 'purpose' to be a
fundamental category of psychology and the stimulus-response
psychologists, the controversy between the Gestalt and emergent
evolution theorists and the more analytical psychologists, and
the controversy betwen introspectionist and behaviorist.

It is the purpose of this paper to point out wherein certain
current psychological theories conflict with a natural science
approach to a study of the functioning of human beings and
to sketch briefly a type of theory which adheres rigorously to
natural science methods and assumptions. It will be convenient
to have a designation for this type of theory. Although both
'behaviorism' and 'institutionalism' have been used in many
senses, they have quite frequently been used to designate the
natural science type of theory in psychology and in social science
respectively, and I shall arbitrarily adopt that usage here.

Behaviorism, so conceived, is neither the use of a particular

11

methodological device nor a partial and incomplete psychology
—a view that omits the consideration of important parts of the
subject. And it may be added that the 'thinking behaviorist' is
no paradox. Behaviorism shares with other psychological viewpoints the study of those phases of human activity which on the
naïve level we call thought and emotion, will, desire, choice and
purpose, awareness and attention, perception, memory, and
imagination, meaning and evaluation. It is interested in them
both ontogenetically and phylogenetically and in both their
normal and their abnormal development. And it proposes to
study them by all the methods appropriate to scientific inquiry.

The behaviorist does not claim to offer a final solution for
these difficult problems. Rather he offers a formulation which
he believes is both promising and consistent with scientific hypotheses in other fields. Behaviorism—let us be frank—is a particular Weltanschauung, or rather the working out of that
Weltanschauung in the field of the study of individual behavior;
its counterpart in the field of group behavior, as already noted,
I shall refer to as institutionalism. The behaviorist and the institutionalist are particularly concerned that their formulations
shall conform to two important canons: (1) that they shall be
consistent with hypotheses in other fields, especially with the
natural-evolutionary hypotheses in geology and general biology;
(2) that they shall leave the door open to the solution of all
psychological problems by methods of scientific observation and
scientific reasoning. Behaviorism is not primarily a scientific hypothesis capable of empirical test; it is primarily a faith that
scientific hypotheses capable of empirical validation can be made
in the field of psychology and can be made consistent with scientific hypotheses in other fields.

It will doubtless be urged that many schools of psychology
share with behaviorism this scientific faith. It may be in order,
therefore, to attempt first a brief formulation of a natural science
creed. I shall put this creed, so far as it directly concerns us here,
into four articles:

I. Observable objects and events are approximately uniform
and predictable, if appropriately analyzed and classified.

II. A complex whole is scientifically understandable (*i.e.*, predictable and controllable) from a knowledge of its parts and their structural and functional relations.

III. In the case of the simpler objects and events with which physical science deals, prediction may be either forwards or backwards in time, but control is always from antecedent to consequent—never conversely.

IV. Scientific observations and descriptive generalizations should be sharply distinguished from appraisals and normative judgments.

On the first of these articles hang all the 'laws' of science. A scientific descriptive generalization ('law' or hypothesis) is possible because of the approximate uniformity of nature. It is unnecessary to assume precise uniformity. It is sufficient for purposes of prediction and control that scientific generalizations should be of a statistical character, approximate fits to the observations. It is a prime object of science to formulate generalizations useful for prediction and control. In any scientific inquiry it is to be assumed that there are more such generalizations possible than have yet been formulated. New analyses and classifications (*i.e.,* new definitions of terms) may yield new generalizations.

On the first word of this article, 'observable,' hangs also the issue between the behaviorist and certain, at least, of the introspectionists. The issue is, What are observable objects and events? For the present it may suffice to note that in the non-anthropological sciences the observer of an object or event is never uniquely specified by the object or the event. Any particular object, condition, or event may be observed by any one of a number of persons. Upon this possibility of substituting one observer for another rests what may be called the objectivity of scientific observation.

According to the second article of our creed science proceeds in large measure by analysis.[1] A given whole—object or event— is presumed to be capable of a variety of analyses. The scientific value of an analysis consists in its fruitfulness in yielding generalizations useful for prediction and control. If generalizations are

[1] For a fuller discussion of this article and its bearing on the Gestalt theory see "An Instrumental View of the Part-whole Relation," *J. Phil.,* 1927, 24, pp. 96–104.

made about a class of objects or events upon the basis of an analysis, and if generalizations are made about the same class directly and without analysis, the two sets of generalizations should yield observable agreement (*i.e.,* be consistent) at least within the limits of accuracy of the generalizations.

The word 'control' in Articles II and III calls for a word of comment. The use of scientific generalizations for purposes of control, is primarily a technologist's task. But the scientist is interested in control [2] for the purpose of testing his generalizations, and the concept of control is important in defining whether one event is antecedent to or subsequent to another. Even where actual control is not feasible, control may be employed hypothetically. Thus an astro-physicist may inquire what changes in a system the near-approach of a star would involve, *subsequent* to that near-approach. He cannot control his condition, the near-approach of the star at a particular date, but he assumes that, if he could, control would be from antecedent to consequent, and not conversely. So also the social scientist employs control hypothetically, when he inquires how a given social change would affect *subsequent* events, other conditions remaining the same.

Before commenting further on the four articles of our creed it will be convenient to consider some more specific aspects of science. Physical science deals with certain uniformities which it assumes to hold for all time. The properties of chemical elements, of electrons, and protons are assumed to be the same today as in the planetesimal period and long before. Physical science also deals with the origin and history of the earth as a changing complex—a set of events which it assumes to be analyzable into its uniformities which are independent of time. Geology and paleontology tells us the approximate dates of the appearance of life and of man upon the earth. Biology finds that living organisms, some directly, and some indirectly through other organisms, convert inorganic objects into parts of themselves, as they grow and multiply their kind. In view of all this the behaviorist believes that the safest assumptions for him to proceed upon are (*a*) that a man is a special case of a living organism, and (*b*) that a

---

[2] *Cf.* the frequent use of a 'control' in biology.

living organism is a special case of physical object—a special type of complex of electrons and protons, or if you prefer, of chemical elements.

The first of these more specific assumptions may fairly be said to be a biological commonplace. The second, if less generally accepted by biologists, is certainly a working hypothesis for many of them. Some biologists and philosophers, however, while paying lip-service to both of these propositions, have sought to avoid their implications by adopting a doctrine of 'emergent evolution.' A common formulation of this doctrine has it that some wholes are not mere aggregates of their constituent parts, in the sense that a new property emerges from the combination—an emergent—which could not have been predicted from a knowledge of the parts. Thus aqueousness emerges in the combination H_2O—it could not have been predicted from a knowledge of hydrogen or oxygen. And, similarly, life and consciousness are emergents. The corollary of this doctrine is that the new property, or emergent, invalidates any attempt to apply generalizations derived from a study of the parts in predicting the behavior of the whole.

A man may be a special case of living organism, but generalizations about the human nervous system, muscles, glands and receptor organs cannot, according to this theory, be used to predict the behavior of the total organism, because consciousness is an emergent which influences behavior.[3] And similarly, it is held that the behavior of a living organism can never be predicted from a knowledge of its inorganic constituents alone, because of the emergent, life.

To my notion such a doctrine is a mere rationalization of compartmental-mindedness. And the rationalization rests on a confusion of two quite different statements: (1) "Some present generalizations about living organisms are not deducible (predictable) from the present generalizations of physics and chemistry," and (2) "Some generalizations about living organisms can never be deduced from any generalizations of physics and chemistry that will ever be made." This is the perennial resort of the mystic —the leap from "science has not yet" to "science can never."

[3] *Cf.* H. S. Jennings, "Diverse Doctrines of Evolution," *Science,* 1927, 65, p. 25.

The behaviorist believes that 'can' is a more promising working hypothesis than 'can't,' and 'can' is specifically asserted in the second article of the behaviorist creed, "A complex whole is scientifically understandable (*i.e.*, predictable and controllable) from a knowledge of its parts." Let us apply this article to our propositions (*a*) and (*b*).

If (*a*) a man is a special case of a living metazoan organism, a special complex of special types of cells, human activity is understandable (predictable and controllable) from a knowledge of the behavior properties of the structural parts of the human organism—muscles, glands, nerves, receptors, etc.,—not necessarily present knowledge of course, but knowledge hoped for, at any rate. Willing, thinking, feeling, etc., are ways of behaving comparable to walking, eating, and the begetting and bearing of children. Mind is a behavior trait of the observable human organism, as life is a behavior trait of animals and plants in general, and if (*b*) living organisms are a subclass of the class, complexes of chemical elements, then mind is a behavior trait of the human body in the same sense as magnetism is a behavior trait of a magnet. And mind, as a behavior trait of the human body, is presumably understandable by analyzing it into the behavior-traits of the structural parts of the body.

It is, of course, a corollary of this view that human psychology and social science are branches of anthropological physiology, and further, that biology is a branch of physical science.

At this point certain introspectionists will doubtless bring the charge of 'incompleteness' against the behaviorist. The charge is sometimes put in ontological terms, "mental states and processes are omitted." In this form the charge implies that *in addition to* the condition and activity of the human body there are certain human mental states and activities which require scientific consideration. If this means psychophysical parallelism, it is to be noted that the mental states are necessarily *ex hypothesi* mere parallels of bodily condition and activity, and so, for purposes of prediction and control, mere duplicates—they can add nothing to the possibilities of prediction and control which rest on observation of bodily condition and activity. And Occam's razor suggests they are for scientific purposes just so much excess baggage. If, on the other hand, a non-parallelist relation is assumed between mental and bodily states and processes, so that both are necessary to prediction of behavior, then unless infants, dogs, and many abnormals and primitive peoples fall in a sharply different class from normal, civilized adults, the charge of incompleteness necessarily denies for them the approximate uniformity of observable objects and events assumed in Article I.

Another possible ontological variant of the charge of incompleteness is to hold that all observations are observations of mental states, and that behaviorism omits some, rather than all, mental states. To this form of the charge, at least a partial answer is afforded by considering the methodological question, "Does the behaviorist omit some relevant observations?" By way of a start at answering this question we may consider the case of *P*, a psychologist, who has designed an experiment in which *S*, his subject, participates. In the course of the experiment *P* asks *S* certain questions. *S* answers these questions and possibly makes other comments. As a behaviorist, *P* would observe and record the words of *S* as faithfully as if he, *P*, had been an introspectionist. *P* would also record other phases of *S*'s behavior, but the charge of incompleteness of observation presumably lodges against the omission of *S*'s verbal activity. *P* does not omit the observation of this, but it should be noted that the behaviorist does not ordinarily class what *S* says as 'scientific observation.' Nor would *P* be likely to design an experiment in which *S* would have to be trained in any particular psychological lingo, if *P* were studying general normal adult psychology. Such a qualification would presumably make his sample of *S*'s biassed, unless indeed he were studying the psychology which is peculiar to the kind of man we call a 'psychologist.'

This view raises further questions. May not *P* be his own subject? Are there not some phases of a man's behavior and condition which he alone can observe? Practically, as a matter of convenience and of the limitations of our present technique of observation, the behaviorist's answer to both of these questions is 'yes.' But the behaviorist would prefer to assume that there is no phase of a man's condition or activity for which it is necessarily impossible to devise a technique which will make it open to the observation of others. And in view of the fact that in the non-anthropological sciences there is always the possibility of substitution of one observer for another, he feels that observations in psychology and in other branches of physiology, for which such a possibility of substitution is not a present practicability, are not upon a par with other observations in respect to objectivity. He feels less certain of their reliability than he does of those where substitution is possible. The behaviorist, then, to sum up, omits nothing which the introspectionist would class as observation, but he does not evaluate the validity of these items in the same way as would some introspectionists.

It has been said that "mind as a behavior trait of body can presumably be analyzed into the behavior traits of the structural parts of the body." This requires the behaviorist to make his formulations about mind consistent with the possibility of such an analysis. But it does not confine him exclusively to this type of analysis. Other analyses are possible, and in the present state of our knowledge perhaps more fruitful. To say that human activity consists of thinking, perceiving, remembering, willing, feeling, etc., is precisely to make another sort of analysis. And similarly, in studying group behavior, the institutionalist may find it more fruitful to analyze social organization into property, language, leadership, and other institutions than into individual behavior, although he aims to keep his hypotheses consistent with the possibility of the latter type of analysis.

Thus far we have considered what may be called the behaviorist question proper, the issue of behaviorism versus introspectionism. The attempt to make psychology consistent with Propositions (a) and (b) and with Articles III and IV raises another important issue, which has sometimes been called 'teleology versus mechanism.' Article III holds that the physical sciences in dealing with chemical elements and their constituents and simpler combinations find that control is always from antecedent to consequent, never conversely. But there is no blinking the fact that in animal behavior reward and punishment influence learning. And there are numerous other phases of human activity in which the end-result appears to control the selection of means. But if (a) a man is a special case of living organism and (*b*) a living organism is a special case of physical object, a special type of complex of chemical elements, then it becomes a problem for the behaviorist (and for those introspectionists who take a similar view of this second issue), so to formulate their views of desire, will, choice, purpose, etc., as to be consistent with the possibility of analyzing these types of human behavior into constituent sequences in which control is from antecedent to consequent. The problem, as I shall presently formulate it, becomes one of understanding purpose and desire in terms of stimulus, response and inhibition. From a natural evolutionary point of view teleological terms like purpose are not properly fundamental terms in a scientific description. The tendency to use them as such is a survival of primitive anthropomorphism and anthropocentrism. The general problem of understanding in non-anthropomorphic terms sequences which have hitherto been interpreted teleologically is a pervasive one in biology. Darwin's theory of natural selection aimed to deal with it as it occurs in the study of (chiefly anatomical) phylogeny. And embryology will have much to do before it has handled the anatomical ontogenetic problem in terms of a non-teleological character.

It should be added that the behaviorist does not rule out teleological interpretations altogether. He rules them out, except as temporary expedients, from scientific description. But the biologist is not satisfied with a mere description which can be used for prediction and control. (And psychology and the social sciences are, according to a natural-evolutionary view, biological sciences.) The physiologist, for example, specifies the ends or functions which the various organs of the body serve; and this is part of his job as a scientist. 'Function' in this sense is to be distinguished from purpose. The function of an organ is a result which the observing scientist expects the organ 'normally' to bring about and in terms of which he *appraises* its behavior. It is not an end which guides or influences that behavior. Nor is the result expected of an organ directly dependent on what actually occurs either in the individual case or typically. As a teleological interpretation it does not purport to 'explain' or even describe the behavior of the organ, but rather it tells what the result *ought* to be. It still remains necessary to make a scientific description of the behavior of the organ, a description both of the normal functioning and of the functioning of the organ which fails to realize the result expected. Such a 'description' is wrong if it leads to wrong predictions; but it is no less truly the function of the stomach to digest food, when the stomach is 'out of order.' The teleological interpretation supplements but can never be a substitute for objective description. Appraisal of the behavior of an organ as appropriate to the performance of the organic function is not part of the description that makes possible prediction and control of behavior. This is the point of Article IV—scientific observations and descriptive generalizations should be sharply distinguished from appraisals and normative judgments.

II

So much for the general viewpoint of behaviorism. I shall now endeavor briefly to consider the terms employed in a typical behavioristic analysis and also a characteristic institutionalist term, and to employ these terms in a few illustrative problems.[4] It should perhaps be emphasized that a behavioristic account of such an activity as human thinking or choice, if purely psychological, is necessarily incomplete in a sense somewhat different from that discussed above. It deals primarily with the ontogenetic aspects of the problem, and requires to be complemented by a sociological and institutionalistic consideration of human functional phylogeny and group behavior, for common-sense terms like thinking have reference to more than the behavior of any single individual taken by himself, however typical he may be.

We have said that the behaviorist regards thinking as comparable to walking, etc. As a biologist he studies these two forms of activity in the same general way—a way in which also the physicist studies the magnetism of the magnet. (1) He defines his problems in observational terms, preferably in terms which permit the substitution of one observer for another. The ob-

---

[4] The brevity of the treatment necessarily involves a good deal of over-simplification.

servations include the condition and activity of *S*, his subject, and of *S*'s environment in successive intervals of time. If *S* is learning a maze, he thinks it pertinent to observe the maze as well as *S*. To omit the environment in studying *S*'s intellectual activity is certainly to run a chance of an incomplete account. (2) He may infer the occurrence of events and conditions which he does not observe directly. So does the physicist. The validity of such inferences, of course, is determined by an observational test: Do they lead to the *prediction* of activity or conditions of *S* which he can observe? (3) He endeavors to analyze human activity into temporal sequences in which he can control the consequent by the antecedent.

To define his problem in observational terms, then, is either to define it as the study of a type of behavior which he can identify directly by observation, or as a type which he infers to take place between a given observable antecedent situation and a predictable and observable resultant activity—the inferred intermediate being conceived as a consequent of the observed antecedent and as an antecedent of the observed consequent. Thus thinking may be defined roughly for observational purposes as the sort of activity which takes place between the oral or written confronting of *S* with a problem new to *S* and *S*'s oral or written answer. This does not, of course, preclude the possibility of inferring similar activity on *S*'s part when the problem presentation or the answer is not directly observable.

In endeavoring to analyze human activity into temporal sequences in which control is from antecedent to consequent, the behaviorist analyzes the behavior of *S* into parts, which he calls responses. A response is a part of human behavior which the behaviorist hopes to correlate with some antecedent condition or activity either in the organism or its environment, called a stimulus, so that he may, given the stimulus and other appropriate conditions, predict the response or, through the stimulus, control its occurrence, or given the response 'predict' or specify the stimulus. Because he believes that the behavior traits of *S* can some day be understood by analyzing them into the behavior traits of the muscles, glands, etc., of which *S* consists, the behaviorist defines the response as a specific pattern and sequence of receptors, nerves, muscles and glands in operation. And when he has correlated a stimulus and response, the behavior trait he attributes to S is called a response-pattern. On the negative side it is to be said that a 'response-pattern' is not to be defined in terms of results, as 'stirring one's coffee.' This procedure leads to teleological interpretations rather than scientific descriptive generalizations. The response-pattern is stirring one's coffee with the spoon in the right hand and with a very special type of position and movements of that hand and arm.

Nor is the stimulus-response relation a single-valued one in the mathematical sense. More than one stimulus may call out the same response. And while an appropriate stimulus is a necessary condition to the response, according to the behaviorist's hypothesis, it is not a sufficient condition.

The key to this complication may be sought in inhibition; *e.g.,* if two response patterns are so related that they cannot function simultaneously, and if these two are simultaneously stimulated, one will function and the other will be inhibited. Thus, the external stimulative situation or the condition of the organism may be such that any given response-pattern will not go off when stimulated. Indeed this is typically the case for most of the response-patterns the adult human being possesses. The typical human being has a vastly greater number of response-patterns for which appropriate stimuli are present at any one time than could in the nature of the case function simultaneously, since many of the responses to these stimuli are mutually exclusive (*e.g.,* standing and sitting). We may speak of the group of response-patterns which are on the threshold of readiness to function at any one time, *i.e.,* not inhibited, as a dominant complex of response-patterns, and a stimulus which calls out any of these responses as being in the focus of attention or awakeness or awareness.

I shall take as the three chief categories of behaviorist psychology, then (1) stimulus, (2) response, and (3) dominant complex—the group of response-patterns which at any time are on the threshold of readiness to function, if stimulated.

If we take birth as a convenient date at which to make an inventory of the behavior traits of a human organism, we may say that native traits fall largely under three heads. (1) A human being begins life on his own account with certain response-patterns. Some of these are more or less rigid, particularly on the effector side, reflexes. With most of these the pattern of response remains recognizably constant throughout life, although some alterations in their muscular and glandular make-up may take place, and on the receptor side there is the possibility of substitution of one set of receptors for another. (Some reflexes, of course, develop in the postnatal period.) Other native response-patterns are highly modifiable, instincts in the Watsonian sense. (2) The new-born infant has also certain complexes into which these initial response patterns are organized. The clearest case of this is a complex in which relatively few patterns are potentially functioning—a complex which remains of a fairly constant type throughout life, sleep. (3) In addition to patterns and complexes of patterns, the infant organism possesses certain capacities for the development of new patterns and complexes, or on the negative side certain limitations to the adult behavior traits which he is capable of developing. It is under this third caption, capacity, that the chief distinctions between man and other mammals are to be found, and incidentally between idiot, moron, and normal human being. Some capacities are dependent on gross structural traits, such as the human hand; for others no structural basis is at present clearly identifiable.

While change of behavior traits (response-patterns and complexes), or learning, continues throughout life, the flexibility of traits diminishes with age, and in early childhood some of the most important phases of the growth of the human personality take place. The learning process has a dual aspect. On the one hand it involves the development of new response-patterns, the building up of new combinations of effectors and the breaking down of old ones, and the regrouping of receptors with the various central nervous processes and effector combinations, leading to a more or less minute sensitivity to differences of stimulus. The phase of this process which has received chief attention is the substitution of one set of receptors for another, called conditioning or association—a new set of receptors and a new or substitute stimulus may come to be associated with a given effector pattern, by repeated presentation of old and new stimuli together.

On the other hand, the learning process involves new combinations of response-patterns into complexes. As a new inhibition develops or an old one disappears, a response-pattern may be taken from or added to a complex. Each of these aspects of the learning process affects the other. The change in form of a response-pattern means alteration in a constituent of various complexes. And the possibility of altering a pattern, *e.g.,* by conditioning, depends on whether the new stimulus comes adequately within the range of attention, *i.e.,* whether it sets up an activity of receptor organs and nervous system which may be associated with the other pattern.

So much for our hurried survey of the outlines of a possible behavioristic analysis of human activity. This process of growth of the personality takes place in an environment of which other persons form a most important part. While social groups differ widely from time to time and place to place, there is a feature common to them all which calls for a word of comment, the *mores.* No known human society is without mores. A *mos* is a type of response, not necessarily a specific response-pattern, which a given situation calls for. If S fails to respond in the socially established way, other members of the community will respond to his failure in ways that have the effect of punishment. How it comes about that all human societies have mores or that any particular society has a particular set of mores, is a question which it is an important part of the institutionalist's task to try to answer. No adequate survey of this problem is possible within the limits of this paper. It involves a detailed inventory of human functional native traits, an application of the natural selection hypothesis to mores as group traits of survival value, and a detailed study of the phylogenetic process of cultural evolution. Suffice it to say that our mores are numerous, and that they prescribe in minute detail much of human activity. There are legal mores, mores of grammar, spelling, etc., mores of politeness and style, mores of sex and family life, mores of friendship and loyalty, mores of leadership and social grouping, professional mores, mores of humor and art, mores of health (physical and mental), mores that we call morals, and mores of reasoning and belief. To the institutionalist, social organization consists of mores. The growth of the human personality during childhood is very largely a process of education or inculcation of the habits and complexes dictated by the mores. For the child, learning is predominantly learning to mind the mores. And in this process we are assuming as an established fact, though one perhaps not adequately accounted for scientifically by present psychology, the efficacy of punishment in learning.

III

We may now pass in hurried review a few sample topics in psychology (and social science). If the outline just completed is tentative, these specific formulations are more tentative still. I hope, however, that they will help to make clearer the behavioristic approach and to illustrate the general type of analysis which is consistent with a behavioristic formulation of psychological problems. Perhaps they will serve in some measure also to substantiate the view that behaviorism is as complete a psychological view as introspectionism in that it deals with all the phases of human activity that introspectionism does. It is not, of course, complete in the sense of claiming to have achieved a final solution of all psychological problems. It does not, *e.g.*, claim to offer a complete and satisfactory scientific description of all telic behavior in non-teleological terms. But a behaviorist can deal with this set of problems at least as satisfactorily as an introspectionist, so far as they accept the same criteria of scientific accomplishment. An introspectionist like McDougall, who takes teleological categories as fundamental, will no doubt have a more complete solution of his problems, but only because his problems are less inclusive.

Perception. To a behaviorist the term perception is ambiguous. (1) In the broadest sense perception is coextensive with response. Any response to a stimulus involves perception of it. Perception of an object is reception of a stimulus. The perceived object is the stimulus, and the perception of it is the activity of the receptors and afferent nerves. (2) In a somewhat narrower sense perception is the functioning of such a reception-pattern as will enable the organism (person) subsequently to report on or specify the stimulus if asked to do so. (3) In a still narrower sense perception is a response of a symbolic sort—a response which may serve as a substitute stimulus for the responding organism or for other persons. If it serves as a substitute stimulus for other persons, it commonly conforms to certain established conventions—to the mores of language. A report is precisely such a response. If it is merely a substitute stimulus for the responding organism, it may or may not be a language response—depending on the organism's habits (learned response-patterns).

To a behaviorist the introspectionist's view of perception often involves not only a confusion of these three meanings of the term, but also a confusion of stimulus and response, a 'stimulus error.' In the third of the three senses perception is a knowing response, and this is the type of knowing response which has received chief attention in the hands of epistemologists, the subject-object relation. For the behaviorist the subject-object relation is not ubiquitous, but is a special case of the stimulus-response relation. The knowledge is the response-pattern, and the known is the stimulus. The common confusion of the older associationist view, which still persists in such forms as the attempt to regard the object (stimulus) as a part or resultant of the psychological functioning of the organism, is well brought out by reversing the Berkeleyan proposition to read *percipere est esse*. For a behaviorist, to perceive an object is not to be it, but to respond to it as a stimulus. The stimulus is the *Ding an sich*.

An illustration may be in order. *P*'s subject, *S*, is driving a car. The light at the corner is red and *S* brings his car to a halt. An appropriate question may bring the response "I had a red sensation." *P* accepts this report, introspection if you will, precisely as he might the report "I saw a ghost." Either report throws an interesting and valuable light upon the language habits of *S*. But *P* reserves the right to infer from the former report a case of stimulus error. It was presumably the stimulus and not *S*'s condition (mental state, if you prefer) that was red, though *S*'s responses may have included one which symbolized the redness of the light *e.g.,* the verbal response, the word 'red.'

It has been alleged that the behaviorist denies images. He does deny that knowledge is made in the image of its object (response in the image of stimulus) except perhaps in the case of sympathetic and imitative responses and of onomatopoetic words. But in the second and third of the senses above assigned to perception a conditioned perceptual response is of course admitted and insisted upon. At least a part of a visual or auditory reception pattern, or a symbolic response, may be called out by some stimulus, internal or external, other than that which arouses the original visual or auditory receptors. Much human thinking presumably involves such conditioned responses.

Desire and purpose. Desire and purpose may be taken to illustrate what I shall call 'telic behavior.' In this connection it is important to distinguish between the terms 'telic' and 'teleological.'[5] The word 'telic' designates behavior in which antecedent responses appear to be determined by the consequent 'end.' The word 'teleological' applies to terms or statements which imply that consequent does determine antecedent in telic behavior. It is sometimes felt that to describe telic behavior in non-teleological terms is to deprive it of its telic character. This is precisely analogous to the theory that to understand man and monkey as descendants of a common ancestor is somehow to dehumanize man. Man is no less man for being known as a primate, nor is a human purpose less purposive for being understood as a special type of animal, and even of bodily behavior in general. Telic behavior itself is not altered by altering the scientist's language behavior about it. The most that can be asserted is that a description of telic behavior in non-teleological terms will inevitably be a wrong description—which is equivalent to assuming that human behavior lacks the uniformity which makes a scientific description of it possible. This may possibly be true; but it cannot be proved a priori, and we are more likely to make progress in anthropological science if we assume as a working hypothesis more uniformity than has yet been discovered. (Article I.)

[5] This distinction was elaborated in *Psychol. Rev.,* 1926, 33, pp. 254 *ff.*

The task of accounting for telic behavior in non-teleological terms may be formulated as that of understanding such behavior as consisting of stimulus-response sequences. The key to the present attempt to deal with the case of desire and purpose lies in the conception of the dominant complex; most of the response-patterns of an organism are inhibited, so that only a few are potentially active at any moment.

If a complex includes chiefly responses which happen to be more or less appropriate to bringing about a determinate result, the complex continuing to consist of these responses until the result occurs and then shifting, the behavior of the organism would properly be designated as telic—a series of responses each of which appears as a 'trial' and each but the necessary ones as an 'error.' We may call this type of dominant complex a 'drive.'

The problem of describing drive behavior in non-teleological terms involves accounting for (1) the continuation of a drive complex until the consummatory response occurs or the end is achieved, (2) the shifting of attention when the consummation occurs, (3) the variability of the preparatory responses, (4) the appropriateness of the preparatory responses to bringing about the end-result.

(1) In some cases a continuing stimulus may account for the continuation of the drive-complex, as in the case of a dog on the trail of a fox. But the complex may continue of its own momentum unless attention is shifted by the presence of some new appropriate stimulus; the dog may lose the trail, and pursuit-responses nevertheless continue. (2) Some responses included in the complex may be inappropriate to the end—*e.g.,* the end of catching the fox—and if called out may inhibit the pursuit responses, thus shifting the dog's attention. Again, the consummatory response may eliminate the inducing stimulus, *e.g.,* eating may eliminate the arousing condition (empty stomach, etc.) for a food-getting complex. (3) The variability of response is an essential characteristic of most complexes, whether or not of the drive type. The stimuli in the range of attention (foreconscious) call out their appropriate responses one-at-a-time. The several patterns are mutually inhibitory. The functioning of one pattern may change either bodily or external conditions (or

both), thus bringing a new stimulus into the focus. (4) The most difficult part of the problem is to account for the inclusion in the complex of responses which are appropriate to bringing about the result on other grounds than their appropriateness as such. If we were to explain the inclusion of these responses in the complex on the basis of their appropriateness we would still be giving a teleological account of telic behavior.

A partial non-teleological account of this inclusion of appropriate response-patterns may be made by an adaptation of a suggestion of Watson's: On previous occasions the shifting of the complex must have required some of these responses so that they tend to occur on the whole more frequently than inappropriate responses and so to continue in the complex. Once a complex (inhibition of a large group of reaction-patterns) induced by a particular condition has begun to develop, it will tend to continue to function until this condition is removed, and so responses which will remove it tend to occur each time the complex becomes dominant and to become conditioned to stimuli which commonly accompany the inducing stimulus. On the other hand responses not appropriate to eliminating the inducing stimulus need not occur if the complex is to cease dominance, and their less frequent occurrence makes it less likely that they will be conditioned to stimuli which commonly accompany the inducing stimulus. It may further be noted that some inappropriate responses may have become inhibited by conflict with appropriate response-patterns which are included.[6]

[6] "Desire, Choice, and Purpose from a Natural-evolutionary Standpoint," *Psychol. Rev.*, 1926, 33, pp. 257–8. [This article also contained the following argument against the widely accepted view that preference is a transitive relation:

["An inherited division of scientific labor has left the economist in the rather awkward position of having to develop a psychology of choice somewhat apart from the main current of psychological thought. Without attempting a detailed discussion of this psychology of choice, commonly called the Marginal Utility Theory, we may say that it treats desires, or more accurately, desirednesses (utilities) as given teleological magnitudes or quantities not changed by choice, the origin of which the economist need not investigate. The price offered for an article according to the more accurate formulations of this view is a ratio of two 'marginal' desirednesses.

["Clearly such a theory of choice is in conflict with an attempt at a natural-evolutionary account like that outlined above. If choice is a process of alteration of complexes, including drives or desires, it will not do to regard desires as given

This treatment is intended not to be exhaustive, but merely to indicate the nature of a behavioristic account of this complicated problem of drives. It should be noted that a drive may include many definitely 'inappropriate' responses along with more plausible 'trials.'

Thus far we have considered the general case of a drive or desire. Purposive behavior may be conceived as a special case of drive, in which the inducing stimulus for the complex is a language-response which represents or symbolizes the end, or in which the inducing stimulus is a *conditioned* sensory response (image), the 'original' stimulus to which is a part of the end-situation. This inducing stimulus (language response or conditioned sensory response symbolizing the end) is thus the 'conscious purpose.'

Values: Meaning and beauty. Only a few comments on these

---

magnitudes unaltered by choice or to neglect their origins. Moreover, the relation between price-offer, as the result of a choice or change in desire, and utility as a state of being desired to a given 'extent' is not, as many economists have supposed, one between a quantity of utility (desiredness) and a ratio between two such quantities. Rather price-offer is one of the responses of which the desire consists; and choice is a process of changing desires, as a result of which there is not a relation between two unaltered desires but rather one changed desire. Price is not a relation between two desires, since desire itself is a relative; desire is a desire for one thing rather than others and so in effect a completed choice. Desiredness is preferredness. Choice does not take place between two desirednesses, since what is desired is changing during the choice-process; choice is rather a conflict between two reaction-patterns and a process of survival of one of them in the complex.

["Moreover, there is nothing in such a theory of desire and choice to show why response A should not inhibit response B, in one situation, response B inhibit response C in another, and response C inhibit response A in a third situation. Yet the marginal utility theory of choice seems to require just this (in assuming that desires differ from each other quantitatively) so far as choice is 'rational' in the sense of choosing that which one desires 'most.' If desire A takes precedence over (is more intense than) desire B, and if B takes precedence over (is stronger than) C, it would seem to follow (from this assumption of the quantitative nature of desire) that desire A would take precedence over (be stronger than) C. In other words, preference is assumed by this view to be what has been called a 'transitive' relation. On this point also there is a possible conflict between this assumption of transitiveness which is necessary to the marginal utility theory, and the present position on the nature of drives and their development, according to which there seems to be no reason to suppose that behavior is 'rational' in the sense that preference is a 'transitive' relation, that preferring x to y, and y to z involves preferring x to z" (pp. 262–263).—EDITOR] topics are possible in so brief a survey. While evaluation is not properly a part of scientific description, it is a part of the descriptive task of science to describe the type of human activity we call evaluation. It is the essence of the present contention that this task can be only partially accomplished by psychology, *i.e.*, by a study of the individual. Psychology requires to be complemented by a study of group behavior.

Upon the psychological side it is to be noted that the value of an object differs from its physical or observable properties in something like the way in which secondary and primary qualities were once supposed to differ. The value of an object is peculiarly dependent upon the response-patterns and complexes of the particular person who happens to be evaluating it. Its value may mean its capacity for calling out a particular type of response; *e.g.*, it is funny if it calls forth a smile or laugh. Or it may mean that it plays a particular part in the type of complex called a drive, *i.e.*, it is the condition or event which eliminates the inducing stimulus.

But the psychological side is not the whole story. If it were, the behaviorist-institutionalist would be a mere sophist. There is a certain objectivity about beauty and funniness. To say that the mores prescribe in some detail the modes of action of an individual and compel him to develop certain habits and drives is to say that within limits they determine what he shall laugh at and what he shall appreciate æsthetically. In the case of the humorous object, the form of the response is largely determined by heredity, it is a laugh or a smile reflex. But even here the mores are a factor in determining which of these reflexes shall be set off, and in a measure also in modifying the pattern of the reflex itself—*e.g.*, a laugh may be either raucous or refined. In the case of beauty, the mores are largely influential both in determining what objects are to call forth an esthetic appreciation, and in determining what type of response constitutes appreciation. Native traits affect artistic activity chiefly in that the activity prescribed by the mores of art appreciation and creation may exceed the capacity for discrimination and performance of many organisms that pass as normal persons.

Meaning, properly speaking, is a value attribute not of objects in general, but of that specific class of objects or stimuli which comprise language behavior and other symbolic responses. The meaning of such a symbol or combination of symbols is in part the object or group of objects for which it is a symbol or substitute-stimulus, and in part its appropriateness in a given context of other symbols, *i.e.,* its appropriateness as a response to other symbols or as a stimulus to other symbols. It will doubtless be felt that this makes meaning a very complicated affair. So it is. Language is an extraordinarily complicated institution, consisting of an elaborate and minute set of mores of grammar, diction, rhetoric, punctuation, spelling, pronunciation, vocal inflection, and logical sequence. Meaning, so far as language activities go, is closely prescribed by these—in the English language —easily a million mores.

Knowing responses and thinking. Thinking is a type of activity that involves the functioning of knowing or symbolic responses. The knowing responses are not necessarily verbal, nor are they necessarily confined to the functioning of the nervous system, the vocal apparatus and conditioned reception-patterns; they may include readily observable behavior of a non-vocal sort—tool-manipulation responses, such as drawing or writing on a paper. Not all functioning of symbolic responses, however, constitutes thinking. Thinking may be conceived as the working out of a drive in symbolic form—a symbolic process of trial and error, almost literally 'making one's head save one's heels.' The inducing situation to the drive may be put symbolically as a question. If the answer is not a verbal perception and is not a habitual language response (memory), a drive may be induced in which the answer is worked out by a process of trial and error. This working out, the symbolic trials, is the thinking; and the response which eliminates the inducing stimulus is the 'answer.' Whether or not the question arouses this type of activity depends upon the language habits of the subject and the complex which happens to be dominant when the question is put.

Phylogenetically it seems appropriate to conceive this thinking process as originating under conditions where the inducing stimulus is concretely present in something more than symbolic form and where the answer is immediately translated into overt, non-symbolic action. But this does not require, as some Pragmatists have seemed to say, that thinking should always eventuate in overt action; thinking may become a game pursued for its own sake, as in cross-word puzzles, or in science.

Much of human thinking proceeds largely in the form of language behavior. So far as this is the case the process tends to conform to the mores of which language consists. The question is often derived from social inheritance, *i.e.,* from the mores. The terms in which the thinking proceeds are largely determined by the mores of language; *i.e.,* the categories of thought, the methods of analyzing and classifying things, come largely from the mores. Many truths are ex-cathedra or more strictly ex-more truths. And the sequences which are accepted as 'logical' are the sequences which the mores prescribe. Upon this aspect of human thinking rests its objectivity, rests the possibility of persuading others by argument. Thinking in a manner which has more than individual validity is as much conforming to the mores as behaving politely.

Pain, fear and anger. We may indicate briefly the nature of a behavioristic conception of emotional activity by a few comments on these three types. They have in common an activity of the adrenal glands, inhibition of digestive activity, an increased activity of the heart and respiratory system, and to some extent a heightening of overt bodily activity. And typically they share with certain other forms of emotional activity, weeping and laughing, an inhibition of the type of activity just discussed, thinking. Hence, no doubt, the common sense opposition of reason and emotion.

Of the three, only pain is clearly an activity of the drive type. For a behaviorist pain is the stimulation of the specific pain receptors. The ensuing nerve impulses commonly take precedence over others. Pain responses are part of nearly every dominant complex. Typically they include activities of major skeletal muscles, movements of the stimulated part, or touching it, and general bodily movements such as walking the floor. In some cases the result is removal of the inducing stimulus, as when one comes in contact with a hot object, and moves away. In some cases the drive fails to achieve a consummatory response. It should be noted that certain gesture responses (responses, the function of which is to stimulate other persons) are often incorporated in the pain complex, the groan reflex and facial contortion reflexes.

A fear complex may also include vocal and facial gesture-reflexes. Sometimes it involves trembling and a somewhat general paralysis of overt activity—sometimes a heightened overt activity. Suddenness is a frequent characteristic of the stimulus, but the appropriateness of a situation or event as a stimulus to fear behavior is largely a matter of individual habit formation.

Anger is not so much a drive as a potential phase of any drive. When a drive continues for a time without a consummatory response, the organism gets, as we say, 'out of patience.' Tone quality of voice, flashing eyes, the set of the jaw and facial muscles are common observable features of such a condition. The grosser movements become quicker and more violent. Muscular coördinations are less nice and precise. But the concrete reaction-patterns that function are for the most part a matter of the individual's habits. To this it must be added that in anger, and in pain and fear as well, the mores are an important factor both in determining the habits the organism possesses, and in determining which habits and reflexes are appropriate to the occasion. It is a common current practice to resort to oaths, when 'out of patience.' And our language affords a special part of speech appropriate to emotional conduct.

Scientific observation. Because of its peculiar importance for the issue between the behaviorist and the introspectionist, a closing word may be said about the type of human activity we call 'scientific observation.' To the institutionalist science is an esoteric cult comparable to the monastic cult of the medieval Catholic Church. Its ritual and its faith are different, but they are no less truly ritual and faith. Scientific observation is part of the cult ritual and its revelations are part of the cult faith. A scientific observation is, of course, a special case of perception in our third sense, verbal perception, a symbolic verbal response to a stimulus. But to be scientific the response must conform to the mores of science. Rigorous training is necessary to acquire this type of language habit. To be scientific the verbal response must employ certain types of categories of thought, certain methods of classifying objects. Scientific observation differs from the verbal perceptions of primitive man, *e.g.*, in that it does not classify fire, weather, rivers, and mammals together as animate beings. Again, to be scientific, an observation must be what the scientist regards as descriptive. "It is a beautiful day" is doubtless a frequent observation, but clearly not a scientific one. It evaluates rather than describes. (See Article IV.) It is of the essence of the present view of perception that it is selective. It is selective not only because the dominant complex determines to which of the stimuli for which the scientist possesses correlative response-patterns he will respond. It is selective also because the response-patterns he has developed determine what differences in the stimulus situation can call out different verbal perceptions. Many verbal perceptions, verbal responses to many aspects of a situation, are doubtless possible that would not class as scientific. To be scientific an observation must have relevance to some part of the scientific faith in which the observer is concerned as one of the high-priests; it must have relevance to a scientific hypothesis. There is nothing inevitable about the truth of a scientific observation. It is true merely because the mores of science prescribe belief in those revelations which are made according to the ritual of scientific observation. Observations are true not because they are logically deducible, but because they conform to observational ritual. They are the dogmas of the scientific cult. If scientific observation is thus a matter of language-habits and the mores, a product of social evolution which itself has evolved and is evolving, we might expect occasional conflicts within the esoteric cult of science as to what constitutes a scientific observation. And this is precisely what we find today. Are observations in which there is not the possibility of substitution of one observer for another on the same plane of scientific validity as those in which substitution is possible? Does one observe external stimuli, or is the object of observation a phase or resultant of the psychological functions of the organism? Are scientific observations mere language habits and cult ritual? To some it may seem that such an attempt as this last question suggests—an attempt by social science and psychology to study science scientifically, to deal with science as a product of social evolution—is to call in question the validity of the scientific faith. But to understand that the basis of scientific truth is sociologically and psychologically similar to that of religious truth is not to give up the scientific faith, but to follow it to its logical conclusion. The mores of scientific observation are no less current mores for being understood as such. And as mores they are enforced by a penalty. The penalty for unbelief in the revelations of scientific observation, like the penalty for unbelief of the medieval cult, is excommunication. As a devout mos-fearing behaviorist I subscribe to the scientific creed, respect the ritual of observation, and claim membership in the cult of science.

· III ·

Economic Theory and the
Natural Science Point of View
(1931)

IS economics a natural science? Ought the economist to deal
with his subject-matter on the basis of natural science assumptions? Ought he to use natural science methods? Ought he to be
concerned that his hypotheses shall be consistent with hypotheses
in other fields, such for example as the hypothesis of biological
evolution?

In discussing these questions I shall consider chiefly that part
of economics which was once the whole but has become a specialized branch, "economic theory" in the sense of theories of
price, production, and distribution. In this connection I shall
have occasion to refer to certain theories as "neo-classical." I
shall mean by "neo-classical" most of the theories of such economists as Cannan, Carver, J. B. Clark, Ely, Knight, Fetter,
Fisher, Laughlin, Marshall, Pigou, Seager, Seligman, Taussig,
Taylor, Wicksteed, Young and, with one important doctrinal
exception, Davenport. I propose to consider briefly how the
following topics might be treated from a natural science point
of view: (1) standards of social policy; (2) the marginal utility
theory and the ultimate determinants of price; (3) the law of
supply and demand; (4) the productivity theory; (5) Say's law
that real supply is real demand; (6) theory of taxation.

The suggestion that economists should adopt a natural science viewpoint is certainly not new. But there is the possibility that natural science method has not been read aright by the founders of economics. Moreover, much has happened in the field of science since the main outlines of neo-classical theory were laid out by the classicists. Evolutionary biology and geology have developed. Psychology has expanded its domain from perception, memory, and imagination to the behavior of the individual organism as a whole. And finally the subject-matter of economic theory, our system of prices, production, and distribution has been changed and is being changed by an industrial revolution that was scarcely begun in 1776, and that was only well under way in this country a century later.

Whether economics is a natural science, is, I think, a question not so much of achievement as of method and of relationship to other fields. I cannot pause to discuss the nature of scientific method and the relationships among the sciences at length.[1] I shall offer only three comments which are especially pertinent here.

(1) It is a prime object of natural science to formulate hypotheses, or descriptive generalizations *relevant* to the subject-matter of science, which are capable of empirical test. Scientific theories should not be mere truisms, or be so abstract as to be incapable of factual disproof. They should be useful in enabling one to say *a priori* what he expects to find under certain specific conditions, within the limits of accuracy of the generalization, and they should be such as to be invalidated if he does not find *empirically* what he expected to find *a priori*. Moreover, a scientific hypothesis should be so formulated as to fit existing data. The economist will do well to put generalizations about price and cost into the terms that are used in keeping business records —into accounting terms. And this theory of wealth should reckon with existing legal categories.

(2) As a natural science economics is first of all a social science. It is not primarily concerned with individual behavior. It presumably deals with certain aspects of our social system not

---

[1] For elaboration, see "Psychology and the Natural Science Point of View" [pp. 11–36].

sharply marked off from the aspects with which other social sciences deal. Secondly, economics is a biological science—it studies group relationships among living organisms of the genus *homo sapiens*. As such its generalizations must somehow make peace with the general theory of biological evolution. They can only be true of and relevant to some definitely specified periods of social evolution. For some specifiable antecedent period in human or pre-human evolution they should be either untrue or irrelevant. Any economic generalization, if scientific, aspires only to historical validity. And the historical limits of its validity should be carefully specified.

(3) The biological sciences do not confine themselves to description. They are normative as well as descriptive. Pathology deals with abnormality. Physiology is concerned about the functions of organs. Function is a normative, not a descriptive category. Social pathology and the functions of elements in our economic system are properly the concern of economists. But it is very important to accurate thinking that we should not confuse a statement of what is with a statement of what ought to be.

With these brief comments on scientific method and the relationships among the sciences in mind, let us consider the topics I have listed.

I. *Standards of social policy.* As an evolutionist I should expect to find no sharp line between the neo-classicists and those who take a natural science view of economics. Many classicists have treated the efficient and economical use of human effort and social wealth in the production of goods and services as the main objective of our economic system. Natural science offers, it seems to me, not a conflicting view here, but the possibility of defining this objective empirically, and of measuring the performance of our economic system statistically. Fisher has made a careful formulation of this objective in empirical terminology.[2] He has accurately adhered to the accountant's distinction between real and nominal accounts, between social wealth and social income or production. And he defines social wealth and income in terms of a consolidation of individual accounts. He is careful to state that there are certain ultimate items which do

[2] Irving Fisher, *Nature of Capital and Income,* 1906, esp. chaps. 6 and 9.

not cancel out. These include ultimate equities in tangible assets, consumer benefits, labor sacrifice, foregone immediate consumption. The selection of these as ultimates involves passing judgment on our economic system. It is equivalent to asserting that the interests of the consumer, laborer, and ultimate property holder are the ends of economic organization, and that business profits are a means thereto, and not conversely,

King has offered us statistical measures of our national wealth and income,[3] and in doing so has made certain amendments of definition. King has also attempted to deflate his income estimates to show the physical volume of income or production. The Stewart-Day-Thomas indexes measure a part of this production more directly, and their technique can be applied to other parts of the production field. These techniques can also be used to show the physical volume of wealth and labor, whose services are required in production. We should shortly be able to measure approximately the general efficiency of our economic system in achieving the neo-classical ideal.

While these measurements are by no means perfect—production includes some things that perhaps should class as illth—they can point the way to many possible improvements in our economic system; and as our system improves our measures will improve also.

II. *The marginal utility theory and the ultimate determinants of price.* For purposes of appraisal it seems well to consider the consumer as ultimate and the business enterprise as intermediate. But when the neo-classicist makes consumers' choice ultimate in his description, or explanation of actual price determination, he flies in the face of the facts. He has confused description and appraisal here. Consumers' choices are effects as well as causes of business policy or it would not pay to advertise. Physicists long ago left the search for ultimate determinants or ultimate causes to metaphysics. Economists would do well to follow suit. Moreover, the neo-classicist is in an embarrassing position. Psychology has expanded its domain—the theory of

[3] W. I. King, *Wealth and Income of the People of the United States*, 1915; *National Income and its Purchasing Power*, 1930; and joint author of *Income in the United States*, 1922.

choice is now distinctly the concern of psychology. The marginal utility theory under any of its names is a psychological theory of choice which conflicts with Gestalt psychology and with the Dewey variety of behaviorism. Moreover, there is no empirical basis for the theory. Marginal *desirednesses* can only be measured objectively through the price offers they are supposed to explain. Finally the alleged law of diminishing utility is not needed to explain the failure of some to buy as much of a good after a price increase as before, when the price increase would require giving up other things if they did, or to explain the honorific value of certain scarce objects.

There is a definite issue here between the neo-classical and the natural science formulations of the price problem—between those who "would know why the price of pig is something big" in terms of ultimate determinants at the time and those who would investigate the historical "behavior of prices." In place of a static, quasi-psychological, tautological theory of the factors behind demand, the natural science view would substitute specific socio-historical theories. Veblen's *Theory of the Leisure Class* offers some interesting explanations of changes in consumers' demand. We can state the problem statistically in terms of changing family budgets. Sales campaigns, public education in hygiene and home economics, changes in household technology, the rise of feminism, are sample historical factors to be reckoned with.

And for the theory that the supply of labor is to be explained by the varying amounts of labor each individual will supply at varying wage rates, the natural science viewpoint requires a similar substitution of specific socio-historical theories. The factory-system has standardized the working time. That time has been affected by business policy, and often by trade-union or government policy. The fatigue and routine of factory employment have tended to bring limitations of workng time in the interests of public safety and health.

III. *The law of supply and demand.* Neo-classical theory has considered chiefly two types of markets; (1) a perfect competitive market, in which demand and supply are functions of a single variable, the current price of the commodity in question, in which competition serves as a regulative agency, and in which price is uniquely determined; (2) a perfect monopoly on one side of a market and competition on the other. The "law of supply and demand," accurately stated, applies only to case (1); the "law of monopoly price" to the second case. Both laws are definitely historical. They are not relevant to interpreting the facts of many primitive societies. Nor does any actual present market conform to the conditions under which either is true, except as a rough approximation. Thus, under perfect competition there could be no widespread unemployment, no important differences of bargaining power, no incentive to sales effort, no significant influence of price policy on market price.

Both laws deal with the conditions of static equilibrium in an isolated time interval. The empirical data for such a study are necessarily confined to a single pair of observations of price and amount marketed—no basis for scientific generalization is afforded, unless we take a dynamic view, unless we add to the two variables quantity and price a third variable, time, and concern ourselves with the historical behavior of prices. When we do, there are striking differences between different markets—also between different times. Mills has shown that commodity price variability exhibits a secular decline, temporarily reversed by the war.[4] While for static purposes competitive supply and demand are coördinate—I have pointed out that dynamically they are not [5]—in peace time supply changes commonly are more important than demand changes in producing changes of commodity prices.

The organized commodity and security exchanges approximate perfect markets in many respects. Price fluctuates from moment to moment with changing conditions of demand and supply. For certain crops it has been possible to construct statistical demand schedules on an annual basis using yearly average prices. The law of supply and demand is useful as an approximation here.

The price quotations of most manufactured commodities are

[4] F. C. Mills, *Behavior of Prices*, 1927, chap. 3, and *Recent Economic Changes*, 1929, chap. 9.
[5] *Journal of American Statistical Assoc. Proceedings*, Mar., 1930, p. 168.

"producer prices." These quotations often do not vary at all for
months at a time, though one may suspect special concessions
from the quoted price before an official cut. But hour-to-hour
changes in demand and supply presumably do not cause price
variations here. The short-time changes in supply and demand
are offset by business policy. The law of supply and demand
may here describe only the swings of, say, a 12 or 24 months'
moving average of prices.

The law of supply and demand conceives demand and supply
as functions of a single price. But every market competes with
the future of itself. An *expected* rise or fall of prices may cause
changes in present demand and supply and hence a rise or fall
of *present* prices. There is, as Taussig has pointed out, a measure of indeterminacy in competitive price determination,[6] important for price fixing during the war and important also for
understanding certain cumulative speculative swings of the market. This indeterminacy helps to make the prices on organized
exchanges among the least stable elements in our price system,
in spite of the stabilizing function of the specialist in specula-
tion.

The law of supply and demand treats the quantity of a
commodity or service passing through a market as capable of
measurement on a single scale, pounds, bushels, or labor-hours.
Recent developments in business price and wage policy have
taken account at what J. M. Clark calls the "different dimensions" of an economic good.[7] We have incentive schemes for
wage payment and two- and three-part utility rates. Both the
quantity marketed and the money remuneration are affected by
the form in which the price is stated, and that form may be
altered by private or public policy. The occurrence of "economic
goods" with more than one "dimension" is presumably more
widespread than is yet recognized in our price system.

Many actual markets do not closely approximate either the
perfect competitive market or the perfect one-sided monopoly
of neo-classical theory. They are mixtures of monopoly and com-

[6] F. W. Taussig, "Is Market Price Determinate?" *Quart. Jour. Econ.*, vol. 35, pp. 394–411.
[7] J. M. Clark, *Overhead Costs*, 1923, chap. 10.

petition and not necessarily like either of the polar ideals. Such a market as the labor market or the market for a good sold in several grades and under a variety of brands may perhaps best be conceived as consisting of a group of little markets, each a monopoly, but each in competition with the others, subject to a certain frictional resistance in shifting from one market to another. In such a case differences in bargaining power are important, differences in ability to wait or to enter an alternative transaction, differences in market information and in the ability to employ a marketing specialist or a lawyer.

So long as we conceive of competition as competition purely on a price basis, it may be a fairly adequate regulative agency. Most competition, however, involves qualitative differences in the commodity and differences in terms of sale. Slichter has analyzed the inadequacy of competition as a regulative agency, under these complex conditions.[8] The consumer may be unable to judge quality, may take price as a criterion of quality. And in the labor market competition may deteriorate the level of conditions of labor, the plane of competition, if we rely solely on it as our regulative agency.

Furthermore, in a market consisting of a group of competing monopolies, offerings and takings at the going price may not be equal. Unemployment may be a permanent condition, though its volume may vary.

Again, in an imperfect market there is an incentive to exert sales effort, directed both toward the distribution of certain market information and toward developing consumers' tastes. Indeed, sales effort may be an essential condition of competitive business survival.

And finally, in an imperfect market business or public policy may be an important influence in fixing prices. Thus wage rates have been known to rise in the face of a stable labor supply and a declining demand. I can only pause to mention the increasing importance of price policy in connection with new monopoly elements in our economic organization, the rise of trusts, trade unions, and trade ethics, the development of public utility

[8] S. H. Slichter in the *Trend of Economics*, 1924, "Organization and Control of Economic Activity."

regulation, the growing practice of branding goods and of resale price maintenance.

It seems fair to say that the Industrial Revolution and large-scale enterprise have greatly increased the significance of four important exceptions to the law of supply and demand: disparity in bargaining power, unemployment, sales effort, and price policy.

IV. *The marginal productivity theory.* The marginal productivity theory assigns to each of us a portion of the social income equal to what we and our property have contributed to the social income, reckoned on the basis of the marginal productivities of the several "factors" or ingredients contributed. It suggests that natural law provides a scheme of social cost accounting and incentive payments, such that there is an accurate allocation of social costs against social revenues, and such that profits are a managerial bonus to society's functional foreman —a bonus for producing only what is socially worth the cost, for producing it as efficiently as possible, and for improving the technique of production. No general manager for society is needed, competition selects the most efficient functional foremen and directs their energies into the socially most desirable channels. As a statement of an ideal system of social organization there is much to be said for this theory.

But as a description of our present order the case for the marginal productivity theory is not so clear. In the course of social evolution (in which governmental policy has played a part) we have developed a complex scheme of property and contract rights and rules of association, a currency system, the institutions of specialization, trade and production for sale, a complex of business organizations and of markets, a system of prices. These institutions so organize our society that most of us are compelled to contribute to the social income in order to share in it. In the rough, our economic system conforms to the competitive ideal. But only in the rough. As a description of our present order the productivity theory is altogether too simple to be accurate—so simple that it can throw little light upon those phases of our economic system which give rise to economic problems. If "productivity" is the rule, a natural science theory of our economic system that is relevant to current problems must be chiefly concerned with the exceptions to that rule, with understanding the causes of economic waste and inefficiency in our present system, the phases of our present system that create financial incentives to private policies that conflict with social policy. And if we are to test the marginal productivity hypothesis empirically, we must be concerned with the types of accounting and statistical information that are needed to measure the performance of various units in our economic system and to compare performance with remuneration.

The productivity theory cannot be both a statement of what ought to be and a statement of what is, if it is to be a useful scientific hypothesis for public policy. I propose to consider briefly some exceptions to the productivity theory considered as a scientific description of what is, exceptions which are apparent even on the basis of our present inadequate information. The marginal productivity theory involves three assumptions that I wish to call in question. (1) It presupposes perfect competitive markets. (2) It treats social wealth as hired by entrepreneurs from the ultimate equity holders on short-term contracts, much as wage labor is hired. (3) It assumes a static unchanging legal system, in which there is no ambiguity or overlapping and conflict of property rights. The correlative theory of profits as in part wages of management assumes individual or entrepreneurial enterprise.

Under the conditions assumed the entrepreneur might wisely confine his efforts to accurate anticipation of demand and to technological efficiency in the use of labor and social wealth. But none of the three assumptions of the productivity theory holds. As Veblen,[9] Davenport,[10] and certain socialists have pointed out, in our competitive society making money does not necessarily involve making goods. It is by no means clear that sales effort contributes to social income in proportion to its social cost, though it may pay in terms of private profits. Legal effort, lobbying, bribery, and adulteration of goods are often profitable. Labor cost can be economized by shrewd bargaining

[9] Thorstein Veblen, *Place of Science in Modern Civilization,* 1919, pp. 279–323.
[10] H. J. Davenport, *Economics of Enterprise,* 1913, esp. chap. 9.

as well as by economical use of labor. Business connections, strategic situations in the economic system, and inside information are of paramount importance to successful business. Large fortunes have been made in high finance and racketeering. For purposes of accurate description we must substitute a profitivity theory for the marginal productivity theory.

In treating social wealth as hired by entrepreneurs on short-term contracts, the productivity theory has overlooked an important accounting distinction. Most wage labor and material costs are directly assignable to the output of a given accounting period. Overhead costs, of which capital costs are an important element, are not so assignable. Under the English domestic system most business costs were direct. The Industrial Revolution has greatly increased the business importance of overhead. With the rise of overhead costs in the latter nineteenth century in the United States, free competition inevitably became cutthroat competition. More recently in the fields where large-scale methods are dominant, business has developed various restraints on free competition, pools, trusts, trade ethics, established channels of trade, brand and patent monopolies, communities of interest, etc. Bell has analyzed this situation admirably.[11] These restraints are essential to business stability, but they diminish the effectiveness of competition as a regulative agency. Incidentally, they involve restriction of output, producing at less than capacity a good deal of the time, and as J. M. Clark has noted,[12] the marginal productivity (profitivity) of a plant operating at less than capacity is zero. Marginal profitivity in manufacturing and public utilities evidently does not ordinarily determine factorial shares.

When a manufacturer puts a price upon his output, he includes in that price a charge to cover his overhead. For him the cost is partly direct or avoidable, partly overhead or unavoidable. For the purchaser the entire cost of the purchase may be direct. There is a conversion in the form of costs from what is overhead for the manufacturer to what is direct to the pur-

[11] Spurgeon Bell, "Fixed Costs and Market Price," *Quart. Jour. Econ.*, vol. 32, pp. 507–24.

[12] J. M. Clark, *op. cit.*, chap. 23.

chaser. There is a similar conversion between laborer and
employer. To the laborer his cost of living is largely overhead
or unavoidable—to the employer wage cost is largely direct.
J. M. Clark and I have called attention to the importance and
prevalence of these direct-overhead cost conversions in modern
society.[13] They give the purchaser a profit incentive to curtail
purchases when socially a different policy might pay. I can only
pause to mention the fundamental importance of the theory of
direct-overhead cost conversions for understanding such problems as the business cycle, the behavior of the labor market,
public utility rates, and the functioning of agriculture and the
coal industry.

In the absence of adequate market information intelligently
used, a long production period may give rise to cycles of over-
and under-production—the hog-cycle, the cattle-cycle, the apple-
cycle, the petroleum-cycle, and less clearly a cycle in bituminous
coal.

The productivity theory presupposes an absence of ambiguity
in our legal system—that there is adequate recourse at law for
any party to collect from a second party all pecuniary gains to
the second party for which the first party is responsible and to
collect full indemnification from the second party for pecuniary
losses incurred by the first party through actions of the second. In
a complex and changing society we can hardly expect such per-
fection. There are many cases of what I have called *de facto*
torts,[14] damages for which no legal remedy is now available. In
the "wild animal" theory of mineral rights we find an incentive
to wasteful extraction of petroleum. Zoning ordinances imperfectly eliminate *de facto* torts in urban realty. The depreciation
of a laborer is not necessarily a cost to his employer. Many lease
contracts, as Pigou has noted, provide inadequately against depreciation or depletion of leased property. Wherever there are
de facto torts there is a profitivity incentive not to take full
account of social cost.

The theory that profit (including the monopoly profit derived

[13] J. M. Clark, *op. cit.*, chaps. 2, 18, 19; Copeland, *Trend of Economics*, 1924,
"Communities of Economic Interest and the Price System" [pp. 201–246 below].
[14] *Trend of Economics* [pp. 205–206, 213, 231 below].

from a patent) offers a socially efficient managerial incentive payment is obviously more applicable to the period before the Industrial Revolution than to the present era of large-scale corporate enterprise. The allocation of corporate profits to minority stockholders not only means that such profits are not received by management, it has also facilitated the capitalization of monopoly profits into the valuation on which public utilities have a constitutional right not to be deprived of a reasonable return. In public utilities (and perhaps some other lines) we are beginning to get the accounting information necessary to measure economic performance. And for public utilities consequently we are beginning to face the problem of reconstructing the institution of profits into a managerial incentive payment that shall go to management and that shall more accurately reflect economic performance.[15] But the problem of getting accurate accounting information and of remodeling the institution of profits is clearly not confined to the public utility field. One-half of our national income is now produced by nonentrepreneurial forms of enterprise.

V. *Say's law.* The theory that real supply is real demand and that the value in exchange of a commodity is independent of the exchange value of money is a reaction to mercantilism that goes too far. It tends to minimize the rôle of money in the national wealth and welfare. Yet oddly enough it leads to overstatement of the rôle of money in the business cycle and the price level. If we allow for the time it takes money to circulate, it is clear that supply today means demand not today but at some later time. Say's law is not precisely true for short periods. Recognizing this, and recognizing also that for purposes of analyzing the functioning of our pecuniary society the consumer, the worker, and the saver are no more ultimate in the nexus of prices than the business enterprise, Mitchell in his *Business Cycles* traces the cumulative expansion of incomes and expenditures of businesses, families, and governments during recovery and prosperity and the cumulative contraction of incomes during recession. The mercantilists were right at least to the extent that a favor-

[15] *Cf.* the *Bauer-Bonbright Plan*, New York State Legislative Doc. No. 75, 1930, p. 411 ff.

able change in the balance of trade may favor business recovery
or promote business expansion and so increase the national income. Historically we may fairly call Mitchell's theory of business cycles the first triumph of the empirical natural science
method in the study of the behavior of prices and production.

The corollary of Say's law, that value in exchange is independent of the exchange value of money, has helped to sustain,
in the face of conflicting facts, purely monetary theories of the
level of commodity prices—the various quantity and commodity
theories. We know that the relations between M and P are complicated by V and T. We know that for short periods the equation of exchange is not precisely true—the shorter the period,
the less accurate the equation. We know that in seasonal movements and trend the variations of V and T do not offset each
other. The offset in cyclical movements is probably only a rough
approximation. We know that seasonally M is elastic, adjusting
itself to the money work to be done. I have shown elsewhere
that a larger proportion of money work is created by transactions that cannot well be treated as P x T, taxes, insurance
premiums, etc., and that commodity price transactions account
for but a fraction of money work.[16] We know that the connection between gold and prices in the United States today is
extremely tenuous, bank reserves are one factor in interest rates,
interest rates are one factor in price changes. The behavior of
the level of commodity prices from late 1925 to 1929 is difficult
to account for on the basis of monetary and credit conditions.[17]
Specific factors affecting specific commodities appear to account
for this period satisfactorily. The natural science point of view
suggests that we should define the price level in the way in which
it is measured, as a weighted average of a specified set of prices,
and that we should deal with it for what it is—a mere average
of prices. There may at times be a pervasive common influence
on prices such as a credit stringency, or a cumulative movement
of prices. At times special factors working on special prices may
be of paramount importance.

[16] See "Money, Trade, and Prices" [pp. 95–107].
[17] *Journal of American Statistical Association, Proceedings*, Mar., 1930, p. 164–9.

VI. *Taxation.* The neo-classical theory of value and cost applies to prices but not to taxes. It distinguishes taxes sharply from prices. Governmental accounting lies outside the neo-classical scheme of social cost accounting, although government fiscal policy makes contact with our so-called natural economic system at many points and through these contacts it necessarily directs the functioning of that economic system into one channel or another.

When we revise the theory of price and cost to take account of overhead costs and real and nominal accounts, the theory is broad enough to include the field of government accounting as well as business accounting—not as a description of what is, but as a statement of what ought to be. It is time our governments kept more businesslike accounts. Accurate distinction between capital and revenue accounts would conduce to wiser fiscal policy. The levying of taxes is essentially a cost accounting problem —the problem of distributing social overhead. Social overhead can often be directly assigned to a given class of beneficiaries, although within this class it must be distributed by pro-rating on some arbitrary basis. But the application of cost accounting methods to taxation has not gone very far as yet. Thus, we are still far from making the users of our highways support our highway systems. As a class they are responsible for highway costs, though the allocation of responsibility within this class can only be approximate. The adoption of cost accounting procedures by the government in such cases as this would do much to improve the economical functioning of our social system.

In this hurried review of developments in the theory of prices, production, and distribution—developments in the direction of adopting a natural science point of view—we have seen that a reformulation of the price problem has been in process. Natural scence does not concern itself with ultimate determinants, it studies the behavior of prices and the unending incidence of price changes. Much of the structure of neo-classical theory remains, but its applications need to be carefully delimited—a clear distinction must be drawn between its use as a description of the present order and its formulation of a Utopia, and as a description it must be taken as a first and very rough approximation. The law of supply and demand describes many of the movements of some markets fairly well; in other markets it does not apply to hourly, daily, and weekly movements; and in yet others like the labor market and the markets for branded goods it offers little more than a convenient classification of factors and policies affecting price into supply and demand factors. The productivity theory, as a description, describes in the rough such coördination of specialists as existing institutions achieve, but it needs to be supplemented if we are to understand the conflicts of interests and the economic waste that characterize our present system. A vigorous government policy directed toward realizing the neo-classical cost accounting Utopia would probably resemble Russian communism more than it would laissez faire. The newer phases of economic theory aim to take account of certain features of society that the Industrial Revolution has made prominent, disparity in bargaining power, sales effort, a variety of restraints on competition, overhead costs, changes and ambiguities in our legal system. It rejects Say's law for short-time movements of price and production and substitutes the cumulative expansion and contraction of incomes of business, family, and government. And it finds a variety of factors influencing the price level. Again it would extend the scheme of social cost accounting suggested by the older theory to include government fiscal policy. To the fuller working out of this newer theory we shall need vastly better accounting and statistical information than is available today.

Neo-classical economic theory is value and distribution theory. From a natural science view hypotheses concerning industrial government or the organization of our railroad system are economic theories as truly as hypotheses concerning variations in price, production and distribution.

The neo-classical theory of economics offers, on the whole, somewhat scanty contacts with other social sciences. For a natural science theory there are no sharp lines between economics, political science, and sociology; and the historical approach is common to all of them. The legal system, government organization and policy, social institutions, market organization, the organization and policy of the business enterprise and the trade union are all involved in understanding the behavior of prices and changes in the amount of distribution of wealth and income. Economic theory is necessarily only a special phase of social theory.

· IV ·

Institutional Economics and Model Analysis

(1951)

INSTITUTIONALISM has two main phases: one concerned with the process of cultural evolution; the other with the here and now. The line between these two phases is, in one sense, a line between the long run and the short run, but not in the sense familiar in model analysis. The institutionalist thinks even the long-run considerations of the model analyst ought to be fitted into his here-and-now category. By and large the longer-term cultural evolutionary phases of institutionalism and model analysis belong to separate universes of discourse. There can be no real clash between them.

But the subject matter of the here-and-now phase of institutionalism and that of model analysis somewhat overlap. There has been and still is a sharp clash between these two approaches to the study of economics.

The "has been" part of this statement needs a slight qualification; the "still is" part clearly calls for elaboration.

When I say there has been a sharp clash, I refer to the debate that reached its peak during the twenties. It is true we did not talk much of model analysis in those days. At the time, the proponents of this rather mathematical mode of thought called it simply "economic theory" or "economic analysis," as if this approach to the study of economics were the only logical one. The institutionalists, to distinguish it from their own mode of theorizing, called it "system theory." But it will probably be conceded that what they meant by system theory was essentially an implicit form of model analysis. Let me say then that there was a sharp clash between the implicit model analysis of twenty or more years ago and institutional economics, and that during the past fifteen years model analysis has become explicit and much less has been heard of the clash.

Why has less been heard of the clash? Have the differences between model analysts and institutionalists really been ironed out? Prior to the mid-thirties economists in the English-speaking world used mathematical symbols somewhat sparingly. The change-over from system theory to model analysis marks a much more liberal use of algebraic and calculus notation. Certainly this change-over did not placate the institutionalists. But it was accompanied by model changes.

I think the main reason why relatively little has been heard from institutionalists of late stems ultimately from these changes. The models—or some of them—have become more realistic. I want to consider this development in a moment. It is more complicated than it sounds. No doubt revising models in a realistic direction did something to decrease the theoretical differences between model analysts and institutionalists. However, it was not because these theoretical differences became small that little institutionalist criticism of model analysis was heard during the forties.

Before taking up the quieting effects of the revised and more realistic models let me note a second factor that has helped to reinforce these quieting effects. This reinforcing factor may be called the propensity of economists to buy their theory by the package.

Model analysis has thus far been confined to quantitative relationships and it has invariably involved a great oversimplification of the real world. Institutionalism has been concerned to emphasize the complexity of reality and the importance of qualitative as well as quantitative facts.

A simple, neat, schematic answer to a question has always had a survival value quite out of proportion to its real merit. It is easier to remember than a more complicated one and easier to communicate to others.

The answers that model analysis provides to theoretical economic questions are often somewhat intricate. But they are usually neat and schematic. Also, however intricate they may be, they necessarily oversimplify reality by largely excluding qualitative facts; and they commonly oversimplify it by dealing with a very restricted number of variables. Model analysis answers are enough like simple answers to enjoy the same advantages: they are easy to remember and easy to communicate. Moreover, they have an advantage that a simpler answer does not—a prestige value. Mathematics has come to be regarded as part of the ritual of science. Economic model analysts have been able, by practicing this ritual, to command an economic rent through the principle of merit by association.

Because they are easy to remember and communicate and because they sound scientific, the answers model analysis offers to theoretical economic questions have a survival value greater than they deserve. Let me push this point a step further. Certainly the merit of an answer depends upon its meaning. But a model analysis answer in the field of economics can have—or at any rate so far has had—survival value, even when economists have not agreed on its meaning. Various forms of words have gained wide currency among economists, forms that can be translated into algebra, particularly forms that can be visualized in geometric diagrams. I say "forms of words" because it appears to be the form, not the content, that has acquired currency. To be sure they equate algebraic symbols with quantitative economic terms, but only with loose terms that different economists can construe quite differently. Let me cite just one of several possible examples. There is a fair consensus on the proposition that marginal revenue tends to equal marginal cost. There are sharp differences on the meaning of cost and the way to measure it. It is the formula, not its empirical meaning, that has gained currency.

If during the past decade or so institutionalist answers to

economic questions have lost ground in competition with model analysis answers, I suggest that it is partly because they have not been put up in the same kind of package. Clearly this is only a partial explanation, for institutionalists presumably lacked neat and impressive packages for their theories twenty or more years ago. Still the lack is a significant factor in the history of economic thought during the past two decades. And it seems a fair question whether economists are well advised to buy a theory so largely on the basis of the neatness and impressiveness of the package in which it comes.

The major factor to which I attribute the silencing effect on institutionalism is the change in models. During the "teens" and twenties the models in vogue were highly unrealistic. Further, they had never succeeded in purging themselves of certain ethical implications. On the whole they were in the laissez faire tradition. Veblen characterized this type of implicit model analysis as bourgeois homiletics. Institutionalism objected to it both because it was unrealistic and because it tended to support a hands-off public policy. Implicit model analysis was rightist in political orientation; institutionalism challenged it from the left.

Just twenty years ago before a round table of this Association I attempted a summary statement of the here-and-now phase of the institutionalist position.* Let me quote some propositions from that summary:

1. A scientific hypothesis should be so formulated as to fit existing data.
2. The theory that real supply is real demand . . . is a reaction to mercantilism that goes too far. . . . A favorable change in the balance of trade may favor business recovery or promote business expansion.
3. The consumer, the worker, and the saver are no more ultimate in the nexus of prices than the business enterprise.
4. Mitchell in his *Business Cycles* traces the cumulative expansion of incomes and expenditures of businesses, families, and governments during recovery and prosperity and the cumulative contraction . . .

* See preceding article.

during recession. . . . We may fairly call Mitchell's theory . . . the first triumph of the empirical natural science method in the study of the behavior of prices and production.

5. We should define the price level . . . as . . . a mere average of prices. There may at times be a pervasive common influence on prices such as a credit stringency, or a cumulative movement of prices.

6. The behavior of the level of commodity prices from late 1925 to 1929 is difficult to account for on the basis of monetary and credit conditions. Specific factors affecting specific commodity prices appear to account for this period satisfactorily.

7. Such a market as the labor market or the market for a good sold in several grades and under a variety of brands may perhaps best be conceived as consisting of a group of little markets, each a monopoly, but each in competition with the others, subject to a certain frictional resistance in shifting from one market to another.

These seven propositions were leading points in the here-and-now phase of institutionalism twenty years ago, and on each of them institutionalism has made something of a sale. Since 1940, developing an aggregative model that will be a good statistical fit for purposes of annual or quarterly forecasts of the national income and product account has come to be a major occupation for a number of economists. Current Keynesian models constitute what may fairly be called a version, though a somewhat expurgated version, of Mitchell's theory of business cycles. Also they treat consumer demand as passive rather than as ultimate prime mover, recognize the cyclical impact of the export balance, and leave ample room for factors other than money and credit to account for changes in the level of wholesale commodity prices. Still further, shortly after 1930 monopolistic-competitive models—thanks to Chamberlain and to some extent also to Robinson—became a generally accepted part of model analysis.

What happened to the seven quoted propositions suggests that the institutionalists gained a signal victory. But really they succeeded in selling to the model analysts—or to a good many of them—only those planks in the institutionalist platform that could most readily be translated into the language of model analysis and put up in neat geometrical or algebraic packages.

With the rest of their platform they did not have much success. Their victory was of very limited scope.

However, one result of this limited victory was a right and left movement. In the twenties implicit model analysis had been predominantly rightist in its outlook. By the forties the center of gravity of model analysis had shifted somewhat to the left. During the twenties most of the criticism of the prevailing form of economic theory was leftist. During the past decade most of it has come from the other side of the aisle. It would be an overstatement to say that, with the shift in the center of gravity of economic theory, there is no left left. Rather, the voices of those who objected to this shift and to the model changes underlying it have been raised so loud that they have almost drowned out the voices of the institutionalists.

Such a political way of speaking emphasizes the policy aspect of this development. I think rightly so. It is true that each of the seven institutionalist propositions I have listed refers not to economic policy but simply to the way our economy operates. And to the extent that model analysis has made concessions to these institutionalist propositions the changed models mean changes in the prevailing way of describing economic behavior. It is true, too, that the critics from the right have, for the most part, directed their attacks against these revised descriptive generalizations. Nonetheless, I think the policy aspect of what has happened should be emphasized.

If relatively little has been heard from the institutionalists during the past ten or fifteen years, it is not because they succeeded in selling a major part of their platform. They did not. Nor is it because the critics from the right have succeeded in attacking the revised descriptive generalizations so cogently. If there were time, I should like to take apart some of the criticisms that have been most favorably received. They are not peculiarly free from logical fallacies. More importantly, they depend on premises that are currently points at issue. And certainly they make little attempt to argue the case on the basis of statistical findings of fact.

One cannot account for the right and left movement of the past two decades in purely objective terms alone. One cannot

overlook the changed policy implications of the prevailing
school of model analysis. The criticisms from the right during
the forties were not well received because they were especially
well presented. Rather it was because they found a receptive
audience. And the audience was receptive mainly because it dis-
approved the policies the new description implied. If this finding from the most recent chapter in the history of economic
thought is correct, it is a sad commentary on the aspirations of
economists to make their inquiries truly objective and scientific.

But this is not the end of the chapter. Institutionalists did not
find the new descriptive generalizations an unmixed improvement. On at least one count a number of them joined in the
criticism. Veblen, it is true, propounded a secular stagnation
hypothesis. But many of his followers did not go along with him
in this respect. During the twenties and forties and even during
the thirties they regarded such a view of the way our economy
operates as a form of historical myopia.

Under the circumstances it is little wonder the voices of institutionalists have not stood out clearly during the past ten years.

Thus far our examination of the recent history of economic
thought has proceeded without regard to the division of academic labor. Keynes proposed a radical change in this respect—a
change that has found wide support. I refer to his distinction
between macroeconomics and microeconomics.

By and large, institutionalists are disposed to welcome this
proposal. However, they tend to feel about it as they feel about
many other Keynesian proposals: that it is something of an oversimplification. Economic theory has three broad aspects. The
Keynesian proposal for a revised academic division of labor
deals with these aspects somewhat unequally.

Let us note what these aspects are and how the Keynesian
proposal impinges on each. Then let us briefly reconsider the
recent history of economic thought under each of these three
heads.

First, economic theory must be concerned with its relations
to political and social theory. Economics is a part of the field of
social science, and economic theory must deal with the relations
of the part to the whole. The Keynesian proposal is silent here.

Second, economic theory must be concerned with its relations to the special branches of economics. The Keynesian proposal has implications for this phase of economic theory; but the implications have not been spelled out. Microeconomic theory must have a particularly close relationship with the special branches of economics, because for the most part these branches deal with microeconomic facts. Keynes did not say what this relationship should be. Should the theorist tell the special branches what questions to study, or should he try to build generalizations out of the common elements in their several findings?

Third, there is an area between these two in which economic theory ought to be pursued on its own account. Keynes's proposal narrowed this area by assigning a part of it to microeconomics, and broadened it by including in it the major operations of our monetary and credit system. The broadening, though not the narrowing, was clearly suggested by some of the seven propositions quoted above. But most institutionalists will enthusiastically support both proposals.

Now let us briefly re-review the recent history of economic thought under these three heads.

First, as to the relations of economic theory to social theory broadly conceived, we have said that implicit model analysis has become explicit. Of course this change has been one of degree. Many economists still abstain from expressing themselves in algebraic and calculus terms. And many who use them do not feel this way of putting things is adequate to express all they have to say. Nonetheless, the change has made economic theory a much more esoteric subject for workers in our sister social sciences. No doubt this situation has been aggravated by the fact that frequently economists who have used algebraic symbols for economic quantities have not identified these quantities with concrete statistical facts. Cultivation of the borderline areas between economic theory and the rest of social theory has thus been hampered. Further, economists have done less such cultivation. Let me illustrate. During the twenties there was a great deal of interest in the legal foundations of our economic order. Commons made significant contributions to our understanding of this important borderline area. But latterly economic the-

orists have given little attention to it; they have been too pre-
occupied with mathematical model analysis.

On the level of the relations of economics to other social sciences, the institutionalists have lost ground during the past
fifteen or twenty years. Let us take up next their record at the
macroeconomic level. They have done much better here. In
fact, practically all the gains in connection with six of the seven
propositions cited above are on the macroeconomic level. On
the whole it is easier to translate institutionalist contentions into
the language of model analysis at this level than on the higher
one just considered or at the level of microanalysis.

So far as macroeconomics goes, the prevailing school of model
analysis and institutionalists are in broad agreement on two
points:

1. Hypotheses should be put in a form that will fit existing
data.

2. Equations that do not lend themselves to empirical exploration are commonly lacking in objectivity and definiteness of
meaning; it is unwise to depend extensively on such subjective
equations in economic analysis.

Institutionalists and empirically-minded model analysts agree
on these two points. But what I propose to call "nonempirical"
model analysts do not. For the most part, but not entirely, nonempirical model analysts can be identified as the critics from
the right.

It is ungracious to give only a single illustrative quotation to
make clear the nature of the issue here, but time presses and
at least one illustration is needed. Let me quote from Fellner's
chapter in the *Survey of Contemporary Economics*. I am sure he
speaks for a significant number of economists. In reference to
models designed to provide a theory of aggregate demand and
employment he says: "The savings-investment approach . . . . ,
if expressed in terms of simultaneous realized magnitudes, either
. . . possesses no significance *per se* . . . , or it implies that the
. . . *ex post* (realized) magnitudes equal the *ex ante* (planned
or expected) magnitudes."

I disagree. If every aggregative model in simultaneous variables were true by definition, as this statement and its context

clearly imply, they would all be perfect statistical fits. None of them is. We do not yet have one that is a really good fit. And as for the aggregative *ex post–ex ante* equation, this has quite a number of proponents, but it seems to me another case of agreement on a form of words without much concern for what the words mean. Certainly we need data on plans, commitments, and expectations in business conditions analysis. In recent years substantial progress has been made in assembling such information, but we are still a very long way from having enough of it to make an aggregative *ex post–ex ante* equation really objective and definite in meaning.

This quotation, however, is only an illustration. More broadly the issue seems to be precisely that posed by Mitchell in his presidential address over a quarter of a century ago: shall we aim to make economics an empirical, scientific study of the way our economy and other similar economies operate? Empirical model analysts and institutionalists say yes. The main alternative to so doing—the alternative I think most nonempirical model analysts advocate—is to make it an exercise in deductive reasoning—in reasoning the relevance of which to our present economy must necessarily be a moot point.

This issue, of course, involves microeconomics as well as macroeconomics. But I have incorporated it here because it is on the macroeconomic level that most of the clashes between the two schools of model analysis have occurred.

I think the agreement between institutionalists and empirical model analysts on the two basic points just mentioned may eventually compel them to get together in other respects. But there are at present sharp differences—differences that have come out especially in discussions of current business conditions analysis and forecasting. The basic issue in these differences is both old and broad: how much of the field of economic theory does model analysis encompass?

Empirical model analysts would like to discover a model in n variables and n equations that gives a good statistical fit to a series of business cycles—as long a series as possible. Of course no one expects to find a perfect fit—only to minimize the errors by getting a best fit. Further there are great difficulties in making the number of equations equal to the number of variables. Efforts at statistical fits have been almost entirely confined to models that treat some variables as exogenous. Both the use of exogenous variables and the recognition that fits will not be perfect suggest that no two cycles are just alike.

During the twenties a number of the critics of Mitchell's theory of business cycles said that it was not a theory. Presumably they meant he did not express his theory in terms of a model. He refused to do so because he was impressed with the differences between one cycle and another.

Empirical model analysis can do something to account for such differences—something but not much. Its main recourse is to introduce a secular trend into each of the parameters in the model.

This suggests two phases of the basic issue between empirical model analysts and institutionalists. First, is it part of the economic theorist's job, in analyzing business cycles, to try to account for what goes on outside the model? Institutionalists answer yes. Nonempirical model analysts answered no in the twenties and presumably still do. Empirical model analysts surely hope to take account of some of these outside facts by improving their models so as to cover them. They are less clear how far the economist should deal with such facts before the models are improved.

The second phase of the issue is this. How much of what goes on in business cycles goes on outside the model? The candid answer is: at present most of it. But when models are improved, it may be much less.

Still I think it is well to note four restrictions under which empirical model analysis operates:

1. It cannot do much with the secular trend. Trend extrapolations are too hazardous.

2. One reason why Mitchell insisted that cyclical history does not quite repeat itself was that sporadic variations in economic time series play a significant part in business cycles: wars and strikes, bumper crops and crop failures, floods and droughts, etc. Empirical model analysts cannot do much to forecast the progress of a war or a strike. At best they can trace the effects of

sporadic variations in time series by making them exogenous variables.

3. If one seeks a model that will give a reasonably good fit to the data for a series of years or quarters, he must restrict the number of variables he employs. Such a restriction is partly one of expediency. A complicated model becomes unwieldy. But to some extent it is inherent. He must employ the same number of variables for each year or quarter covered by his data.

Institutionalists insist on using in cycle analysis a very much larger number of time series than can easily be handled in a formal model. They insist also on taking account of new series as they become available and on resolving aggregate quantities into different components in different periods so as to isolate the significant factors in each period.

4. Finally, empirical model analysis can do very little to take account of pertinent qualitative facts. The years of wartime rationing are awkward to fit into a consumption function. The establishment of the U. S. Steel Corporation as a market leader and the inauguration of the Federal Reserve System have undoubtedly had significant effects on the way our economy operates. Empirical model analysts cannot hope to do much toward tracing these effects.

Nonetheless, we can and should confidently expect that empirical models will someday do a good deal more to tame the unruly facts of business cycles than they have to date. But there remains the question what to do in the meantime. For the immediate future I think we will do well to recognize that the analysis of business cycles must be largely a form of historical analysis. It must analyze developments of a qualitative nature, analyze sporadic variations in time series, and analyze the behavior of exogenous variables. It must work with a large and ever changing set of time series.

So much for macroeconomics. Microanalytic models are not markedly more realistic today than they were twenty years ago. The empiricists have concentrated so much energy on the aggregative level that there has been relatively little exploration of microeconomics through empirical models. The chief concession to institutionalism has been the development of the nonempirical monopolistic-competitive model. But this is only a gesture to realism. What it means is that those who go in for intellectual gymnastics now have a new piece of apparatus in their intellectual gymnasium.

Unfortunately, this new piece of gym apparatus is much more familiar today than the general theory of cost and price which Clark built out of findings common to the study of railroads, taxation, and other special branches of economics. He did not put what he had to say in a neat mathematical package. But he said a great deal that was new and important: about how to measure and estimate cost and what is a unit of business; about the typical long-run cost curve and the typical production function; about the bearing of cost differentials on price differentials; about private versus social cost accounting; and on other subjects.

Clark's *Economics of Overhead Costs* is not the only institutionalist contribution to a realistic microeconomics; nor is it confined to microeconomics. But it is much the greatest institutionalist contribution at this level.

In conclusion, let me add a brief injunction to this review. I think it is urgent that economists should again turn their attention to those phases of economic theory that lie outside the scope of present model analysis. On the highest level, this means that economic theorists should once more cultivate intensively the borderline areas of their subject, such as that between law and economics. At the aggregative model level this means, so far as empirical current business cycle analysis is concerned, that they must tackle the whole job, not just the small part that present models can deal with. And particularly at the microeconomic level it means that they should emphasize the empirical meaning of their findings and give somewhat less consideration to the neatness and impressiveness of mere forms of words.

· V ·

Statistics and
Objective Economics
(1955)

ONE could argue that the history of economic thought has long been shaped—at least in part—by statistics. In the nineteenth century value theory was strongly emphasized, the theory of production rather slighted; at that time price statistics were far more plentiful than production statistics. Again laissez-faire was bolstered by a price, wage, and interest theory that largely ignored the government as a customer, as an employer, and as a borrower; at that time the government budget was small in relation to national income. Further, international economics emerged as a special field; international trade statistics and foreign exchange rates loomed large among our earlier economic time series.

This is by no means all there is to the earlier influences of statistics on economics. But the major statistical impact has come since World War I, and it is that impact we are concerned with here.

Let me begin by considering the nature of the stimulus that has been applied to economics. Really there are two stimuli. On the one hand, there is statistics as a scientific method of making observations and drawing inferences, particularly a method of inferring the characteristics of a population from the characteristics of a sample which is in some sense random. Modern statistical method is a widely applicable technique of scientific investigation that embraces the planning of the pattern of observation as well as the mathematical logic of inductive inference.

On the other hand, we have statistics in the sense of the facts of observation themselves, or rather, since we are here concerned with economic statistics, the facts which emerge from what is called statistical collection and compilation. Statistical collection and compilation necessarily goes farther than mere observation; it involves logical inference and trained judgment. Moreover, this kind of fact-finding is commonly beyond the capacity of any one individual. It takes an organization to find the population of the United States, and more than one organization to find the gross national product. Yet such findings of quantitative facts are for the economist the nearest available analogues to the measurements of physical science. Possibly they are much closer analogues than has sometimes been supposed, despite their inferential nature. At all events economic statistics are the empirical measurements the economist has to work with.

Since World War I there has been a very great increase in the stock of economic measurements economists have at their disposal. There has also been a very great development in statistical method. But the impact of statistics on economics has come almost entirely from the measurement side; the greatly improved mathematical-statistical method has made but little impression on the recent course of economic thought.

The reason why statistical measurements have exerted a substantial influence is not far to seek. Economists had long aspired to make their subject a genuine science. For a time they had looked to Newtonian mechanics as an example of what a science ought to be. The aim was a mechanics of the market place, but the result turned out to be more like Euclid than Newton. Presently there were some that argued that geometry, rather than mechanics, was the proper model for economic science. But there were others who regarded the so-called laws of economics as too static, too deductive, and too remote from the real world, and who yearned to make economics an objective empirical study of our actual economy.

Wesley Mitchell was a great leader in this latter group. In addressing the American Economic Association as its President, he outlined what he thought quantitative analysis, aided by "the increase of statistical data, the improvement of statistical technique, and the endowment of social research," might do to—and for—economics. He predicted that "the men now entering upon careers of research may go far toward establishing economics as a quantitative science." And he anticipated that moving in this direction would require "a recasting of the old problems into new forms amenable to statistical attack." Further, contrasting the Newtonian or mechanical and the statistical conceptions of nature, he said the latter "may be expected to make more radical changes in economics than it makes in physical theory." He commented too on the prospect for the traditional type of economics which he characterized as "deductive" and as involving "excursions into the subjective." He thought it "unlikely that the quantitative workers will retain a keen interest in imaginary individuals coming to imaginary markets with ready-made scales of bid and offer prices. Their theories will probably be theories about the relationships among the variables which measure objective processes. There is little likelihood that the old explanations will be refuted, . . . much likelihood that they will . . . drop out of sight in the work of the quantitative analyst." [1] Mitchell's address was delivered in 1924.

Before World War I there had not been very much in the way of statistical measurements on either side of the Atlantic to implement the kind of objective quantitative inquiry Mitchell expected to see develop. And in many respects American economists had been less well off than their European colleagues. To be sure our Statistical Abstract was a substantial octavo volume, and it was literally then, as it is today, only an abstract. But the quantity of statistical measurements is not a matter of weight and tale alone. They must be apropos.

Economic statistics, like other measurements, are by nature comparative. A single measurement can be quite useless; usually you need other measurements with which to compare it. In the

---

[1] *American Economic Review*, March 1925, 1–12. There are various other quotations from this address below.

case of economic statistics there is one type of comparison that
has long been recognized as particularly important—comparisons in time. Economic time series, such as the series on our
wheat crop each year, are a particularly useful class of economic
statistics. And within this class there is one subclass that possesses
far greater utility than the others—economic time series that
are on a current quarterly or more frequent basis. This kind of
measurement is essential for analyzing the current business situation. Before World War I we had only a thin, scattered assortment of such series, e.g., imports and exports, foreign exchange
rates, stock, bond, and wholesale commodity prices, bank clearings in leading centers, freight-ton-miles, business failures, pig-
iron production.[2] There were no comprehensive current figures
on employment and unemployment, on inventories, on construction, on retail trade or retail prices, on bank credit. The
idea of an index of physical production was widely deemed not
feasible. Monthly measures of total personal income would have
been thought an idle dream. The gross national product was
only a theoretical concept mentioned by Adam Smith and then
largely forgotten. It had not yet been given even an annual or
occasional statistical significance.

This listing of gaps in the current quarterly and monthly time
series available before World War I makes it clear that our area
of ignorance was much larger than our area of knowledge. In
terms of annual, decennial, and other noncurrent compilations
we were considerably better off. Such compilations covered
agriculture, mining, manufacturing, railroads, banks, government, and several smaller industry sectors. In the decade 1904–
13 about three-fifths of our national income originated in these
sectors. Moreover, there were clues to what was going on in the
others, notably the clues in the decennial census of occupations.
But it should be added that the statistical record of our pre-
World-War-I economy is substantially more complete today
than it was in 1918. A good deal of what we now know has been
pieced together in the meantime. Piecing together is an essential

[2] See *Historical Statistics of the United States, 1789–1945*, Washington: Bureau
of the Census, 1949, Appendix I.

part of the work of statistical fact finding, and a part that has come to be performed far more adequately in the last thirty-odd years.

This building up of the retrospect has meant a significant addition to the stock of statistical measurements at our disposal. But most economists would rate as far more significant what has been accomplished by way of building up the current picture. With regard to the magnitude of this accomplishment it can be said that we now have what we lacked before, an effective working stock of current time series, a far better one than that possessed by any other country in the free world. There are still gaps to be filled, and there are shaky figures that need to be made firm. But it is a sufficiently well-rounded and reliable stock to make effective empirical economic analysis possible.

The measurements of physical science are mostly *ad hoc* measurements. When an investigator needs a measurement he finds a way to make it. Scientific curiosity is in general the motive that provides such measurements. Scientific curiosity has played a part, too, in making our stock of economic measurements what it is today. But its role in this connection has necessarily been a modest one. I have noted that the retrospect has been improved by a process of piecing data together. This piecing-together process is responsible, also, for vast improvement in our current statistical picture. Without it that picture would still be a very spotty one. And scientific curiosity has been a main motive in the development of the piecing-together techniques. However, without the basic current and less frequent periodic reporting services that have come into being since World War I, there would not be much that could be pieced together. And scientific curiosity has hardly been the main promoter of these services. Probably the most that can be said is that it has abetted curiosity-with-an-axe-to-grind. But even curiosity-with-an-axe-to-grind has played a modest role. It is true that *ad hoc* collection services provide a substantial part of our basic data. The various censuses, the monthly payroll and employment reports to the Bureau of Labor Statistics, and current trade association reports are cases in point. But there is a much larger body

of basic data collected or recorded for some administrative purpose. For example, there are tax returns and the accounting records of businesses and governments. In the vast assortment of
basic data we rely on today the statistics that are by-products of
administrative record keeping and administrative reports bulk
far larger than do those that result from *ad hoc* collections.

We will not attempt to explain how our stock of by-product
measurements has come to be what it is today. Such an inquiry,
however intriguing, would be a digression. But the comments
just made on the role of scientific curiosity in adding to our
stock of measurements have been offered because they help to
answer a directly pertinent question that has surely occurred to
you: If the economic measurements accumulated since World
War I have exerted a substantial influence on the course of economic thought, because there was a group of economists who
yearned to make their subject an empirical science, how comes
it that the greatly improved mathematical-statistical method,
which now offers to all fields of science a plan of inductive inquiry, has made but little impression?

Let us consider this question under two heads, one relating
to the problems of the accuracy of economic measurements; the
other, to the problems of constructing economic models.

If we think of statistics as a genus of quantitative facts, it
would seem that economic statistics should be regarded as a
species of that genus. Now the proponents of modern statistical
method regard the members of the genus as numerical character-
izations of what they call a population or universe, or of a sample
of a population or universe. Presumably the figure $365 billion
for our gross national product in 1953 is a numerical characterization of a particular universe, the 1953 national product, and
since to some extent sample data were used in arriving at this
figure, it is natural for the proponents of statistical method to
ask, "Why not use the theory of sampling to provide a measure
of its accuracy?"

Certainly it is not the practice to say that GNP was $365 bil-
lion $\pm x\%$. In fact national income figures were often published
in this form thirty-odd years ago, but the practice has gone out.
Most economic statistics are now published without any attempt

to specify the error quantitatively.[3] There are exceptions to this rule, of course. But the rule is against such a specification.

The ground for this rule is surely not that the degree of accuracy attained by economic statistics is so high—quite the contrary. One reason for the rule is that the errors modern mathematical statistical method has enabled us to measure are not the only errors to which economic statistics are subject. Often they are relatively unimportant. For one thing there are sampling errors that have a time dimension that is not yet covered by probability theory—I mean errors which arise because a sample-universe relationship derived from study of a benchmark year is applied to sample data for subsequent periods, and in these subsequent periods the sample may have gotten out of line with the universe to an extent not reliably measured by any available statistic. There are conceptual errors too—thus the articulation of the parts of a total like GNP may not be quite correctly designed. The articulation of the parts may be imperfect for this reason. It may be imperfect also because the basic data do not fully conform to standard specifications, e.g., the basic data used in putting together a consolidated balance sheet for our banking system may not all refer to exactly the same date; or they may not all define foreign banks in the same way. Further, there is always the possibility of sheer mechanical errors. And of course there are incomplete and doubtful data that must be used in some of the steps taken in arriving at a comprehensive total like GNP. Again, the data available are continually changing—probably no two successive annual estimates for a total like GNP are exactly comparable. This is not a complete catalogue of sources of error, but it is perhaps enough to indicate why attaching a single percentage error measure derived from a probability calculation to many current economic statistics would only be misleading. Instead, in the case of time series, the prevailing practice is to mark some figures p and others r.

But, as it applies to time series, there is another reason for the rule against showing the percentage error. The main interest

[3] Thus none of the current monthly figures regularly appearing in the *Survey of Current Business* is accompanied by such a specification, although many of them are based on sample data.

here centers not on one absolute error but on various relative errors. What counts is not so much the absolute level of a comprehensive total like disposable personal income but its year-to-year and quarter-to-quarter movements and its relations to other totals, e.g., personal consumption expenditure and personal saving. Attaching a separate percentage error figure to each quarterly estimate of disposable income would not be a satisfactory way to indicate the accuracy of either quarter-to-quarter or year-to-year movements in this series. Nor would separate percentage error figures attached to both disposable income and consumption estimates be too helpful in appraising the accuracy of a measure of the relation between them.

These comments indicate why the scientific error measuring technique that has been elaborated by modern mathematical statistical method has not made much impression in the field of economic statistics. They also have an affirmative implication that deserves attention here. Every basic compilation of statistical data and every set of pieced-together economic measurements ought to be accompanied by an adequate descriptive statement. Such a statement is the best available substitute for a quantitative appraisal of errors; but it should serve a still more important purpose too. It is needed to tell the user exactly what the figures mean.

This affirmative implication has two edges—it asserts an obligation on the producers of statistics, and a corresponding obligation on those who use them in economic analysis.

The producer has an obligation to provide an adequate description of his product. In the case of those basic data that are by-products of administrative records or reports this obligation may rest on the processor, if the primary producer has not met it properly. And with respect to the processing or piecing-together, the obligation should read like this: Specify what you have done so fully that you could expect others to repeat the process and come out with substantially the same findings. If economists want to aim at something like the kind of objectivity in their measurements that attaches to the measurements of physical and biological science, this is surely the sort of standard they should set for themselves. But it suggests a material qualification on what has been said above about our progress in developing economic measurements. We now have a lot of measurements but with regard to many of them, if we are candid, we must admit that we do not know enough about them to reproduce them. Undoubtedly there has been substantial progress in statistical specification statements, but to conform to the objectivity canon proposed there is still a long way to go. And there are pressures that work against going that way very rapidly. The preparation of a statistical specification statement is a tedious job that cannot well be delegated to a clerk. Time and money can be saved by slighting it, and there are both time and money pressures. Only a fraction of the statistical public will object if the specification is delayed a few years, or if it is quite brief and vague. Very few will object if they cannot repeat the process and confirm the results. However, those few do something to bring about the correction of errors in economic time series. And they exert some pressure—perhaps disproportionate to their numbers—toward better specifications.

The other edge to the implication from my comments on the nature of the errors in economic measurements relates to the users. Those who use such measurements in economic analysis have an obligation to understand the meaning of the figures they use, i.e., to know what they are doing. No doubt this statement will strike many noneconomists as an unnecessary amplification of the obvious. But, unfortunately, a kind of division of labor has grown up under which some people make it their business to know in detail how concepts like GNP, personal income, and personal saving are defined, and to play a part in the piecing-together process of constructing economic measurements; others prefer to concentrate on exploring the relationships among these economic variables. With such a division of labor, one can contemplate the possibility that Mr. X may find a new and better formula for predicting what is currently called "personal saving" from "disposable income" and yet not realize that what he has learned to predict is really not personal saving but a mixture of household saving, institutional saving and additions to noncorporate business surplus, a mixture that does not necessarily reflect all of household saving. It can be argued that such an unhappy possibility is a necessary cost of progress in economic inquiry; both the constructing of statistical measurements and economic model-building can be very time-consuming occupations. But the validity of this argument is open to question. Economic model-building is still a kind of job that can be done by people who are not full time specialists. I think those who concentrate on analyzing relationships among variables whose meanings they have not really stopped to investigate are unnecessarily impatient to get results. They may get results by impatience; but for the longer pull the obligation to know about the figures they are using remains.

The other part of the question posed above as to why the recent developments in mathematical statistical method have exerted but little influence on the course of economic thought relates to model-building. Present-day statistical method offers a kind of guidebook to model-builders. Why hasn't this guidebook done more to shape the course of economic model-building? One reason is quite simple. The guidebook proposes a plan for taking observations. It tells how to sample a universe so as to get a reliable model for it. Economic measurements are the quantitative observations the economist wants to get, and he particularly wants time series. What he wants is not a sample of a time series, but the whole series for a period of years, if he can manage to get it. Often he would like it for a longer period than circumstances permit. In taking time-series measurements he takes all he can get. The guidebook is no help. It is true there are areas of economic investigation where *ad hoc* observations can advantageously be made and a plan of observation is needed. It is true, too, that there are other fields of inquiry in which the possibilities of *ad hoc* observation are more narrowly confined than in economics, e.g., history and paleontology. Nonetheless, the part of economics that is not helped by a mathematical statistical plan for taking observations is a substantial part of the whole.

But there is a second and more fundamental reason for the somewhat limited usefulness of the new mathematical-statistical guidebook in economic model-building. This reason involves both the nature of the guidebook and the nature of economics.

The guidebook aims at general applicability to all fields of inquiry, and general applicability implies that the problems of the various fields—say physics, biology, and economics—conform closely to a single pattern. We contend that they do not, and that the guidebook, since it has been designed mainly for the physical and biological sciences, is not particularly well designed to serve the purposes of the economist. The economist's inquiry problems differ from those of the physicist and biologist because of two special characteristics of many of the time series with which he has to work. These two characteristics apply peculiarly to social and economic statistics. They are of special concern to the economist, because economic time series constitute the vast bulk of social and economic time series. It will be convenient to refer to series in which the two special characteristics are prominent as one-culture time series.

Per capita disposable income in the United States at 1947 prices, 1929–53, may be taken as an illustration of a one-culture time series. Let us contrast this type of series with such a series as total annual precipitation at Chicago, 1929–53. The first special characteristic that distinguishes the former is that the geographical specification is more than a mere geographical specification; it is a culture specification as well. And culture specification is important, because cultural differences can pose major obstacles to making interspatial comparisons. Thus while there are doubtless serious difficulties in saying what per capita income in the United States in 1929 would be equal to $1500 in 1950, such a comparison seems quite safe and simple when we face the problem of trying to say how many dollars of per capita income in the United States in 1950 would be equal to a per capita income of £200 in the United Kingdom in that year. But cultural differences do not hamper the making of interspatial comparisons of meteorological or other physical measurements. Because the geographical specification is partly a culture specification in the case of many economic measurements, and because one-culture intertemporal comparisons of such measurements are often so much easier and safer than intercountry comparisons, one-culture time series are today the outstandingly important category of economic measurements. Hence, too, economic

model-builders—to the extent that they have operated empirically—have inevitably devoted most of their attention to
time-series or period analysis models.

The second special characteristic of a one-culture time series
is that its meaning may be gradually changing as the culture, of
which it is an aspect, evolves. So, too, if we think of a set of one-
culture time series as a set of variables, the relations among these
variables may be gradually changing. Because of this characteristic the economic model-builder faces a theoretical dilemma.
Theoretically he can attempt to develop a period analysis model
that will describe the course of cultural evolution. Alternatively
he can assume that the evolutionary process is sufficiently gradual so that he can get useful results if he ignores it. The first alternative offers no prospect of early success; it is strictly a theoretical alternative in the present state of our understanding.

The second and only practical alternative today is rather awkward. The economic model-builder necessarily works with time
series covering a finite period and fits his model to the observations for that period. He would like to assume that these observations constitute a representative sample of a longer period,
and to use his model to draw inferences about that longer
period. But because he is following the second alternative he
cannot get out of the past a random sample of a period that includes the future. He cannot use the methodological guidebook
of mathematical statistics to appraise the validity of such inferences. Instead he adopts a rule of thumb to determine the confidence with which a stable relationship among variables during
the period for which observations are available can be used to
draw inferences about a longer period. The rule is that confidence diminishes as the length of the extrapolation period increases.

In view of the gradual-evolution characteristic of one-culture
time series the rules of mathematical statistical inference can not
be applied to extrapolations. But the economic model-builder
can still use various statistical techniques much as if they did.
He can and does. In particular he uses mathematical best-fit
techniques to determine his parameters and on occasion he
postulates probability distributions for his error terms and

makes his parameters functions of time. On the other hand there are many rather mundane techniques employed by statistically minded economists to the development of which mathematical-statistical theory has made negligible contributions. Some of these are used in the piecing-together process of statistical fact-finding and in designing and operating index numbers (e.g., splicing); others in analyzing time series variations (e.g., calendar adjustments). Such mundane techniques may well have done rather more for scientific method in economics than the mathematical-statistical guidebook.

The restrictions on the applicability of mathematical statistical method we have been considering relate to time-series analyses. With respect to cross-section analyses I shall stop only to say that the usefulness of mathematical statistical method varies with the problem. There are problems for which it seems ideally designed. There are problems for which its applicability is even more seriously restricted than for those connected with time series. And there are many problems in between.

We have attributed the very limited impact of recent improvements in mathematical-statistical method on the course of economic thought to the fact that that method is not well adapted to the problems of inquiry in the field of economics. The direct impact would, in any case, be limited to those problems which lend themselves to statistical treatment. Even within this area it is further restricted because there is a group of economists engaged mainly in statistical-economic research, who feel modern mathematical-statistical techniques to be malapropos and make a point of avoiding their use. Still, so long as there is a substantial group who do use them, one might well look for a significant impact.

There is, indeed, at least an incipient change in economic thought that can properly be attributed primarily to statistical theory. In the older—still widely held—deductive, subjective conception of an economic model the endogenous variables were all uniquely determined. With the error terms that characterize the statistically fitted equations of empirical model analyses some measure of indeterminacy is beginning to replace this older absolute determinism.

So much for the slight impact of statistical method on the course of economic thought. What has been the nature and extent of the impact of statistical measurements? Have they given economics the sort of objectivity Mitchell had in mind? In considering this question I must in fairness note that I omitted some of the qualifications he attached to his forecast. One of them suggests a kind of obduracy in the deductive, subjective approach. He expected "quantitative analysis (to) produce radical changes in economic theory" but he warned us that it "does not promise a speedy ending of the types of economic theory to which we are accustomed." We have had radical changes; the "excursions into the subjective" continue, although the rationalizations it is their purpose to provide have no proper place in the theoretical framework of any true behavioral science.[4]

Following Keynes the problems of economic theory have been recast. The field is now divided into two main parts, macroeconomics and microeconomics. In macroeconomics, quantitative analysis has made great progress. Quantitative workers now have at their disposal an impressive array of basic economic concepts which have something like the objectivity that attaches to the concepts of physics, in that they are defined operationally, i.e., in terms of the way they are measured. Among these are production (i.e., deflated GNP), wealth, personal income, personal consumption expenditure, gross private domestic capital formation, money (i.e., the total currency and deposit liabilities of the banking sector to other sectors), bank credit, the wholesale price level, unemployment, the labor force. These operationally defined macroeconomic concepts have given economists a set of objective variables whose behavior they can investigate empirically.

Quantitative workers conceive the task of macroeconomic theory to be to develop equations which relate these economic variables; to use these equations as well as a vast amount of detailed facts, to analyze the past behavior of our actual economy as it is reflected in changes in the aggregative variables; and, on the basis of such analyses to form opinions about the future.

---

[4] It would of course be scientifically appropriate to investigate, on the basis of an operational definition of rational behavior, how much of human behavior is rational.

Consider one of these equations, the consumption function. This equation is not as yet a very perfect instrument; while a number of improvements have been made in it in the past decade, much work still remains to be done. In contrasting the mechanical and the statistical conceptions of nature, Mitchell emphasized "imperfect approximation" as characterizing the latter. The consumption function is unmistakably an imperfect approximation. But quantitative analysts have found it very useful nonetheless. It is what is called a behavioristic equation, i.e., it is a statistical best fit to the available measurements. Historically it is interesting that when Keynes proposed the consumption function he indulged in subjective analysis; it is interesting, too, that this kind of rationalization of consumer behavior has dropped "out of sight in the work of the quantitative analysts" on improving the consumption function and that these quantitative analysts have introduced lags and stickiness factors commonly slighted by those who stress subjective rationalizations. But these quantitative analysts do not have the field to themselves. And their neglect of the subjective has not gone without protest.

Many a macroeconomic theorist, who has been accustomed to defining his basic concepts in terms of individual choices and expectations, has continued to prefer such subjective definitions to objective, operational ones. Quite possibly he feels the latter to be lacking in logical precision; certainly they smack of "imperfect approximation." And the shift from subjective to operational definitions would require a fundamental change in habits of thought that is not easily made except when one is young.

Those who prefer subjective definitions in general prefer a corresponding type of economic analysis. Thus there is today a considerable group of economists who see no merit in a purely behavioristic equation like the consumption function. They argue that there are "in fact two concepts of propensity to consume." One they characterize as "formal," "aggregate," and "*ex post*." [5] This is the one we have been considering. Though they call it *ex post* it has been used in making projections into

---

[5] Gotfried Haberler, "Mr. Keynes' Theory of the 'Multipler,'" reprinted in *Readings in Business Cycle Theory*, Philadelphia: Blakiston, 1944, 193–202.

the future. It might, therefore, be better to call it objective. The other concept is not amenable to statistical investigation. The economists who insist on it distinguish it as "psychological," "individual," and "*ex ante*." They tend to deprecate the objective, statistically determined propensity as "the tautological concept of the marginal propensity to consume," [6] and to say that a theory of business cycles that depends on it reduces to "a definitional proposition of no significance." [7] There is also a slightly milder condemnation of this kind of quantitative cyclical analysis which asserts that it tends "to submerge the process of economic change" in static or "instantaneous pictures." [8]

These reactions are of course reactions to Keynesian model analysis. Those who have labored to construct and to improve a statistical model along Keynesian lines are quantitative analysts. And the criticisms of this type of analysis just cited are in effect criticisms of any purely behavioristic analysis, Keynesian or otherwise. Those who bring the charges of tautology and static pictures appear to hold that a theory of the cycle must be something more than an hypothesis that approximately describes or fits the observed facts and that can be used in making projections; that it must indeed explain or rationalize what happens in terms of hypothetical individual expectations and preferences. On this ground Mitchell's own hypothesis for the cycle was long ago criticized as not a theory. Of course this was mere name-calling; not an intellectual criticism. But the recent critics of behavioristic quantitative economic analysis would have been better advised to say "not a theory" than to say "tautology" or "static." They are vulnerable on the truism count themselves. Besides, the charges of tautology and statics cannot be sustained against a Keynesian statistical model. Whatever else may be said about this type of model it is not a definitional proposition devoid of empirical significance and not a static picture. No tautology could possibly lead logically to a

[6] Fritz Machlup, "Period Analysis and the Multiplier Theory," reprinted in *Readings in Business Cycle Theory*, Philadelphia: Blakiston, 1944, 203–18.

[7] William Fellner, "Employment Theory and Business Cycles," Section 6, in *A Survey of Contemporary Economics*, Philadelphia: Blakiston, 1948, 53–5.

[8] John H. Williams, "An Appraisal of Keynesian Economics," *American Economic Review*, Supplement, May, 1948, 288–9.

wrong factual conclusion as did the model which produced the VJ Day forecast; nor could a static model. It takes a period analysis model to produce a prediction.

Perhaps these comments on behavioristic quantitative analysis and its critics suggest that economic theorists can be classified as either behaviorists or subjectivists; they cannot. There are not a great many quantitative analysts today who are—as Mitchell thought they some day would be—"chary of deserting the firm ground of measurable phenomena for excursions into the subjective." And plenty of those who insist the role of hypothetical individual expectations and preferences in economic analysis is a basic one, themselves engage extensively in the work of analyzing objective economic measurements.

I have used the statistical consumption function as an example of a behavioristic equation. But the class of aggregative equations it illustrates is not yet very large. There are, of course, a considerable number of current input equations in the Leontief model. Also there are the import function (a kind of stepchild of the consumption function); the personal income size distribution pattern (the equation formerly used to state this pattern was called Pareto's Law); and the secular pattern in the functional distribution of national income. There are few others.

These not too stable behavior patterns may be contrasted with another much more stable type of equation that I propose to call conceptual. Conceptual equations do not contain parameters that have been determined as statistical best fits as do behavioristic equations; and most such equations can be applied to future periods with great confidence.

More economists have disparaged conceptual equations than have disparaged the consumption function. It is because they have used the designation "definitional" in this connection to imply tautology that I suggest the substitute word, conceptual. Despite disparagement, conceptual equations are today the mainstay of quantitative economic analysis. And despite the implication of tautology a number of them are not quite true— each of these imperfect equations contains an error term much as does the consumption function. There are three broad classes of conceptual equations: those that assert that a whole equals the sum of its parts; those that assert that product equals multiplicand times multiplier; and those that assert a balance of debits and credits.

The second kind of conceptual equation is used in analyzing a dollar volume time series into a price-index series and a physical volume series. This form of factoring analysis was somewhat widely used in the early 1920's; it was also somewhat widely and seriously abused. With the vast increase in available data and with a better dissemination of the necessary know-how, the use of this kind of quantitative analysis has been greatly extended during the past thirty years, and it has in general been tightened up by far more attention to detail. Abuses have not disappeared; but the grosser ones are now quite generally recognized as such.

Before taking up the other kinds of conceptual equations, let me call attention to an issue—or rather a group of issues— that the increased use of statistics has injected into economics. If these issues can be summed up in a single question it is this, "Which should the quantitative economic analyst emphasize, his models or the complexity and ever changing nature of the world he is investigating?" One of the issues that stems from this question has already been noted, i.e., How fully should the quantitative analyst understand the economic measurements with which he works? Another and deeper one is, Should he devote his efforts to developing and improving a comprehensive model—say one along Keynesian lines, or a Leontief model? Alternatively, should he assume that such a schematic approach would be likely to impose unwise constraints on his inquiries? Or should he take some middle ground? I shall not stop to list other issues that stem from the basic question of what to emphasize in quantitative analysis. Suffice it to say that together they divide the quantitative workers, not into two distinct camps, but rather into something like a spectrum.

Equations that assert the whole equals the sum of its parts make possible an obvious but basic type of economic analysis. Thus one who wants to understand the behavior of a total like the Federal Reserve index of industrial production may wish to resolve it into its various industry components, and may, to bring out some influence at work during a particular period, focus his attention on a specially designed grouping of the components that are sensitive to this influence. Economists who emphasize the complexity and changing nature of their subject are likely to rely heavily on this kind of quantitative analysis, and to feel that preoccupation with a comprehensive model might be a serious handicap when it comes to discovering significant special purpose groupings of components. Equally, those who emphasize models may hold that preoccupation with *ad hoc* component analyses and a detailed historical approach is prejudicial to the discovery of stable economic behavior patterns. Probably both groups are right.

Aggregative debit-credit equations are social accounting equations. Most of the development of this type of equation— and it has been a substantial one—has come in the last thirty years. Hardly anybody has bothered to call either component equations or factor equations tautological. This charge has been directed against the social accounting equations. And the fact that they have been singled out in this way seems to be a tacit recognition of their high theoretical importance.

There are two reasons why a social accounting equation should not be considered a definitional equation. First, every variable in a social accounting equation is either actually or potentially directly measurable, and thus has or can have an operational definition that is independent of the equation.[9] Second, a social accounting equation is significant theoretically because it expresses a significant economic adjustment. Thus the gross savings and investment account (gross S = gross I), against which the charge of tautology has most frequently been brought, reflects the equilibrating of supply and demand in the loan and security markets, although in the form in which it appears in the Department of Commerce national income and product accounts the supply of and demand for funds are not

---

[9] Admittedly when a social accounting equation is used to provide a residual estimate of a variable, it serves *pro tem* as a definitional equation. But this is not its main purpose; indeed its analytical usefulness may well be increased when a direct estimate or measure of the variable is developed.

brought out very clearly.[10] Anyhow it should be obvious that this equation is not merely true by definition; the error term in the 1948 account for the United States was 5 per cent of gross investment.

Because social accounting equations have substantial theoretical significance, the recent rapid growth of social accounting has exerted an important influence on the development of economic thought. Let us consider briefly how.

For one thing, it has helped to correct a formerly somewhat prevalent misconception. Before we had much in the way of social accounting measurements it was frequently supposed that aggregate demand might be less than or greater than gross national product. This misconception took various forms, but I shall cite only one of them, a theory of the cycle that had many adherents in the late '20's. Its authors, Messrs. Foster and Catchings, stated it in terms of what they called "the annual equation" or "balance of output and demand." This is clearly a social accounting equation. But they held, "The year is the shortest period of time within which we may reasonably hope to approach closely to a balance." And, "The annual equation may be upset. As a matter of fact, every recession in business activity is marked by this kind of overproduction or by the fear that it is imminent." [11] With the growth of national income and product statistics and of the practice of assigning these measurements a central place in aggregative analysis, economists have become cautious about suggesting any imbalance in a social account except a statistical discrepancy. Causal hypotheses involving a social accounting imbalance have been largely replaced by causal hypotheses depending on an imbalance in the subjective realm of hypothetical individual plans and expectations.

But the really important influence of social accounting on economic thought has been the constructive one. Before we had much in the way of social accounting measurements,

[10] The writer has discussed this point more fully in *A Study of Moneyflows in the United States*, New York: National Bureau of Economic Research, 1952, especially pp. 246–60.

[11] William Trufant Foster, and Waddill Catchings, *Profits,* New York: Houghton Mifflin Company, 1925, 249–50.

aggregative analysis was rather like a ship without chart and compass. Current business analysis it was called at the time. It lacked a central core of basic concepts around which inquiries could be organized. The available current time series were appraised as business indicators or business barometers; the primary considerations in the appraisal were somewhat mechanically determined properties—cyclical lags and leads and cyclical sensitivity. Various selections of series with approved properties were combined according to various more or less arbitrary formulas into indexes of business activity. During the last 20 years the system of social accounts has come very largely to replace these indexes. Today a major consideration in appraising a time series is its relation to this system—the GNP account and the sector or demand accounts that interlock with it. The system portrays the economic circuit which, at least since the time of Quesnay and Smith, had been recognized as playing a central role in allocating resources and determining the composition and distribution of product in the more industrialized countries. The accounts have added precision to our understanding of the circuit, and they have given us measures of the main component flows of which it consists. Some time series report component flows, and are appraised on the basis of their roles in the circuit. Others, like prices and interest rates, are appraised in terms of the way they influence the circuit flow. Still others, like employment and unemployment, are regarded as resulting from the operation of the circuit. Thus the social accounts have helped to give aggregative economic analysis a sense of direction and a balanced perspective.

Note that I say, "helped"; they have not done this all alone. A statement of an accounting balance is not a mere truism; but it is a rather colorless assertion, even when it asserts a balance of supply and demand. It reports a correlation; it does not, by itself, indicate causation. Aggregative analysis has more of a sense of direction—and a sharper focus, too—than mere statements of accounting balance could impart. This improved direction and focus are to an important extent the results of a wide acceptance of a causal hypothesis proposed by both

Keynes and the Stockholm school—the hypothesis that changes in the level of GNP are brought about mainly by changes in aggregate demand. Thus time series that report components of aggregate demand have a central place in aggregative quantitative analysis, and interpretations of the government account, the S and I account, the rest of the world account, and the personal account are directed toward explaining the behavior of the four major components of aggregate demand—government demand, private domestic investment, net foreign demand, and personal consumption expenditure. Without the social accounts there could be no such interpretations; without the hypothesis of the general primacy of aggregate demand the interpretations would not focus in this way.

Mitchell's forecast suggested that "the men now entering upon careers of research may go far toward establishing economics as a quantitative science." Despite the lingering defects in our statistical specifications and despite the persistence of subjective rationalizations of economic behavior there can be little doubt that the advance in quantitative aggregative analysis that has already taken place represents a long step toward the development of a quantitative economic science. And the period of the forecast still has twelve or fifteen years to run.

Progress has been substantial; but it has also been lopsided. Superficially, at least, microeconomic analysis seems to have been largely immune to the transforming influence of statistics, and empirical explorations of this phase of theory have not been very numerous. It is true something has been done toward developing statistical demand and cost curves; but there was rather more interest in statistical demand curves thirty years ago than there is today. And the most significant development in microeconomic model analysis that has occurred in the past thirty-odd years, that relating to monopolistic competition, has not to date proven very amenable to statistical exploration.

It is tempting to suggest a kind of cumulative disequilibrium theory to explain this lopsidedness. The progress of quantitative empirical analysis in the macroeconomic field seemed to offer a prospect of more progress. Consequently the field attracted those economists who had an aptitude for quantitative analysis, and they neglected the cultivation of microeconomics. To the extent that such a theory has merit—and it seems to fit the declining interest in statistical demand curves—the lopsidedness is a defect that time should help to cure, perhaps is already in process of curing.

But this is probably only a partial explanation of the lopsidedness. The push to divide economic theory along the macro-micro line came from persons interested in macroeconomics. The division facilitated work in macroeconomics; it was in some ways awkward for the microeconomist. His concern is presumably with the various parts of the economy rather than the whole. But most of these parts had long before been assigned to various special fields, e.g., labor problems, agriculture, transportation and public utilities, private finance, industrial combination and competition. And the effective application of quantitative analysis to a particular microeconomic problem is likely to call for detailed familiarity with one of these special fields. The bulk of the statistical work on microeconomic problems that has been done during the last three decades has been done by workers in the special fields. Certainly the result has been a substantial improvement in our understanding of the several parts of the economy, but the accomplishment here is a piecemeal affair that consists of a multitude of scattered bits of new knowledge. The cobweb theorem and the Federal Reserve elements analysis are striking, though hardly typical examples. It would be difficult to give a reasonable summary characterization of what has been accomplished, and I shall not attempt one. But it seems fair to say that the many scattered bits do not yet add up to a radical change comparable to that in macroeconomics.

These comments, so far as they go, attribute the contrast between macroeconomic and microeconomic quantitative analysis to influences that derive from the existing division of academic labor. But I suspect the contrast is due partly, too, to subject matter. In the macroeconomic field a problem has been singled out that is peculiarly amenable to statistical investigation, the problem of quarter-to-quarter and year-to-year changes in aggregate demand. The question is, "How do you account for the cyclical behavior of this aggregate quantity?" And a very large part of the answer can apparently be given in terms of the behavior of other economic variables, i.e., in quantitative terms. A very large part of the answer, but not all of it. Qualitative factors, such as technological or legal changes, often have to be taken into account. Still I think the fact that workers could afford to rely heavily on quantitative analysis in investigating business cycles has been a highly significant contributing circumstance in the progress this type of analysis has made. And since the progress has been lopsided, it is pertinent that the circumstances are lopsided, too. In the microeconomic field qualitative factors loom much larger. Witness the amount of time a specialist in labor, in railroads, in banking, or industrial combination and competition devotes to a study of the law as it impinges on his field. If the progress of micro-quantitative analysis has not been very spectacular, it is partly because many of the problems of the special fields of economics do not lend themselves to a predominantly quantitative approach.

Mitchell's address was primarily a forecast of the development of objective quantitative analysis. But he took care to emphasize the complementary relationship between qualitative institutional analysis and quantitative analysis and the bearing of both on questions of policy and economic welfare. He said in part, "quantitative work cannot dispense with distinctions of quality. . . . Indeed qualitative work itself will gain in power, scope and interest as we make use of . . . more reliable measurements." Out of "quantitative economics . . . we may expect to come a close scrutiny of our pecuniary institutions and our efficiency in producing and distributing goods. . . . Economists will concentrate . . . to an increasing degree upon economic institutions. . . . Quantitative analysis promises . . . to increase the range of objective criteria by which we judge economic welfare."

This portion of his forecast, to date at least, seems to have been wrong. During the first third of the twentieth century economic theorists did a large amount of valuable work on the qualitative analysis of pecuniary and other economic institutions and their significance for economic welfare, but there has been very little of this type of inquiry since the appearance of Keynes's *General Theory*. True, a good deal has been accomplished in detail in the special fields, but statistics do not appear to have contributed any special impetus to the accomplishment. And in the field of theory they have, if anything, helped to divert attention from qualitative, institutional inquiries.

Recently, however, the outlook for this type of work has brightened. We now have a new division of academic-economic labor. An increasing number of economists are concentrating their efforts on the problems of economic development and on comparing the institutional structures of different economies. In this area of research the complementary relationship between qualitative, institutional analysis and quantitative analysis is particularly close. It is too early yet to appraise the impact of statistical measurements here for we are only beginning to assemble a stock of this kind of information, and the field is still very new. But its problems clearly call for a balanced combination of qualitative and quantitative analysis, and this combination may some day have important repercussions on general economic theory. Quite possibly there are to be found here the makings of a delayed response to the statistical stimulus somewhat along the lines Mitchell visualized.[12] Certainly he was right when he said "qualitative analysis . . . cannot be dispensed with."

[12] Cf. comment by Evsey D. Domar, "Methodological Developments" in *A Survey of Contemporary Economics*, Vol. II, New York: 1952, 455.

TOWARD BETTER

MEASUREMENT AND TESTING

· VI ·

The Equation of Exchange: An Empirical Analysis

(1929)

A

Money, Trade, and Prices—A Test of Causal Primacy *

THE relation between changes in the quantity of currency in circulation and general rises or falls of prices is, as Fisher's equation of exchange makes clear, complicated by fluctuations in the rate of circulation or velocity of currency and in the physical volume of trade. Many hypotheses which attempt to state the relation between currency and prices have been formulated in terms of Fisher's equation in order to take account of these complications. Among them, two important conflicting hypotheses have been selected for study here. The present paper aims to test these two hypotheses empirically, using for the purpose the results of a statistical inquiry published elsewhere.[1] It is hoped that the tests will throw valuable light on the fundamental question—the relations of currency, velocity, trade, and prices.

---

* Substantially condensed; detailed empirical discussion omitted.

[1] Monthly indices for the principal items in the equation of exchange for the United States from 1919 to 1927 were presented in the *Journal of the American Statistical Association*, June, 1929. [Extracts from this paper are presented in part B.—EDITOR.]

The limitations of the available information have required certain modifications in the equation as formulated by Fisher. The new form of the equation is $MV = k(PT + R)$. MV and M'V' of Fisher's equation (cash and check payments) have been combined, because it is not possible to separate payments by check and cash withdrawn from banks (which reflects cash payments) in the data now existing. M (cash and checking accounts) = Fisher's M + M', while V (velocity) is a species of average of his V and V'. And k is an arbitrary constant and equals one, when both MV and (PT + R) are expressed as relatives to 1919 as 100 per cent. R represents obligations incurred to make money payments which cannot be conveniently expressed as "p" $\times$ "t" (price $\times$ volume of trade). R includes interest, dividend, and tax payments, etc. MV, T, and R all represent volumes per working day per month.

Neglecting R for the moment, we may say that the relations between P (conceived as an average of prices) and M are complicated by V and T. Fisher sought to eliminate these complications [2] by resort to a concept of normal value for the complicating factors. Since he does not define "normal" empirically, his theory of the causal primacy of M does not seem to be an hypothesis capable of statistical test.

Perhaps the most plausible empirical argument for the causal primacy of M is that advanced by Holbrook Working. He holds that for purposes of the business cycle the average of the prices charged during any month, P, is a passive factor. Cyclical fluctuations in P are caused chiefly by changes in the quantity of currency, M, in circulation during that or preceding months.

Changes in the [physical] volume of transactions between periods of prosperity and periods of depression are approximately provided for by changes in the velocity of circulation. . . . Changes in the volume [of currency] . . . act upon the price level . . . without substantial interference from the changing physical volume of transactions.[3]

---

[2] Also that of the ratio of M to gold in monetary uses.

[3] H. Working, *Review of Economic Statistics*, viii, 131. Working says "volume

W. C. Mitchell has taken an opposite position. According to his view, the relation between changes in P as an average of prices, and changes in the quantity of currency in circulation, M, is considered in connection with changes in the volume of trade, T, and changes in velocity, V.

Most of the time, P and T are the "active factors" in the equation of exchange. . . . Modern monetary and banking systems provide a considerable measure of elasticity. . . . But when the pecuniary volume of trade [i.e. PT + R] has reached limits which tax MV . . . monetary and banking factors assume the "active" role, and force a reduction in PT.[4]

The first of these writers would break the equation of exchange up into two parts for cyclical purposes, and consider P as a function of M in isolation from T and V; the second would consider the equation as a whole. The first finds the causal primacy with M, for cyclical purposes; the second regards P and T as "active factors" most of the time—for seasonal and cyclical purposes. It would seem that both of these hypotheses cannot be correct *in toto*. At least one of them requires modification. Can we find help in this issue in economic theory by having recourse to the facts?

In selecting these hypotheses for test it is not intended to imply that they exhaust the possibilities of the situation. They have been selected partly as representing opposed views regarding causal priority within the equation, partly as conforming to that important canon for scientific hypotheses that they should be so formulated as to be capable of empirical test. It remains possible of course that, whatever appears regarding questions of causal priority as between the MV and PT sides of the equation, both sides may be "caused" by some condition antecedent to both. Moreover, neither of the hypotheses has direct reference to trends; only the shorter-time movements are included. It must be admitted, to be sure, that something

of bank credit" instead of volume of currency; but his statistical data on this factor are demand deposits, and he treats deposits as the proximately causal factor.

[4] W. C. Mitchell, *Business Cycles* (1927), p. 137. Mitchell's statement does not include R as a separate item.

of a problem may be raised for one who would find a causal sequence for trends contrary to that which appears to hold for shorter-time fluctuations.[5]

Working, in support of his hypothesis which deals with M and P in isolation and regards M as causal for cyclical movements, makes two important points. (1) The cyclical fluctuations of T and V are very similar and practically offset one another, and (2) the cyclical fluctuations of P tend on the whole to lag behind those of M. The second point, regarding the lag of P behind M, has not been fully tested. The P used by Working was wholesale prices, and the M did not include hand-to-hand cash. For the recent period, which is the only period for which monthly data are available, net demand deposits were not corrected by Working to agree with demand deposits at dates of call.

Before drawing general conclusions it should be noted that there are three important qualifications to which conclusions based on the material here considered are subject.* (a) They are limited to 1919–27 and to this country; even tho the analysis which has been employed here may prove useful elsewhere, and may have disclosed relations which must be reckoned with

[5] Mitchell suggests a possible reconciliation of his view of the causal primacy of P and T for short-time movements with the proposition that the annual output of gold has "a dominant influence upon the secular trends of wholesale prices, and seemingly some influence upon . . . trade."—Op. cit., p. 138. He assumes that "over long periods of time, prices and the physical volume of trade have tended to expand up to" the limits which the gold supply imposes on MV. It may well be doubted whether the downward trend of wholesale prices during the mechanical changes and geographical expansion of the nineteenth century accords with such a view. Moreover, it is difficult to hold that for the problem of long-period relations "the proposition 'other things being equal, prices vary as the quantity of money in circulation' is both valid and important," and at the same time give due emphasis to V and T as complicating factors. And it is a fair question whether the trend of the pecuniary volume of transactions, $PT + R$, may not have been a significant factor in changes in our monetary and banking systems. Was the decline in P in the nineteenth century connected with the fact that during this period silver was ceasing to be a part of the supply of the standard money metal in important countries? Or were the damping effects on business of the inelastic MV in the United States, 1909–1913, an "active factor" in promoting the agitation for banking reform which led to the establishment of the Federal Reserve system, with its lower reserve requirements?

* Statistical material omitted here.

in dealing with other times and countries. (*b*) Because of the incompleteness of our information, the conclusions are necessarily tentative. (*c*) They have reference primarily to seasonal and cyclical movements. Subject to these qualifications the following conclusions based on the analysis of this nine-year period are offered.

(1) It is possible to state the equation of exchange in such a form that it will be true by definition. But in this form it is practically useless as a means of studying the relation between currency, velocity, trade, and prices. But if the equation of exchange is stated as $MV = kPT$, where MV and PT are empirically determinable magnitudes and where P refers to market prices and T to deliveries, it is hardly too much to say that the equation is measurably false in two [6] important respects:

(*a*) It omits a very large volume of transactions, R, — interest, dividend and tax payments, etc. Both the seasonal and cyclical fluctuations of $PT + R$ appear to differ significantly from those of PT. R is a factor which complicates the problem of relating P and M quite as truly as T and V, and its effects are too important to be overlooked. We cannot assume that $P = \dfrac{MV}{T}$. The equation should be written $MV = k(PT + R)$.[7]

(*b*) The equation of exchange, even when R is included, is probably not precisely true on a monthly basis. On the whole the indices of MV and $PT + R$ are fairly consistent with the view that P, T, and MV do not refer to the same dates—that a part of $PT + R$ leads MV appreciably in some of the seasonal and some of the cyclical movements, while another part of $PT + R$ is approximately synchronous.

(2) Working's hypothesis appears difficult to reconcile with the facts. It does not take account of R as a complicating factor. P sometimes appears to lead M. And the cyclical movements

---

[6] There are other qualifications which may be added: transactions settled by offset and defaulted liabilities falling due need to be subtracted from $PT + R$. The first is difficult to measure; the second is of negligible importance in the total.

[7] Where $k = 1$, it may be more convenient to write the equation for some purposes $MV - R = PT$. But this does not make R any less a complicating factor in the relation of M to P.

of T and V do not entirely offset each other; even for cyclical movements it is dangerous to break up the equation so as to treat M and P in isolation. The indices based on existing information would have to be grossly in error, if this hypothesis were true. Moreover, it is open to the theoretical objection that, even if R, T, and V could be neglected for cyclical purposes, so that M acts on P without substantial interference, we should have to assume a cyclical lead of T/V with respect to M in order to account for a consistent cyclical lead of M with respect to P.

Incidentally it may be noted that in dealing with the problem of measuring the items in the equation of exchange empirically, there were disclosed two further difficulties in breaking up the equation so as to find a direct relation between currency and prices.[8] MV and PT + R constitute two separately and independently measurable magnitudes. But on the basis of Fisher's ideal formula, P and T cannot be measured independently of each other or of an index of PT. Again the distinction between deposit currency (which is most of M) on the one hand, and time deposits and other very liquid assets such as securities and loans on call, on the other hand, is arbitrary. Moreover, business practice with regard to these different forms of "cash" has been undergoing considerable change of late. Any index of M in recent years contains an arbitrary trend. Neither M nor P is a clearly definable, independent empirical quantity. In the case of P the objection can perhaps be set aside—in the case of M it clearly cannot be neglected.

(3) The second hypothesis states that most of the time PT + R, obligations incurred to make money payments, are causally prior to MV, the fulfillment of those obligations, and that MV is elastic and passive except when stretched to the limit. According to this theory we should expect the monthly index of PT + R either to lead that of MV, or possibly (where the actual lead is a fraction of a month) to be synchronous with MV. The typical seasonal variations of MV and PT + R are in agreement with this theory. And while there are in the cyclical movements some appreciable discrepancies with the

---

[8] See *Journal American Statistical Association,* as cited, p. 113 and p. 116.

theory, the agreement is probably as good here as could fairly be expected from the rough data available. Present information about the movements of money, velocity, and the dollar volume of transactions is more nearly consonant with the second hypothesis, which attributes causal priority most of the time to the dollar volume of transactions.

B

Special Purpose Indexes for the Equation of Exchange for the United States, 1919–1927 *

Attempts to test statistically an hypothesis regarding the causal relations between the quantity of currency in circulation and changes in the general level of prices necessarily presuppose a fairly accurate estimate of the principal items in the equation of exchange by months. Yearly figures offer a partial validation of Fisher's general analysis, but they do not enable us to investigate the lags among the items in his equation which are of chief significance for disclosing their causal relations. Figures for deposit currency and "the price level" alone do not afford an adequate basis for such statistical analysis, as Working appears to have argued.[1] It is quite possible, for example for P, "the price level," to lag behind M', deposit currency, and at the same time for $M'V'$, check payments, to lag behind PT, the dollar volume of transactions. If this should turn out to be the case, the causal significance of a lead of M' over P is certainly considerably different from what it would be if $M'V'$, check payments, and PT should turn out to be synchronous, or if $M'V'$ should lead PT.

The recent development of statistical information in this country has made possible the construction of monthly indexes for "the price level" and "the physical volume of trade" for a period which is sufficient to yield results of some significance. These materials have been organized by Snyder to give

* Substantially condensed; statistical tables and detailed methodological explanation omitted.
[1] Holbrook Working, *Quarterly Journal of Economics,* Vol. 37, pp. 229–257; *Review of Economic Statistics,* Vol. 7, pp. 120–133.

an estimate of the changes in "the general level of prices" by months since 1913,[2] and of "the physical volume of trade" by months since 1919.[3] Snyder's indexes, combined with the available data on bank debits and net demand deposits of reporting member banks and of cash in circulation, have supplied us with monthly estimates for the principal items in Fisher's equation since 1919, which place that analysis on a definite factual basis and have thrown valuable light on the cyclical relationships of the several items.

But when one attempts to use Snyder's indexes for a detailed study of lags and leads in the equation of exchange, a number of difficulties appear. Snyder's indexes are general purpose indexes, and it is an old story that general purpose indexes fit any particular problem badly. As a measure of changes in the physical volume of trade with the business cycle Snyder's trade index has many advantages over other indexes of general business, but the very characteristics which make it peculiarly adapted to this purpose are in some respects drawbacks for the purpose of estimating T as an item in the equation of exchange. Snyder's index is a weighted average of relatives to trend with all the prominent seasonal variations eliminated. It thus shows only cyclical and sporadic fluctuations of T. But for a study of the time lags among the items in the equation of exchange, it is highly important to know the seasonal variations. Again, the elimination of trends from the constituent series facilitates the use of a series like chain grocery sales as an index of the retail grocery trade (since the two may be presumed to differ chiefly in trend). But some measurement of the trend of T, made independently of any consideration of the trend of bank debits, is needed for comparing PT with $MV + M'V'$ if we are adequately to check the accuracy of the P and T indexes. Furthermore, while the index of trade, as a measure of the business cycle, is probably improved by the inclusion of deflated bank debits, it is clear that such a series should not be

[2] Carl Snyder, "The Measure of the General Price Level," *Review of Economic Statistics*, February, 1928. (The original index goes back to 1875.)

[3] Carl Snyder, "The Index of the Volume of Trade: Second Revision," *Journal of the American Statistical Association*, June, 1928. Vol. XXIII, p. 154 *et seq.*

included in an estimate of T as an item in the equation of exchange for two reasons: (1) Bank debits are a fairly accurate measure of $M'V'$. They are clearly not one of the special groups of "pt's" that go to make up PT (or $\Sigma\ pt$). (2) In order to include debits in T it is necessary, because they represent no special group, to deflate them with a general index of prices. Thus an important element in Snyder's T is not determined from empirical data independently of the other items in the equation of exchange but as $\dfrac{M'V'}{P}$. This element has a weight of 12 per cent. New Capital flotations, as a constituent T series with a weight of 2 per cent in Snyder's index, are also subject to the objection that they have been deflated by P. Both Snyder's trade index and his index of the general price level are, for purposes of their specific use in the equation of exchange, open to certain criticisms of weighting. And finally, indexes of P and T alone, for reasons that will presently be noted, give an incomplete picture of the so-called "goods side" of the equation.

Certainly none of these points is intended as a criticism of Snyder's indexes as general purpose indexes. But it has seemed desirable, in view of the difficulties in his indexes for the specific purpose in hand, to construct a new set of special purpose indexes upon which a study of the lags and leads in the equation of exchange can be based. The present paper aims to set forth these new indexes, including certain corrected indexes for the so-called money side of the equation.

It has often been said that the equation of exchange is a tautology. If the equation is stated, "the quantity of cash disbursed in any period in discharge of financial obligations = the value of financial obligations discharged in that period," it may be said to be a tautology. But when one substitutes $\Sigma\ pt$ for "value of financial obligations discharged," where "t" means number of units of a good purchased during the period and "p" the average market price charged for the good, the second part of the equation refers more nearly to "obligations incurred to make money payments" than to "obligations discharged." In this form the two sides of the equation are separate, empirically determinable magnitudes, and it even becomes a pertinent question whether the equation is precisely true.

Let us consider first the problems of measurement involved in the "obligations discharged" side of the equation. It has been customary to represent this as $MV + M'V'$, where MV refers to cash payments and $M'V'$ refers to payments by check. The chief source of information on this side of the equation is "debits to individual accounts" in 141 centers. These include approximately 80 per cent of all such debits [4] in the United States. A debit to an individual account may arise from (1) a payment by check; (2) the withdrawal of cash from a bank (either from a time or a demand account); (3) a withdrawal from a time account for immediate transfer to a demand account. Fisher has estimated that a dollar withdrawn from a bank makes on the average less than two payments before it is redeposited. Apparently, then, the debits data include a large proportion of cash payments (slightly in advance of their actual occurrence) as well as payments by check. They also include under item (3) certain debits which do not properly fall either under MV or $M'V'$—debits which are merely changes from one form of deposit to another. To include them and then to include also the checks drawn on the demand deposits so created would be to count these cash disbursements twice.

Because our present information does not enable us to separate accurately on a monthly basis what Fisher called MV from what he called $M'V'$, we will use only the one set of symbols MV for the left-hand member of the equation, as representing all cash disbursements. But we may correct the monthly debits series by more accurate annual estimates to meet the difficulties that have just been noted.

We may consider next the problem of measurement of the dollar volume of obligations incurred to make money payments. Theoretically these data may be compiled on either of two bases: (1) as obligations of business enterprises or other parties, incurred to make money payments, and (2) as claims to receive money payments acquired by the prospective recipients. Actu-

---

[4] See the writer's estimate, *Journal of the American Statistical Association*, September, 1928, p. 303.

ally most of our figures are from the point of view of the prospective payee, representing either cash receipts or additions to his "receivables." If we had complete figures on this basis it would be desirable, in order to avoid double counting, not to include any figures for cash disbursements or additions to "payables." In estimating PT for a single country like the United States, therefore, we should include merchandise and invisible imports as representing sales of foreign exchange, and so receipts of the foreign exchange bankers, but theoretically we should not include exports as a separate item, since these would all appear as sales of commodities, securities, services, etc.[5] As a matter of fact, figures on trade are so incomplete as to make it desirable to include merchandise exports in the monthly indexes, and probably also government disbursements.

In order to determine the importance of the several available monthly series for purposes of assigning weights, and in order to appraise the reliability of an index based on data now available, it is desirable to know approximately the annual dollar volume of money payments to which each main class of transactions gives rise. Crude estimates of this sort have been made for 1919 and 1921. These estimates bring out several important points:

1. Financial transactions are of outstanding importance. The following groups of transactions probably amounted to two hundred billion dollars, or over 30 per cent of the total of cash disbursements in 1919 (about six hundred billion dollars) —short-time loans, resales and repayments, capital flotations and retirements, stock exchange and over-the-counter security sales, commodity exchange transactions, time deposits, foreign exchange sold, interest and dividend payments.

2. Not all obligations to make money payments arise from the sale of a specifiable physical volume of goods or services at a specifiable price. Most taxes and charity subscriptions fit this formula badly. The flotation of a new stock issue involves a sale, but practically it seems hardly feasible to find two time

---

[5] This seems a more logical view than one half (exports + imports), the one Fisher states in *Purchasing Power of Money*, 2d ed., p. 483, especially since he clearly distinguishes the two bases of compilation on p. 373.

series, one to represent prices and one physical volume of sales of new securities. Again, the making of a loan and the payment of interest and principal are not easily to be treated as a "p" × a "t." And there are a number of other transactions that are at least equally difficult to treat as a "p" × a "t." The following items probably amounted to at least two hundred billion dollars in 1919, or over 30 per cent of the total MV—short-time loans, resales and repayments, payments from one checking account to another held by the same depositor, capital flotations and retirements, time deposits made, taxes, insurance premiums and benefits, interest and dividend payments, reimbursements of agents for expenses incurred, cash gifts, receipts of churches and clubs. In view of the importance of these transactions it seems necessary to include them in our indexes for the right-hand side of the equation. We shall designate this general group of transactions R, and write the equation $MV = k(PT + R)$.[6] And our problem is enlarged to include the construction of an index of $PT + R$.

The indexes which are available for the various groups of transactions may be in the form of "p's," "t's," or pt's," a price series, a physical volume series, or a dollar volume series. Any two of these three, referring to the same set of transactions, will suffice. But in a number of cases either only one is available or if two are available, they refer to two partly overlapping but not quite identical groups of transactions. A "t" for real estate sales is available (for 41 cities), but no satisfactory corresponding "p" or "pt." For house rents we have a "p" but no corresponding monthly "pt" or "t." In the case of manufacturing revenues we have a "t" (output) and can adapt existing "p" indexes to represent a manufacturing "p." Moreover, we can correct the resulting "pt's" biennially by the census figures. Wherever a "p," a "t," and a "pt" series were available such a correction has been made in the series employed in the P, T, and $PT + R$ indexes. And more accurate annual data have, so far as possible, been used to correct the monthly figures. The constituent series employed, then, consist of corresponding "p's," "t's," and "pt's,"

---

[6] The k is an arbitrary constant. It enables us to express the right-hand member in index number form on any desired base.

such that for each set "*p*" × "*t*" = "*pt*," and such that the annual averages of the monthly "*p*'s," "*t*'s," or "*pt*'s" agree with corresponding annual data.

In constructing the indexes an approximation to Fisher's ideal formula has been used. This means that the basic index is the $PT + R$ index. This is a weighted average of relatives to 1919, with the weights based on the 1919 dollar volume estimates. Since the monthly data have been corrected by annual figures, this index is not materially affected by the choice of 1919 as a weight-base year.[7] The construction of the P and T indexes is based on the PT constituent of the $PT + R$ index. So-called aggregative indexes of P and of T are first constructed, using the nine-year averages of the "*pt*'s," "*t*'s," and "*p*'s" as basic. The resulting preliminary indexes of P and T are then adjusted to make $P \times T$ equal the PT constituent of the $PT + R$ index. The dependence of the P and T indexes upon the $PT + R$ index and upon each other, both in determining the weights for the preliminary indexes and in making the corrections, raises an interesting theoretical question: It is clearly proper to speak of $PT + R$ as an independent empirical quantity, but is it proper to speak of either P or T as independent? Are they not rather interdependent?

[7] If W represents any *pt* or *r* and the year is indicated by the subscript, we have

$$^b(PT + R)_x = \frac{\sum W_b \frac{(W_x)}{(W_b)}}{\Sigma W_b}$$

where b indicates the base year. In other words,

$$^b(PT + R)_x \times {}^x(PT + R)_y = {}^b(PT + R)_y \text{ and } {}^b(PT + R)_x = {}_x(PT + R)b^{-1}.$$

Both the time-reversal and base-shift tests are satisfied. The factor reversal test, of course, does not apply.

· VII ·

The Capital Budget and the War Effort[*]

(1943)

THE term "capital budget" stands in contrast to "annual budget." The one suggests long-range fiscal planning and the other short-range fiscal planning.

Our present federal budget system emphasizes the short-range type of planning. Although the system is not much more than twenty years old, capital budgeting has been under discussion for some time. Short-range fiscal planning is a logical first step to longer-range planning.

There is a sense, however, in which short-range and long-range planning are opposed. Professor F. R. Fairchild, writing in *The American Economic Review* for June 1941, says, "Budgetary *theory implies* that the *entire financial program,* including all expenditures and all revenues, shall be embraced in the *annual* budget." [1] Those who, like Professor Fairchild, emphasize the annual aspect of budgeting or fiscal planning are apt to feel antipathy to certain aspects of long-range planning. The reason is not far to seek. If it be held that the basic fiscal period for which we should seek a balance of the budget is not a year but, say, five years, or the period of the business cycle (if

[*] Somewhat condensed.
[1] P. 284. Italics added.

that can be sufficiently precisely determined), then, it will be held presumably that, if we go into debt during a part of this longer fiscal period and get out later, the budget is not out of balance during the period. From this longer-term point of view, borrowing to meet current expenses during any one year is to be regarded as "budget borrowing." But from the annual point of view such borrowing clearly involves budgetary unbalance.

The emphasis which Professor Fairchild places upon the annual aspects of fiscal planning leads him to object to so-called permanent appropriations as hampering the development of a "single unified plan" of federal finance for each year. In spite of his implication that there are many important instances of obnoxious permanent appropriations, the principal instance of this type of appropriation having the features to which he objects is an appropriation representing a certain percentage of customs revenue and amounting to about 140 million dollars this year (fiscal 1943).

If all appropriations be put on a fiscal year basis in order that the "entire financial program" may be "embraced in the annual budget," the permanent appropriation device is not the only device useful in long-range budgeting which is likely to be questioned. Appropriations which may be obligated over a period substantially longer than the fiscal year are clearly needed for long-range fiscal planning. Such appropriations or their equivalent have been an urgent necessity in connection with our war effort. The First Defense Aid appropriation applied to a biennium. There has also been extensive use made of "no year" appropriations.

Whatever may be said against the school of thought which emphasizes an annual basis for fiscal planning, there is one strong point in its favor: it has grasped the simple truth that, if we are to achieve budgetary balance over a period of years, we need to assume responsibility for budgetary balance in each separate year. If one can always put off the task of achieving budgetary balance until some indefinite future date, budgetary balance is extremely unlikely ever to be achieved. When a rule can be relaxed under many special circumstances, special circumstances are likely to become the rule.

On the other side of the picture it may be said that it is widely held today that there are two major functions of the federal government which are incompatible with fiscal planning on an exclusively annual basis. (1) The encouragement of the smooth functioning of our economy and the relief of persons unemployed when that economy does not function smoothly have come to be recognized as major functions of our federal government. To any one who accepts the relief and moderation of business depressions as a federal function, it is clear that budget balancing on an annual basis is entirely impracticable. (2) The provision of national defense is a universally recognized federal function. Although most economists today urge greatly increased taxation, there are few who believe that a complete pay-as-you-go policy is compatible with a maximum war effort.

Our inquiry thus far has revealed various conditions to which a long-range fiscal plan should conform. It will be well to recapitulate these conditions at this point:

1. It should be possible to make long-term commitments.

2. Without deviating from the fiscal plan it should be possible during any short period, such as a year, either for expenditures to exceed revenues or for revenues to exceed expenditures.

3. A satisfactory fiscal plan must provide for a very great increase in cash expenditures during a war emergency or during a business recession, an increase not limited by any necessary relation to increased revenues during the same period. Particularly during a business recession it should be possible to expand expenditures more, and more quickly, than they can readily be expanded under present arrangements. The plan should also provide for the prompt contraction of expenditures as soon as the need for large expenditure has ceased.

4. On the other hand, the plan should be so constructed that for each separate year it is perfectly clear whether or not the plan has been fully adhered to.

5. A satisfactory fiscal plan should provide for a prompt increase in taxes levied during periods of business expansion; *i.e.*, taxes should be allocated as between peacetime years on

the basis of the year-to-year variations in our ability to pay them.

It would seem that developments thus far in the direction of long-range fiscal planning have involved modifications in our federal annual budgetary procedure which are in the nature of relaxations. We have made marked progress in the techniques of long-range planning of public works. And since June 1940, we have developed something that begins to resemble a production budget system for a very large part of our economy, a system that looks more than a year into the future. Nonetheless, the restraints appropriate to fiscal planning merely on an annual basis have been seriously weakened. No restraints appropriate to longer-range fiscal planning have been put in their place. We have cast aside the fiscal guide line of an annual balance between revenue and cash expenditure. Clearly, to recognize defense and the promotion of economic stability as federal functions is to reject such a standard for fiscal policy. But we have not developed a substitute. We have today no objective standard of fiscal policy by which to judge the relationship between revenue and expenditure.

Seen in this light, the relaxation of restraints which has been associated with the capital budget idea in the sense of a *dual* budget represents a transition stage. If we omit the word "annual," surely Professor Fairchild is right in insisting that budgetary theory implies a comprehensive, *unified* financial program.[2]

It was suggested above that long-range planning might mean balancing the budget at regular intervals of more than a year in length. Unfortunately the contingencies for which we need to plan occur at intervals longer than a year, intervals which are

[2] Professor Hansen, in his book entitled, *Fiscal Policy and Business Cycles* (New York: Norton, 1941), p. 201, holds that, "Double budget accounting requires that the operating budget must carry year-to-year losses or write-offs sustained by governmental corporations or subsidiaries, together with depreciation and interest charges for nonremunerative capital projects." It will be argued below that the inclusion of write-offs, depreciation, and all similar items has the effect of unifying the financial program. It would seem better to apply the term "double budget" only where such a unifying arrangement is either absent or incomplete.

In any case it should be noted that a proper interpretation of the word "unify" does not require that the General Fund shall be the only fund.

definitely irregular. The restraints that are needed should apply annually.

The term "capital budget" as applied to federal finance is suggestive not only of a long-range planning but also of the application of business methods to government. We may fairly ask, Can we by examining business methods find suggestions for restraints which meet these requirements and which are appropriate to long-range fiscal planning? Can we discover procedures which will satisfy our five conditions? It will be argued below that we can, provided proper adaptations are made. Indeed, in various ways, business methods have already been experimented with in government. Among these experiments may be cited the arrangement under which the Defense Plant Corporation advances funds for new facilities, and is subsequently reimbursed from the Treasury General Fund over a five-year period. Provision is thus made for writing off a capital expenditure over a five-year period.

Glossing over irrelevant details, we may summarize the financial and accounting devices employed by business which seem especially pertinent in the present connection as follows:

1. All cash expenditures are classified under one or the other of two heads, current and capital. The particular rules which bring about this classification are not of direct present concern. What is significant is that, in spite of marginal items, a sharp line is drawn.

2. Only a capital expenditure can be assigned against accounting periods other than the period in which it is incurred; and the assignment of any such expenditure must follow a rule adopted either in advance of the time when the expenditure is incurred or at the time when it is incurred. Again, for our present purpose, it is less important to know what rule is adopted for distributing a capital expenditure among various accounting periods than to know that some rule must be adopted at or before the time when the expenditure is incurred.

3. An objective standard of financial policy is provided. If we may oversimplify a bit, we may say that, to accord with this standard, the revenues in any accounting period should equal or exceed the sum of two items: (a) the current cash expendi-

tures of that accounting period, and (b) the portions of the capital expenditures of all periods which have been assigned to that accounting period.

Can these three business practices be advantageously applied to our federal financial system? As steps toward an affirmative answer to this question it will be well to consider a possible objection and a possible misconception. The objection is that government expenditures are different from business expenditures and so do not lend themselves to the same sort of treatment. The misconception is that an improper delegation of legislative function to the executive may be involved.

First let us consider the objection: Are government expenditures badly adapted to the sort of treatment involved? Can they well be classified, before they are incurred, as either capital or current? Can a plan for apportioning a capital expenditure among accounting periods be advantageously adopted at or before the time the expenditure is incurred? The difficulty commonly alleged is that in the case of private business (but not in government) a capital expenditure is typically for the acquisition of a wasting asset, and that the expected wasting and retirement of the asset suggest the plan for allocating the expenditure among accounting periods. But so far as concerns the identification before they are incurred of those expenditures which are to be allocated among accounting periods, and so far as concerns the advance planning of their allocation, government and business would appear to be in the same general situation. There is no reason to suppose that identification of capital items and advance planning of the method of apportioning them by years are either more difficult or less desirable simply because one particular pattern for the planning is less often available.

Second, let us look at the misconception: Does the application of the three business practices we have singled out involve an improper delegation of legislative function to the executive? All that it is intended to propose here is a change in the language of appropriation acts and in the methods of keeping records. It is suggested that those appropriations which are for capital expenditures be identified as such, and that, except where such expenditures are for investment in self-liquidating assets, they be regarded as deferred charges to be written off in subsequent years and the plan of allocation of the accounting charges recording such deferred expenditures be specified in the appropriation act or at any rate determined at the time of appropriation. In order to avoid any implication that these items which are to be written off are necessarily related to tangible assets, it may be well to call them "deferred charges." It would probably be wise to have a statutory definition of such deferred items, the executive being directed to follow this definition in presenting estimates and to assume the burden of proof in classifying any estimate as a deferred item. Presumably an item to be classed as deferred (1) should not be recurrent annually or more frequently and (2) should be large, or part of a large program, such as a works and relief program during a depression or the defense effort begun in 1940. Indeed the statutory definition of deferred expenditure items might confine such items to these two types of program: (1) a public works and relief program during a business recession or depression, and (2) such part of a war, defense, or reconstruction effort as it is not feasible to finance through current taxes.[3]

As a result of these two simple changes in appropriation procedure—the identification of items as either current or capital and the fixing of the write-off plan for deferred items before appropriation—we would have an objective standard by which to judge the relationship between revenues and expenditures. We would know in a real sense, instead of in the present unreal and nominal sense, whether our budget was in balance. There would be a moral force in favor of maintaining a balance, but only a moral force. That moral force would be far better directed than the badly crippled moral force that operates today for a nominal but unreal balance.

Let us turn now to the question: If the three business prac-

---

[3] It would not greatly complicate the definition to give expenditures for tangible durable goods a place in it. There are advantages in so doing, especially in the case of public utility type investments. However, it is far more urgent to treat as capital expenditures the two main types of program listed above.

tices singled out above are applied to federal finance, will we have made material progress toward meeting the five conditions for long-range fiscal planning outlined above?

1. If these three business practices are applied, will commitments for a period longer than a year be permitted? Clearly, these practices would not in themselves remove present restrictions on long-term commitments. However, if restraints appropriate to longer-range planning are provided, the need for retaining restrictions appropriate to annual budgeting would be largely removed. We might expect appropriations for a two-year period—or possibly a longer period—to become more frequent, and devices such as the contract authorization to be dropped.

2. If these practices are applied, will it be possible for total cash expenditures during any short period either to exceed or to be less than revenues? Since revenues will be compared with the sum of (a) cash expenditures on current account and (b) portions of the deferred expenditure items incurred during a number of years, it is clear that the answer to this question is Yes.

3. If these three business practices are applied to federal finance, will there be substantially greater flexibility in expanding or contracting the volume of outlays classified as deferred than there is under present arrangements? So far as a national defense or war emergency goes, the present moral restraints on a great and rapid expansion of expenditures are but weakly operative. In dealing with a depression emergency these restraints have undoubtedly substantially helped to retard expansion of federal works and relief expenditures. The substitution of a new fiscal standard for the unworkable present one of an annual balance of cash expenditures and revenues would help materially to remove the moral pressure which prevails under present procedures, against a quick large expansion of public works and relief expenditures. On the other hand, if a definite day of reckoning must be agreed upon when deferred expenditures are authorized, and if that day is not too far off, the pressure for contraction of deferred expenditures, when the emergency is

passed, would be greater than it is under the present arrangement which permits us thoughtlessly to relegate the day of
reckoning to the indefinite future.

4. If the three business practices are applied to government,
will it be clear in each separate year whether federal finance
has conformed to the new fiscal standard? Here, again, the answer clearly is Yes. "Balancing of the federal budget" will have
a new and truer meaning; and it will be perfectly clear whether
the budget is in balance, *i.e.*, whether revenues in any year
equal cash expenditures on current account during that year
plus those deferred expenditures of various years which are
charged against that year.

Before taking up the fifth question, we may digress a moment.
Whether, in fact, such a plan as we are considering will operate
satisfactorily will depend to some extent upon the wisdom of the
rules for distributing deferred expenditures among different
fiscal years.

There are two basic approaches to the problem of distributing
capital expenditures: (1) such an expenditure may be distributed by accumulating in advance of the time when the expenditure is to be incurred a reserve out of which to meet it;
or (2) a deferred expenditure may be distributed in retrospect.

Properly speaking, the first of these methods is not open to
us at present in the case of federal finance (though it is in the
case of state and local governments, many of which are currently accumulating reserves out of surplus revenues). Our
present concern is, therefore, with the second method. It is not
difficult to set broad limits to the length of the period over
which any deferred expenditure item should be distributed. If
the period is too short, say two or three years for a large program, little flexibility is provided, for we have deviated only
slightly from an annual budget system. On the other hand,
if the period is too long, fiscal flexibility is inadequately counter-
balanced by restraints; the day of reckoning lies so far away
that it might as well be in the indefinite future.

As guides to fixing the write-off period for any capital expenditure within these limits, two principles may be offered:
(1) The smaller the total of new deferred expenditure items,

the shorter the write-off period should be. (2) The greater the likelihood that a deferred expenditure item will be repeated, the shorter the write-off period should be. These principles do not uniquely fix the write-off period. They are intended rather to indicate the nature of the fiscal planning problem involved. The first might be rephrased, "Make the write-off period as short as ability-to-pay will reasonably permit." The second principle clearly opposes an indefinite pyramiding of deferred outlay items.

Let us turn now to the pattern of write-off year-by-year and to question number 5: If the three business practices previously referred to are applied to government, will relatively heavier tax burdens be likely to fall on years of business expansion and relatively lighter tax burdens to fall on years of business recession? Whether the ability-to-pay principle will apply in this sense with the three business procedures in operation depends largely on the pattern of write-off year-by-year. It is not difficult to devise a formula which would provide for writing off deferred charges more rapidly in good years. Thus, for example, the amount to be written off might be made to vary with the Federal Reserve Board Index of Industrial Production. Such a distribution of deferred charges as this suggests should offer a definite psychological pressure for tax increases in years of good business. By the same token, the psychological pressure would be relaxed in years of recession.

Some will doubtless urge against the type of long-range fiscal plan here outlined that the advantages claimed for it are largely theoretical because the Congress could not be expected to stick to such a plan, if it were adopted. It is important to realize that sticking to the plan would mean only not juggling the accounts by changing the pattern of allocation of a deferred charge after the pattern has been set. No Congress can legally restrain successor Congresses from indulging in such a juggling of accounts. But it should be possible in adopting a fiscal plan of the type proposed to bring both a strong moral pressure and a strong force of inertia to the support of adherence to allocation patterns once they are fixed.

The argument that the type of fiscal plan above outlined will not be followed is not so much an argument against this type of long-range plan as an argument against any long-range planning. Because sticking to the plan means merely not juggling the accounts, the argument is less applicable here than it might be to many other types of long-range plans. Moreover, if the plan got off to a good start for a few years, adherence to it might soon become traditional. Further, as contrasted with our present unsatisfactory procedures, the type of long-range fiscal planning here outlined has two great advantages. It provides increased flexibility where increased flexibility is needed; and it offers more restraint at points at which restraint will be called for increasingly in the years to come because of the magnitude of our war effort. Both flexibility and restraint are promised through the replacement of our present nominal and misleading standard of budgetary balance by a truer standard.

· VIII ·

Authority and Reason as Instruments of Coordination in the United States

(1948)

WE depend very largely today on the Federal Government to provide the over-all social and economic measurements which should reveal the operations of the various aspects of our society. Our society is an organic whole; the Federal Government is, to some extent, a divided personality. In particular, the task of providing economic and other social measurements is divided among a large number of Government agencies. It is clear that if our social and economic measurements are to be adequate, either for policy purposes, or for analysis pursued for its own sake, the various measurements must articulate with each other. We must have a balanced coverage, not a wealth of information about one aspect of our society, and little or nothing about another. Again, when we have some major components of a significant total, we need also to know the total. Further, when two series measure related factors, the movement of the ratio between them must reflect a real social or economic change, not incomparabilities in the two series. Above all, statistical pronouncements must not contradict each other.

ON THE MERITS OF A DECENTRALIZED SYSTEM

Can we hope from an agency division of statistical labor to get a coordinated picture of our economy and our society?

It has sometimes been suggested that we could solve the problem of coordinating our statistical information by consolidating all Federal statistical compilation in a single agency. I doubt the wisdom of such a proposal. When the work of collecting and compiling statistics is largely divorced from the work of analyzing them, it is usually bad for the statistics. It may even be bad for the statistics if one agency collects the basic reports and another does the compiling. To be a good compiler of figures, you need to know how they were collected and (what is more important) you need to know what they are good for.

But it would be impossible to have a close association of collectors, compilers and analysts if all compilation were carried on in one central agency. The great bulk of our statistics is basically a by-product of administrative reports; and most administrative reports will have to continue to be collected by the agencies vested with the several administrative responsibilities that give rise to these reports. Tax forms will presumably continue to be collected by tax collectors, etc.

The work of social and economic analysis also will necessarily continue to be distributed among a large number of agencies. When economic analysis is needed as an aid to economic policy it is practically essential to locate the analysis in the agency which has the policy responsibility. Thus, work in bank credit economics needs to be located near those responsible for bank credit policy.

These considerations should make it clear that, if all statistical compilations were made in a single central agency, there would be an ill-advised divorce of statistical compilation and analysis. And incidentally, many important economic series would necessarily remain outside the consolidation, e.g., cash income from farm marketings. There would also be a divorce of the collection of statistical forms from the compilation of the information on them—a divorce that would create numerous difficulties in the resulting figures.

Nor is this all. Economists have often stated a law known as the "law of the size of the firm." This law assumes that when an enterprise passes a given size, its efficiency of operation decreases. I think this law applies with peculiar force to an intellectual operation such as the compilation and analysis of social and economic statistics. Diminishing efficiency sets in at an early stage. As the size of a statistical and economic or social research unit increases, it very soon develops mental compartments; it also tends to become set in its way. A good working organization unit devoted to statistical compilation and analysis is almost necessarily a small one.

There is another objection to solving the problem of statistical coordination by a general consolidation. It does not get at the basic difficulty. Statistical coordination means getting people to work together intellectually. For this purpose, good will is a necessary condition, but it is not sufficient. The basic need is for intelligent leadership, for leadership which understands and will point in some detail the paths to be followed. Mere consolidation of agencies does nothing to provide such leadership. It does not even assure us good will. Consolidation of government agencies cannot be counted on to improve the intellects of government officials; quite possibly it will not improve their dispositions.

I recall some years ago participating in negotiations which eventuated in the consolidation of two machine tabulating units. The consolidation was duly carried out in form; the personnel of the two constituent units were made responsible to a single officer. A year later, I had occasion to inquire into the situation and discovered that the two constituent units were still operating as separate entities. They were as remote physically (space assignments had not been changed) as before the consolidation. They were also as distant intellectually.

If we are to continue our decentralized system of Federal statistical services, as I think we should (and as I think we are likely to in any case), we ought to face certain broad questions. We ought to face the question of how under such an arrangement to provide a coordinated and well-balanced system of reports; how to get a new series when one is needed; how to make sure that an urgently needed improvement is made; how to eliminate contradictions when they arise; how to provide for comparability between related series compiled by separate agencies; how to provide for discontinuing work of relatively slight consequence, when funds are more urgently needed for other purposes.

STATUTORY POWERS CANNOT COMPEL ONE TO BE WISE

If we reject the idea of a general consolidation, a plausible alternative suggests itself. Should we not have a central authority to settle jurisdictional disputes, to direct the discontinuance of some series and the establishment of others, and to direct that needed improvements in series be adopted? If such an agency is to be effective, its orders must be implemented. For full implementation it would need to be able to impound unneeded funds and to make allocations from a statistical reserve fund to finance its affirmative directives; it would need also to be in a position to dismiss an officer responsible for a given statistical operation when he proves incompetent or recalcitrant, and to see that competent people are hired.

In my opinion, such a central authority is also an effective and an impossible solution. In the first place, the implementation I have suggested would mean combining for the statistical services the powers of the Division of Estimates of the Bureau of the Budget with those of the Civil Service Commission, and it would mean delegating to this central authority discretion which the Congress now regards as part of its appropriating power. We are not likely to see such a concentration of authority.

We might, of course, have a single central authority with less extensive powers than those I have suggested. But, unfortunately, it is far easier to clothe such an agency with restrictive powers than it is to provide implementation for its affirmative directives. Yet for purposes of a good over-all statistical picture of our society, it is vastly more important to confer on such an agency the power to get things done than it is to give such an agency the power to hamper or to stop a statistical activity.

Even if a central agency could be given adequate legal authority to get things done, I think such an arrangement would be very unwise. The attribute of statistical work which is most important for purposes of getting a coordinated picture of our society is that such work calls for intelligence. Among the obstacles which impede the making of needed improvements in social and economic information the two principal ones are: (1) Those who should make the improvements do not know what series it is important to create; they cannot visualize a "statistic" we do not yet have, or cannot understand how it will be used. (2) Those who should make the improvements cannot see how to get along with the materials at hand; they are blocked by technical difficulties they do not know how to overcome. A central authority with ample power to direct and inadequate intelligence would not remove either obstacle. Such an agency could do a great deal of harm and probably would not do a great deal of good. On the other hand, a central agency which understands what information is really needed, how it will be used, and how it can be got from existing basic data, can bring about many improvements. Even if it has no power but the prestige which attaches to an important status in the Federal organization chart, it can accomplish a great deal, nearly as much in fact as it could with greater legal powers.

Let me indicate two dangers that I see in vesting an agency with mandatory powers to improve statistics:

1. Such an agency is likely to yield to the temptation to emphasize its prerogatives as a policeman; to devote a major part of its energies to prescribing rules, to interpreting them in particular cases and to searching out infractions and invoking whatever sanctions may be at its disposal. Policing is not conducive to the development of interagency good will. It is a poor substitute for the provision of intellectual leadership with a true sense of values and an ability to help find the way around technical obstacles. But the temptation to make such a substitution is strong.

2. An agency which operates largely in terms of rules and sanctions is likely to get bogged down in a mass of unimportant details.

REVIEW MUST BE DISCRIMINATING

Something can be done toward improving our statistical information and toward coordinating the statistical end-products of various agencies through a review of statistical questionnaires. The Division of Statistical Standards has attempted to serve this objective and at the same time to serve the objective of saving respondents unnecessary burdens in making out report forms. But the two objectives are not entirely compatible. Many proposed questionnaires that are potentially burdensome promise little in the way of valuable data. From the point of view of improving our over-all social and economic information, there are probably at least ninety-nine questionnaires to be reviewed which are of negligible importance to one questionnaire that is really important. But there is no sharp line between important questionnaires and unimportant questionnaires. Hence, it would be difficult to manage a questionnaire review service in such a way that most of the energies would go into the one per cent of really important questionnaires and a negligible part of the staff energies would go into the ninety-nine per cent that are of negligible importance. Moreover, consideration for respondents' burdens militates against a highly discriminating review of this sort. I like to call this type of administration problem the conflict between democracy and the "jay-shaped" distribution. A frequency distribution of questionnaires by social and economic significance is decidedly "jay-shaped"; the least significant are by far the most frequent. But it is difficult to prevent a review staff from regarding all questionnaires as nearly equal before the law. An agency which does not succeed in discriminating ruthlessly between the significant and the insignificant will almost certainly have too little staff energy left for providing intellectual leadership.

WHAT INTELLIGENT LEADERSHIP CAN DO

I have attempted to contrast administrative authority and intellectual leadership as instruments for improving our statistical picture of the operations of our society, and I have urged that intellectual leadership is far more likely to produce good results. I do not mean to say that the obstacles in the way of improved information are always and exclusively intellectual obstacles. Sometimes the trouble is lack of funds; sometimes it is a jurisdictional dispute; sometimes it is bureaucratic cupidity; sometimes sheer official incompetence. The Division of Statistical Standards has done a good deal to provide us with a remedy for such administrative difficulties. I shall presently indicate a direction in which I think it can do more. But first I should like to consider the techniques of intellectual leadership more fully.

If you know clearly some piece of social or economic information which is needed, know why it is needed, and know how it can be got technically, what can you do to put the idea into effect? There is first the direct approach. You can sell the importance of your idea to the proper official and tactfully demonstrate its feasibility. To some extent you should be able to select the most likely customer. This may be the man immediately in charge, the man to whom he reports, or possibly the Secretary. But if you go over a man's head, you must not give him cause to fear you have criticized him before his superior—if you expect to have his good will. After the sale, you will be dealing with the man immediately in charge. When technical obstacles to carrying out the idea are encountered, you must stand ready to be helpful to him in finding the way around them. I would underscore the word "helpful." It would be unwise condescendingly to tell him the way around. If you have made a sale of the idea, the title to it must pass. It must become the idea of the man who is to carry it out. It must cease to be your idea. Your customer must have the credit for the improvement.

You may not make a sale the first time you try it. But this should not stop you. You should have learned how to improve your proposition. In any case provide your prospect with a rationalization for changing his mind. Revamp your proposition thoroughly, rechristen it, and try again.

There is a great advantage in the method of direct salesmanship, particularly when the job involved is comparable to that of developing an index of production, or, let us say, construction. If the man who is to do the job does not fully understand it and its implications for social and economic analysis, if he has not made the idea his own, if he is merely undertaking to comply with a directive, his intention may be compliance, but the result may be nearly worthless.

There are other methods beside direct salesmanship, other intellectual methods. There are always various possibilities of indirect salesmanship, of selling your idea to someone else who can help your cause. I will stop for only one illustration. If it is difficult to persuade a responsible official that he ought to follow an approved line of statistical action, when he seems bent on some other line, it sometimes pays to build a bonfire under him. This means selling your idea to a number of third parties. You must know your Washington to know what third parties you can carry along with you and what third parties can help your objective most. Also, you can burn your fingers on such a bonfire.

Still other methods are available for intellectual leadership, methods that are less spectacular and much slower, but they are methods which nonetheless should accomplish much in the longer run.

One such device which a leadership agency has at its disposal is a very simple one—the power to ask questions. Just asking the right question of the right person at the right time will often help materially to bring about a reform in statistical operations. Very little in the way of authority is needed for this purpose. But to ask the psychologically right question, one must have a well thought out and highly selective program of statistical development, and one must be able to stick to it. Repeated doses of this kind of medicine are likely to be needed. To change the metaphor, the process is one of erosion. Physiographic erosion is directed by the force of gravity; intellectual erosion needs a similar consistency of direction, if a definite pattern is to be achieved.

STATISTICAL CROSS FERTILIZATION

Another important contribution that an agency in a position to give intelligent leadership can make is almost as simple as asking questions: the mere getting of people together to talk over common and related problems is important. If such a policy is followed systematically and wisely it helps to keep each agency informed of related developments taking place in other agencies. And it promotes good will, mutual understanding, and the cross-fertilization of ideas. This device can be supplemented by printed aids. Thus, the Division of Statistical Standards has developed through a system of representative committees and has promulgated several standard schemes of classification. It has also provided the *Statistical Reporter* and the *Federal Statistical Directory.*

An agency in a position to get people together can help to overcome the evil called "layering." For example: Mr. A reports to Mr. B, who reports to Mr. C. Through channels Mr. A cannot speak to Mr. C. Mr. X, in another agency, may be able to talk to both Mr. A and Mr. C, and even to bring them together.

The Division of Statistical Standards does not possess authority in respect to personnel, but it can exert and has exerted an important influence toward the improvement of standards for professional social science personnel. This is a broad subject, and I shall content myself with having called attention to it.

In the bringing of people together and in the encouragement of improved standards for professional personnel, the Division of Statistical Standards has been making an important contribution, a much more important one than has been generally realized.

WHO CAN LEAD

I have spoken of a leadership agency. This is, I think, misleading. No agency has, or can have, a monopoly of the kind of leadership I have been talking about. The Division of Statistical Standards has an important responsibility in this respect and has done much to encourage statistical improvements, but it is by no means the only agency in a position to contribute intellectual leadership.

Indeed, there are other agencies that have an advantage the Division of Statistical Standards does not enjoy—the advantage of a professional staff actively engaged in a broad program of substantive analysis and research. In this respect the Council of Economic Advisers is in a particularly strategic situation. Although it is a recent addition to the family of Federal agencies it has already come to exert a very significant influence toward a better statistical picture of economic conditions and this influence seems destined to increase. Again, an agency such as the National Income Division in the Bureau of Foreign and Domestic Commerce necessarily has a wide grasp of statistical sources, and a keen appreciation of urgent statistical needs. It has furnished important leadership and should continue to do so. Further, the unit in the Bureau of the Census responsible for the *Statistical Abstract* has the point of view of the consumer of statistical compilations and is in a position to look at the statistical services broadly and critically. Especially in recent years it has helped to promote better statistics. We may fairly hope that its leadership functions will continue to grow. There are many other agencies to which we may look for leadership in the development of our statistical information. In fact, private individuals as well as Government agencies can make their contributions; any one who has an idea for statistical improvement to sell may undertake to sell it.

CENTRALIZING RESPONSIBILITY WITHIN EACH FIELD

I have urged that our Federal statistical organization should continue to be decentralized. I do not mean that it should remain unchanged. In its First Annual Report, the Central Statistical Board, predecessor of the Division of Statistical Standards, outlined a plan of organization for the statistical services. It suggested that there should be a focal agency having centralized responsibility for statistical information pertaining to each major aspect of our society. It suggested also that, in many cases, this focal agency should be one primary collecting agency for reports coming from a given industry or group of industries to the Federal Government. In other words, it proposed no over-all consolidation, but a development of as much centralization in each segment of the social and economic field as would be compatible with existing assignments of administrative responsibilities.

The advantages of such a plan should be obvious. Far more in the way of the bringing of related functions together in one unit can be realized by this plan than by a single over-all consolidation. But the segmentalized consolidations can retain the advantages of small-scale operation—flexibility, morale, and the absence of mental compartments. Such an arrangement should also help to lighten the reporting burdens imposed upon respondents. Finally, it would change and clarify agency functions in a way that is particularly important for our present purpose. Today the task of providing the social and economic information we need is, in many respects, not clearly assigned to anybody. As soon as a focal agency has been developed in each broad field, the task of providing most of the information will be stated as a set of clear and definite job assignments.

In 1940, the Division of Statistical Standards gave careful consideration to a broad move designed to implement a development along these lines. It is my belief that this move would have been made, had wartime problems not inopportunely intervened. I believe the time is now ripe to reopen this question. I hope the Division of Statistical Standards will again undertake to implement broadly the development of focal agencies.

· IX ·

Suitable Accounting Conventions to Determine Business Income

(1949)

THE American Institute of Accountants has wisely established a broad Study of Business Income. And this Study has undertaken to consider the views of lawyers, business executives, public officials, and economists as well as those of accountants on the question, "How should business income be defined?"

This question is a timely one. It is also highly controversial and extremely complex. Any short answer is necessarily a partial answer. In responding to this question as an economist let me make two points clear at the outset. (1) Economists differ widely on the subject. To keep my answer short I shall attempt to present only one economist's viewpoint, my own. (2) The Study of Business Income has had under consideration (a) alternative methods of inventory valuation, and (b) the possible application of a price-correction factor to depreciation charges computed on a straight-line historical-cost basis. In the interest of brevity I shall confine what I say about how business income should be defined to aspects of the question suggested by these two considerations.

A contrast has often been drawn between the income of a business as shown in a financial statement summary drawn from its accounting records and the economic income of the business, as if economic income were something independent of accounting records. This is a false contrast. Economists should mean by "business income" in the first instance what accountants say it is; the "income of a business" should be defined basically by a set of accounting conventions. This proposition, advanced with apologies to the legal aspect of the responsibility for income determination, is subject to two qualifications: (1) Economists should be free to use special-purpose modifications of business income so defined, provided they specify the modification. (2) They should also be free to express their own ideas concerning appropriate accounting conventions.

Under the second qualification, I submit two canons for further consideration: the canon of accounting certainty and the canon of economic suitability.

THE CANON OF ACCOUNTING CERTAINTY

If as an economist I accept the accountant's definition of business income as a starting point for economic analysis, I want to know what I am accepting. I would like to have the accounting conventions supply a reasonably certain and unambiguous concept.

One illustration of accounting uncertainty is the practice of setting up general purpose contingency reserves. The use of these reserves is not permitted by generally accepted accounting principles (as set forth in Accounting Research Bulletin No. 28), of course, but some companies still do it. There never were adequate conventions as to how big these reserves should be, the circumstances under which they should be set up, or how and when to get rid of them. Bulletin No. 28 recognized the difficulty of establishing such conventions, and by banning these reserves it made unnecessary any effort to fix rules. But unless the Bulletin is observed, so much discretion is exercised by the individual enterprise regarding the timing and amount of charges and credits to its income account that we do not have accounting certainty.

I think the first consideration in defining income ought to be, How far can you go toward establishing a set of accounting conventions that will define income so that two people working on the same company will come up with substantially the same result? I think that a maxim which has been employed in another field, that of the law, is perhaps more apropos here: "It is more important for justice to be sure than it is for justice to be just." It is more important to have conventions which make the definition of income certain than it is to have just the right set of conventions.

It has been proposed to amend present accounting conventions to provide that depreciation charges computed according to the straight-line historical-cost formula may be corrected by multiplying them by some present-cost-prior-cost ratio as a correction factor. What does the canon of accounting certainty suggest as to this proposal? I think it means that the proposal should be quite fully specified. Perhaps it has been in some of the memoranda submitted by the Study of Business Income, but I have failed to find it. The two main questions that occur to me are these: Just how is it proposed to define the ratio by which the straight-line historical-cost computation is to be multiplied? Just what, if any, are the balance-sheet implications of the proposal?

First, as to the correction factor, some index-number basis of computation appears to be contemplated. Is it intended to make the Bureau of Labor Statistics wholesale-price index the official American Institute of Accountants basis of this computation? If not, how is the proposed accounting convention regarding this basis to read? And how is the time reference for the computation to be specified? I assume the numerator of the correction ratio will be some average price index for the current fiscal period. But what about the denominator? How is the official Institute base period to be defined?

Second, as to the balance-sheet implications of the proposal, it has been made clear that the gross book values of capital assets are to remain on a historical-cost basis. So far as these gross book values are concerned, balance-sheet implications are definitely ruled out. But various comments on what is meant by keeping capital intact that have been made in connection with the proposal leave me puzzled so far as another possible type of balance-sheet implication is concerned. Would the proposal amend the present definition of "keeping capital intact"? Or is it merely a modification of the straight-line apportionment formula? Let me make this question more specific. The straight-line historical-cost procedure sets a definite limit on the reserve to be accumulated against any asset. A constant annual amount of depreciation is determined when the asset is acquired and that amount (or a revised constant amount, where it becomes necessary at some time during the active life of an asset to recognize a radical change in the expected retirement date) is set aside each year until the reserve limit is reached. Does the proposed method of determining depreciation mean that the reserve limit will remain unchanged, and that the proposed depreciation allowance (the straight-line computation times the proposed correction factor) will be set aside each year until and only until this limit is reached?

If the answer is "Yes," there are, I think, two corollaries which should be stated as parts of the proposal: (1) It is intended to apply the correction factor not as a blanket adjustment, but separately to the straight-line depreciation allowance on each separate asset. (2) It is intended that, if during the active life of any asset there develops a radical divergence between its expected retirement date and the date when it is expected the reserve limit will be reached, the basic straight-line depreciation allowance (and if need be the then net book value) will be adjusted accordingly.

If the answer to this question is "No," there is need to spell out just what is proposed in regard to reserve limits. And I should like to suggest that the spelling out be included as a separate proposal. The issues involved in changing depreciation reserve limits are quite different from the issues involved in applying a correction factor to straight-line computations of annual depreciation allowances. But I shall not discuss them here, because no specific proposal amending reserve limits accompanies the correction-factor proposal.

Since the subject before us is changes in the definition of income, it is scarcely necessary to say that the canon of accounting certainty should be so construed as to provide for making, from time to time, changes in the accounting conventions which define "business income." There must be periods during which and areas within which alternative conventions can apply (the alternative elected being set forth in each financial statement). The canon of accounting certainty clearly implies that such periods of transition should not be unduly prolonged. It would be more difficult to restrict the areas of transition, but this possibility should not be lost sight of.

THE CANON OF ECONOMIC SUITABILITY

The second canon I propose requires a consideration of the economic impact of accounting conventions. It calls for changes —radical changes—in present accounting conventions. As between two possible sets of conventions defining business income both of which may be equally certain, it asks: Which one will make the economy operate more satisfactorily? Which one is better adapted to economic analysis?

The implications of this canon are diverse. They include consideration of such questions as: Does the present accounting definition of business income properly segregate the accomplishments of management during a fiscal period from the effects of changes in the general business conditions and other conditions under which management has been compelled to operate? Would the present definition, or some alternative definition (e.g., one that applied an index-number correction factor to depreciation charges as computed on a straight-line basis) have a more salutary effect on dividend policy? on price policy? on wage policy? on the general level of business activity? How should the present definition of business income be changed to make possible a more satisfactory determination of national income? (How should debits and credits to the business-income account be defined to make possible a reasonably accurate consolidation of the separate business-income statements into a national income account?)

Because the implications of the canon of economic suitability are very diverse I can only attempt to illustrate one aspect of them here. I think there are serious questions about the way business income has been defined, assuming that we start in the first instance with the recovery-cost or historical-cost approach. One very important question, it seems to me, is how to work out a better apportionment of income among fiscal periods.

Economists have a great interest in comparative income statements. Show an economist the combined statement for a group of companies for the current quarter, for the preceding quarter, and for the same quarter of last year. He will not be satisfied. He will want to see the combined statement (on as nearly comparable a basis as possible) for a whole series of quarters extending over a period of years. He will want what he calls a time series. And he will want to analyze the net-income time series into four components. A part of the quarter-to-quarter variations in this series he will think of as seasonal in nature, as the reflection of a somewhat regular, recurrent within-the-year pattern. A part of the quarter-to-quarter variations he will attribute to the so-called business cycle, to fluctuations in the general level of business activity. Part of the variations he will regard as reflecting a longer-term trend. But there will be some variations that are neither seasonal, cyclical, nor trend variations. Economists call these sporadic variations.

These four component categories may seem strange to accountants, but I think something like them has played an important part in the development of the accounting conventions which define business income. Consider the difference between what may be called a concern's "net cash inflow" for a fiscal period apart from lending and borrowing operations, proprietorship withdrawals, and changes in paid-in capital [1] and its net income. The difference is wide. But I suggest that the net-income concept has evolved from something like the "net cash inflow" concept. In fact net income might be defined as "net cash inflow" corrected for the sporadic and short-time variations so as to reveal approximately the trend-effect of the year's operations on the financial condition of the business. We call the corrections accrual accounting. Accrual accounting makes

---

[1] "Net cash inflow" is not at present a familiar concept in business accounting. But it is familiar in discussions of the federal budget. In this connection it is called the "cash surplus."

the corrections by anticipating the receipts and expenditures of a given period in earlier periods or by reassigning them to later periods, entering the anticipations and reassignments in the balance sheet as accrued and deferred charges and accrued and deferred credits to income.

Let us assume that business income is to be defined by accounting conventions so as to reveal the trend-effect of the fiscal period's operations on the financial condition of a business. And let us assume that an economist has before him a whole time series of comparable quarterly business-income statements, as income is currently defined. Further, let us assume that he has "net cash inflow" computations for the same concern. What would he make of these figures? And what would he recommend in the way of changes in the present accounting definition of business income on the basis of these figures? He would presumably be concerned with the question, Have the three main types of short-time variation (sporadic variation, seasonal variation, and cyclical variation) been fully eliminated so as to reveal the true trend-effect of a period's operations on financial condition? I think his findings would run something like this:

Sporadic variations. He would find marked sporadic variations in the "net cash inflow" series but little sporadic variation in the net-income series. Accrual accounting has eliminated most sporadic variations. The most important single step in this direction is, of course, the handling of expenditures for wasting capital assets. Through depreciation accounting they are handled as a kind of deferred charge. The practice of segregating capital gains and losses from income attributable to the period in the case of public service enterprises is another such step.

Seasonal variations. He would find that something has been done by accrual accounting to eliminate seasonal variation but that a good deal of seasonal remains in net income as currently defined. He would recommend that accrual or deferment devices be worked out which would get rid of the seasonal, and make quarterly financial statements really meaningful. This does not seem to be too difficult a problem, and it is high time it was cleared up.

Cyclical variations. He would find that very little has been done to eliminate or moderate cyclical fluctuations in business income as it is currently defined. The present determination that we call business income is a hodge-podge of two things. It reflects partly the stage of the business cycle we happen to be in, partly the trend-effect of the year's operations on the proprietorship equity. The present form of income statement does not help us to distinguish these two influences. Income statements would be far more meaningful if the two could be somehow separated. I think a substantial part of the present dissatisfaction with the prevailing definition of business income is basically due to the way it confuses the trend-effect and the cyclical variations. The problem this confusion presents to us is a tough one. I will mention three steps that go part way toward meeting it.

(i) The Lifo method of inventory valuation. Compared to Fifo it results in a smaller net income when business is good; a larger net income when business is declining.

(ii) Something like the Lifo method of valuation for the portfolios of industrials, rails, and utilities. If a revised method of valuation is good for inventories, why not for portfolios? We have already had to move in this direction in the case of banks and insurance companies.

(iii) Applying some correction factor to depreciation as computed by the straight-line historical-cost formula. It has been proposed that this factor be a price-index ratio.

I should like to suggest an alternative type of correction factor based on a statistical determination of the trend of a concern's operating revenues. We may compare the two correction factors thus:

(1) Some price index for this period divided by this price index for some base period.

(2) Operating revenues for this period divided by what they would have been if on the trend line.

Point (1) has some advantage from the point of view of the

canon of accounting certainty, but I think the advantage is very slight. It commends itself at the present time because price increases have been large in the present business cycle. But its base period will be likely to get out of date in a few years, unless some moving base is adopted. Point (2) has two important advantages. The resulting corrected annual depreciation allowance takes account of both price and volume changes, and it takes into consideration the special factors affecting an individual business. It is suggested that the Study of Business Income try out (2) as well as (1) in some of its statistical tests. I have assumed that both (1) and (2) would be employed under present rules regarding the limit of a depreciation reserve. A proposal to change reserve-limit rules would raise important issues I shall not try to discuss.

Improved methods of inventory and portfolio valuation and of handling depreciation charges will moderate the cyclical fluctuations in business income only slightly. It should be possible to develop various supplementary devices. I hope the Study of Business Income will be directed in part to finding other devices that will help moderate the cyclical fluctuations in business income, and that this Study will succeed in finding a good many of them.

SOCIAL ACCOUNTING CONCEPTS

· X ·

National Wealth and Income—
An Interpretation*
(1935)

AMONG the most inclusive summary statements concerning the functioning of our economic system are those which present totals and breakdowns of our national wealth and national income. We should all agree on the basic importance of such summary statements about the operations and condition of our nation's business, information which is analogous to the information a judicious stockholder wants from his corporation.

The terms "national wealth" and "national income" are refinements of concepts which have played a central part in the history of economic thought. Were Adam Smith writing today he would probably feel the need for both of these terms in the title of his great work. Smith, like the Physiocrats, was concerned not only with wealth in a social sense that recognized the double counting involved in assets such as I.O.U.'s, and so confined wealth to tangible resources, but he was concerned also with income as a net total of ultimate distributive shares, after eliminating the duplication involved in payments by one enterprise to another. Without accepting the labor theory of value we may recognize in it, first an attempt to state national income so that it shall involve no double counting, and second an at-

* Somewhat condensed.

tempt to express it as a physical volume so as to be independent of price changes.

So long as the concepts of economic theory such as production, consumption, and savings remain abstract categories, it is difficult to give them the precision necessary to agreement as to their meaning. It is a fundamental of scientific procedure to define concepts in terms of the methods of measurement or observation, in order to secure such precision and objectivity. Statistical determinations of national—or more broadly of social—wealth and income offer economists the chance to make their basic concepts accord with scientific method. Irving Fisher perceived this clearly a quarter of a century ago,[1] but his contribution in this respect has been more fully appreciated by statisticians than by economic theorists. When we define our basic economic concepts in terms of the methods of measuring them statistically, their meaning is clarified and made more precise. The concepts also become less neat, and we may be compelled to recognize certain ambiguities, to reckon with two definite meanings instead of one vaguer one. Finally, relationships that might otherwise be overlooked are made to stand out clearly. It would be interesting to trace parallels in all these respects in the history of sciences that have been longer on an empirical basis.

Although the process of measurement of these basic concepts is partly a statistical one, it is also in an important sense an accounting process, an attempt to portray the economic condition and operation of a society in terms of double-entry bookkeeping, in terms of a set of controlling accounts that at once recapitulate the accounts of the legal persons of which the society consists, and present a consolidated picture clean of duplications. The double-entry system implies that a full statement of financial condition as of any given date would show the net equities of various types, bonds, bank deposits, etc., held by ultimate equity holders, as well as the several types of wealth, i.e., it would be a balance sheet. The double-entry system implies that the income statement should show both the value of

[1] *Nature of Capital and Income*, 1906, New York.

products and the costs of the services of the various factors of production.

Measurement of wealth involves a consolidation of all balance sheet accounts. In this process of consolidation the holdings of intermediate equity holders, such as business corporations, cancel out, and only the holdings of ultimate equity holders remain. In the measurement of income by the so-called "net value-product" method the consolidation process is applied only to intermediate or production accounts. Payments of enterprise A to enterprise B cancel receipts of B from A, but only *intermediate* transactions are thus cancelled. The payments of lawyers to doctors do not cancel the receipts of doctors from lawyers, or vice versa. In estimating national income it is necessary, therefore, to effect a separation of accounts. Intermediate accounts, i.e., accounts portraying revenue from products sold to, and cost of products acquired from, other enterprises must be segregated from ultimate accounts, i.e., accounts portraying personal income, personal savings and the cost of living or of consumption. Unfortunately some of the accounting data used for measuring national income are for a mixture of intermediate and ultimate accounts. In estimating national income, farmers present a particularly troublesome problem of segregating intermediate from ultimate accounts, costs of conducting the farm business from the farmer's cost of living.

The physical volume of statistics required to estimate the national income (aggregate national value-product) for a single year is impressive. But we must not be so impressionable as to conclude that the national income or value-product is therefore a purely factual affair. The question whether production is a descriptive or an ethical category has been frequently considered in abstract theory. An answer to this question on the basis of the method of statistical measurement may be ventured —it *is* a category which partakes of an ethical character.

Let us consider production first in current price terms. The total net value-product of a society is, as Adam Smith pointed out,[2] the same as its total social income. The ethical nature of

[2] *Wealth of Nations,* Book IV, Chapter 2.

social or national income derives partly from the cancelling only of intermediate transactions in the consolidation process. This requires the statistician, or social accountant, to distinguish the productive consumption of a commodity or service from its ultimate consumption, to pass judgment on the purposes to which a good is put.[3] Crops fed to stock represent intermediate or productive consumption. Crops fed to human beings represent ultimate consumption. A slave economy might see fit to class crops fed to slaves with crops fed to stock. Again in assessing the cost of government service the social accountant must distinguish between the farmer's personal taxes and his business taxes, or between that part of a farmer's tax bill which is a business expense and that part which is an item in his cost of living. The total *net* value-product of the industries of a society during a year is equal to the *gross* value of the goods and services used for ultimate consumption plus the increase in wealth during the year. The process of measuring that net value-product, therefore, requires us to determine whether a good is used for intermediate or for ultimate consumption.

The ethical nature of the national income or net value-product derives also from another aspect of the consolidation process used in measuring it. Although ours is a competitive system consisting of a multitude of separate enterprises, we attempt to judge the condition and operation of these numerous enterprises as if they were a single enterprise—we consolidate their accounts. We conceive them as a *system,* hiring the services of labor and the national wealth, and producing commodities and services that are either consumed by ultimate consumers or added to the stock of wealth.

National income, reckoned on a current price basis, may be increased either through an increase in production in a physical volume sense or by boosting prices. The term "net value-product" of an industry, therefore, is misleading, unless we understand "product" in a Davenportian sense, as "proceeds." Were data available we could and should compute the net

[3] It is also necessary to distinguish between payments which are part of the national income and payments which are mere redistributions of it, e.g., between wages on ordinary government construction and made-work wages.

value-product of the racketeering industry. But clearly this net value-product would not represent the part of the national income *produced* by the racketeering industry. Strictly, net value-product means either (1) the net social income distributed by or accruing from an industry or (2) the net social cost of operating the industry. For any single industry net value-product is a fairly good measure of social cost. For an entire society it measures both output and cost *at current prices*. Total *current* value of social output equals total *current* social cost. The debits and credits necessarily balance for each separate industry, even racketeering, but that fact does not establish that the distribution of the total value-product among industries accords at all accurately with contribution.

For comparisons of national income in different years correction for price changes may be needed. Consideration of the problem of making such a correction reveals a further and important ethical significance of national income. Since the national income may be considered either as a debit total representing the remuneration of the factors of production or as a credit total representing the value of production, we can *deflate* the total income using either of two sets of price indexes, one appropriate to yielding a measure of the physical volume of production, and one appropriate to yielding a measure of the physical volume of services of the factors employed, i.e., of national wealth and of labor. Deflated national income may represent either "real social income" or "real social cost." Hitherto in deflating national income attention has centered on measuring "real social income."

Although no published measurements of social cost are yet available and although the published measurements of real social income are not entirely satisfactory, nonetheless, in view of their important significance for economic theory, three comments may be ventured: (1) While total social income and total social cost measured at current prices are necessarily equal in every year, deflated total social income and deflated total social cost will not in general be equal except in the base year. This is because the prices appropriate to the deflation of labor income and income from national wealth (wage rates, property rents, the returns on corporate property, etc.) and the prices appropriate to the deflation of consumed and saved income cannot be counted on to maintain a fixed relationship to each other. (2) If we choose a prewar base, real social income according to very rough estimates made by the writer appears to be significantly above real social cost during the latter part of the decade of the '20's. The physical volume of production apparently increased more rapidly during this period than the physical volume of services of labor and wealth employed. The steeper trend of the production curve offers a crude measure of the increased efficiency of our economic system. (3) If we include unemployed labor and other unemployed resources as a part of the real social cost in each year we can obtain a similar crude measure of the decrease in efficiency of our economic system in depression years. It is admitted that available data permit only very rough measurements. But each of these three observations is what economic theory would lead us to expect.

The ethical significance of the concepts of national wealth and national income has been emphasized. To be sure they are ethical in a somewhat narrow sense—they conceive our society and its organic and inorganic environment in collectivist terms as a system, a system serving exclusively human wants, and serving only those human wants the means of satisfying which can be measured in dollars. Nonetheless, some will object that as ethical concepts the terms "wealth" and "income" are unscientific, that if this is what defining economic concepts in statistical terms means, it is to be avoided.

To this objection three replies may be offered: *First,* statistical measurement of wealth and value-production is not responsible for the ethical nature of these concepts; the concepts of economic theory were just as ethical before data and techniques of measurement were available; the techniques only define the nature of these concepts more precisely. *Second,* biology employs appraisal concepts of a comparable nature, e.g., morbidity, maturity, parasitism. *Third,* measurement of wealth and income is objective. For a large part of total income there is close agreement as to final estimates, and differences in estimates for the remainder of income and for wealth can be largely accounted in one of two ways:

(1) The absence of reliable information covering certain items. In some cases the lack of information is due to the fact that we have not troubled to collect it. In other cases it is due to defects in the existing basic accounting records.

(2) The necessity of using different definitions of income appropriate to the different purposes for which the income measurements are to be used. Thus it may be desirable either to include or to exclude non-money income items, such as the net rental value of owned homes and the stock of other consumers goods. Again, it may be desirable to use different bases of valuation for wealth, e.g., book value, and market value of equities. The corollary of the different valuation bases for wealth is different definitions of saved income.

For the sake of brevity, consideration will here be limited to four concepts of social income, for which over-simplified specifications follow:–

(i) Realized money income, which includes all kinds of income involving money payments—payroll, interest, net income from rents, corporate cash dividends and entrepreneurial profits.

(ii) Total realized income, which includes also non-money income items such as the net rental value of owned homes.

(iii) Total social income on an accrual or book-value basis, which includes in addition to total realized income, book additions to corporate surplus. This is the sense in which total income has been used above, the total net-value-product of a society.

(iv) Total social income reckoning changes in proprietorship equities on a market-value basis instead of a book-value basis.

It is submitted that neither the incompleteness of present information nor the recognition of different definitions for different purposes invalidates the thesis that definition of terms like value-product according to the method of measurement is a long step in the direction of scientific precision and objectivity, and that the existing agreement among final estimates of items representing a large part of national income means substantial scientific progress.

In the absence of good annual estimates of wealth, and of good physical volume data on wealth, saved income—which should equal the increase in wealth during the year *—has been estimated by various shortcuts. In using these shortcuts it is difficult to avoid double counting and still more difficult to know how far the results are affected by market appreciation or depreciation of existing wealth. It is not surprising, therefore, that saved income is still a highly controversial item.

Most attempts at deflating social income thus far have erroneously attempted to deflate saved income directly, dividing through by a price index. For purposes of deflation, total produced income needs to be broken down into two parts, consumed income and savings. Consumed income can be directly deflated by indexes of cost of consumption goods and services and fortunately for existing deflation, consumed income represents the bulk of total income. Saved income cannot be directly deflated by any index—it is a net item, new wealth produced plus appreciation of old wealth less depreciation, depletion and retirements. To deflate saved income we can best apply the deflation index to the year-end figures for total wealth and then compute the increments.

It is important to note that if we set up a consistent set of accounts for the economic system of the United States on any *one* valuation basis, saved income equals both the increase in wealth and the increase in the net equities held by the ultimate owners of wealth. A good deal has been made recently of the distinction between savings and investment to account for business cycles. This distinction appears to be a distinction between increase in wealth and increase in equities. Since these two will be the same if reckoned on the same valuation basis, the distinction is clearly not between assets and equities alone. Either the distinction involves different bases of valuation or else some item, such as change in value of existing wealth, is

* Cf. "A Note on Saving and Investment," at the end of this article.

included in one case and not in the other. If a theory resting on such a distinction is to merit our serious consideration as a scientific hypothesis, it should be clearly stated in terms of the methods of measuring savings and investment.

Unfortunately the effects of using different valuation bases for wealth must be reckoned with when we try to consider the distribution of income. Not only is the proportion of income which is saved involved, but also we must know the valuation basis applied to wealth in considering either the personal distribution of income or the functional distribution—or else we must consider a distribution of something short of total income, e.g., realized income. The item of saved income chiefly involved is additions to corporate surplus if we use a book value basis, and changes in the market value of proprietorship equities and nonbusiness wealth (paper profits) if we use a market value basis. This income is not only *saved* income—it is also necessarily *property* income and it accrues largely to the higher income classes.

One final word may be added to this brief review of our measures of national wealth and income. We have made rapid strides in recent years in the development of the data and the techniques needed for these fundamental measurements of the condition and operation of our economic system. The measurements, still very rough for some important items, have already found important uses both practical and theoretical. These uses are limited today in part by the state of our data and our techniques. But the uses of these basic measurements are limited also by their newness and by the large costs of exploratory use. The next few years may do much to remedy these limitations. It seems probable that we are on the threshold of a much fuller use of national balance sheets and income statements and their detailed breakdowns, a use which may take a direction for the accounts of our national economic system, analogous to the progress from general accounting to cost accounting for the individual business. Development in this direction of social cost accounting should do much to bring about a closer articulation of the theory of value and distribution with statistical measurement.

The analogy to individual business accounting will suggest to some another possible line of development, the progression from accounting as a record of past transactions to budgeting, in other words, to some form of economic planning.

A NOTE ON SAVING AND INVESTMENT *

The total national income conceived as the sum of the distributive shares (payrolls, interest, profits, dividends, and additions to corporate surplus) and the total national income considered as the sum of consumed income and additions to national wealth should be equal. We may state this proposition differently. The total of the distributive shares, payrolls, etc., plus an appropriate allowance for replacement of wealth used up, should equal the total value of goods and services produced. Still another way to phrase this proposition is: Total investments equal total savings; that is, the increase in our national wealth, including our net external credit, is equal to the increase in equities held by all residents of the country in that national wealth. I am aware that a somewhat heated debate has raged over the question whether savings and investment are equal. But I believe the present trend of opinion is to the view that savings and investment, if consistently defined, are equal; and, similarly, that total national income, conceived as total distributive shares, and total national income, conceived as consumed income plus the increase in national wealth—if these two totals are consistently defined—will be equal. However, consistency of definition is not easy to achieve in terms of our existing information.

* Extracted from *The Distribution of Wealth and Income,* Academy of Political Science, March 1938.

· XI ·

Concepts of National Income*
(1937)

I NATIONAL INCOME AND SOCIAL INCOME

THE purposes of this memorandum are first, to indicate the present status of concepts of national or other social income, and to outline the most useful types of income breakdown; second, to consider some of the questions that are now particularly moot with respect to concepts of national income, and to suggest possible answers. It should be fully recognized that this procedure involves taking sides on issues that are necessarily controversial and that may well continue to be controversial for some time.

In the following discussion references will be made to social income and social wealth. For the world as a whole and for parts of it either smaller or larger than an entire nation there may be need for measures corresponding to those designated as national wealth and national income. The terms 'social wealth' and 'social income' are intended to include both these cases and cases of national wealth and national income.

While this memorandum is focused on concepts of social

---

* One section of the original (about one-third) omitted.

income, some discussion of social wealth is unavoidable. The writer believes that several moot questions respecting concepts of social income can be discussed adequately only when their relations to questions concerning social wealth are recognized. Indeed, the world's social income may perhaps best be defined briefly as the total value of goods and services entering utimate human consumption plus the increase in social wealth.

For the purposes of defining social wealth and social income precisely a society should be conceived as consisting of two parts: (a) a producing organization or 'economic system'; (b) the families or individuals who contribute their labor or the services of their property to the economic system, and who receive the benefits of its operation. The concepts of wealth and income are essentially accounting concepts, or more precisely, financial statement concepts. Statements of wealth and income for an economic system correspond closely to the balance sheet and the revenue-income-and-profit statement for any single business enterprise. Indeed, existing methods of estimating social income consist in consolidating or putting together either (a) the financial statements for the businesses and other enterprises of which the economic system consists, or (b) the financial statements for families or individuals conceived as consumers, investors, savers and workers. In estimating social wealth all balance sheets are consolidated simultaneously.

In the consolidation of all balance sheets, assets that are in the nature of claims by one set of parties upon another are canceled by the corresponding liabilities of the second set of parties, so that the vast bulk of remaining assets (or social wealth) at least for the entire world, consists of tangible assets. It is convenient to group these assets under two heads: (1) durable goods for which depreciation or depletion accounts may be assumed to be maintained; (2) short-lived goods which are inventoried annually. Against these assets stand the various accounts held by individuals—bonds, stocks, mortgages, bank deposits, insurance policies, direct investments, etc. The balance sheet may be set up thus:

Concepts of National Income

Social (or National) Balance Sheet

Assets	Equities
(1) Durable goods	(11) Bonds and mortgages held by individuals
(2) Inventories	
(3) to (8) All other assets _____	(12) Stocks held by individuals
(9) Total wealth	(13) Bank deposits of individuals
	(14) Insurance policies for the benefit of individuals
	(15) Direct investments, etc.
	(16) to (18) All other equities _____
	(19) Total individual equities in social (or national) wealth

The process of consolidating income statements is more complicated and calls for fuller discussion. It is well to recognize that social income estimates may be made by attempting to consolidate either the income statements of the businesses and other enterprises of which the economic system consists, or the personal income and expenditure statements of families and individuals.

(1) The commonest method of estimating social income in this country uses the income statements of businesses and other enterprises, putting them together by a process that is known as the net value product method.

a) For most industry groups this method consists in determining and adding up those items which may be regarded as distributive shares originating in the enterprises of which the industry group consists: (i) payroll and other labor income; (ii) interest and cash dividends paid, less interest and cash dividends received, plus additions to corporate surplus; (iii) entrepreneurial profits; (iv) other distributive shares.

b) The net value product of an industry may also be estimated as follows: (i) gross revenues other than interest and dividends received, less (ii) the cost of those goods and services (purchased from other enterprises) which have been used or sold during the year; less (iii) depletion and depreciation.

(2) A short cut for the second form of the net value product method is sometimes attempted. This consists: (i) in identifying those gross revenues derived from goods and services going to ultimate consumers, and those revenues derived from new wealth produced, whether as replacements or as additions, and (ii) in subtracting depreciation and depletion, as measures of the old durable goods used up during the period under consideration.

(3) Social income may be estimated by adding together the incomes received by families and individuals chiefly in return for the services of their labor and property to the economic system.

(4) Social income may be estimated by adding up the expenditures of individuals for consumption goods and services and the increase in their holdings of equities in social wealth.

It is assumed that in consolidating the accounts of families and individuals for methods (3) and (4) transfer payments (or secondary distribution items) such as gifts are canceled out.

In the existing state of accounts it is inevitable that these different methods of estimating should yield different results, each purporting to be total social income. An ideal system of keeping the various types of income accounts can be conceived, such that if followed, it would ensure that the measurements of social income by the several methods would yield a single unambiguous result. In applying the several methods of estimate to existing records, corrections may be attempted to offset the difficulties due to the divergence between ideal and existing accounting practices, so that the results of the different estimates may approximately agree.

The main purposes of social wealth and income estimates are to provide a summary picture of the condition of an economic system or an exhibit of the value of non-human resources available for its use, to portray the changes in this stock of wealth and to set forth the values of goods and services produced by the economic system during the period under consideration, and to indicate the various distributive shares going to families and individuals for the services of their labor and property. Estimates of wealth and income should show not only the totals for a society, but also a variety of breakdowns that will reveal, on the one hand, the shares derived by the various participants in the economic system and their industrial sources, and, on the other hand, the uses to which their respective shares are put. So far as the value of products or the values of consumption goods and services provide measures of public well-being, social income estimates with appropriate breakdowns afford such general measures of public well-being.

For the economic system of the world as a whole social income measures: (a) the value of goods and services produced or the value of goods and services entering into human consumption plus the net increase in wealth; (b) the distributive shares or the costs of operating the system under existing methods as measured by the current hire-costs of labor (including entrepreneurial labor) and of wealth.

Because for the world as a whole total social income represents both (a) the value of products 'turned out,' 'produced' or 'contributed' by all participants or factors of production taken together, and (b) the total of distributive shares, it is too often assumed that the share in the social income derived through any one industry or by any one group of laborers or property owners represents a contribution to the output of the economic system equal in value to the share received. Thus, Simon Kuznets tells us: "any payment for productive services contributes just as much to the national income total as it takes away from it." He also refers repeatedly to the total income produced in the various industry groups, including all legal enterprises but excluding illegal enterprises.[1] Thus, if monopolies, shyster lawyers and fly-by-night promoters who have been careful to keep within the law are classed together as an 'industry group' he would logically speak of the share of national income produced in it. Such statements, in their implication that our existing economic system is fair and just, are strongly reminiscent of the productivity theory. When applied to the shyster lawyer, the lobbyist regardless of what he lobbies for, and the fly-by-night promoter, this view of national

[1] For such ethical implications see *National Income, 1929–1932* (73d Cong., 2d Sess., Senate Doc. 124, 1934), especially pp. 5, 7 and 10.

income requires us to conclude that, provided these gentle-men are careful to stay within the law, they make contributions to the social income as valuable as the claims upon it that they derive from the practice of their callings. In the writer's opinion such assumptions of equality between contribution and re-muneration are gratuitous and entirely unwarranted.

II DISTINCTIONS AMONG INCOME CONCEPTS

Before proceeding to a consideration of the chief types of breakdown used for social income and of various moot ques-tions in the concepts of social income, we may consider three main types of distinction among income concepts.

1 Income 'Derived From' vs. Income 'Received or Receivable In' an Area

For any area short of the entire world, it is important to dis-tinguish between income 'derived from' the wealth and labor employed in it and income 'received or receivable' in it. In the United States since the War the national income received or receivable has been larger than the national income derived from persons and resources employed. The difference, or net income derived from abroad, can be estimated from the balance of international payments statement and certain related in-formation in a manner analogous to that used in estimating the net value product for any individual enterprise.

The distinction represented by the exclusion or inclusion of the item 'income derived from other areas' is usually re-ferred to as 'income produced' vs. 'income received' in an area. Neither term is entirely accurate. 'Income produced' by a na-tion is open to the productivity theory implication just men-tioned, and 'income received' in a nation may not include all income accruing to the inhabitants during the period. The item 'income derived from other areas' may, of course, be either positive or negative.

2 The Receipt and Accrual Bases for Reporting Income

A good many items of income may be reckoned on either of two bases, receipt or accrual. For some items, e.g., payrolls, no substantial difference is involved, at least when the social income for a year or longer period is under consideration. For a good many other items there is, or may be, a considerable difference. Thus, we may consider either actual pension payments or credits to the accounts of prospective pensioners. Again, in connection with interest payments and receipts, allowance may or may not be made annually for the accumulation of bond discount or for a reserve for bad debts.

Dr. Kuznets' distinction between 'income produced' and 'income paid out' might be conceived as a partial application of the distinction between the receipt and accrual bases, since the income paid out excludes the addition to corporate surplus that accrues to individual equity holders without being received by them. However, 'income paid out' is partly on an accrual basis because it considers banks and certain financial enterprises (e.g., life insurance companies) as agencies receiving incomes for the account of individuals.[2] It is probably better, therefore, to consider 'income paid out' as an item in a breakdown of 'income produced.'

For some income items, for example, some employee pension and benefit items, it may be desirable to present income on both accrual and receipt bases. For various items, for example, interest paid, it is probably not worth while in annual estimates of income to attempt anything but a receipt basis. For incomes derived by corporate proprietorship equity holders some effort should surely be made in the direction of estimating them on an accrual basis.

In general the accrual basis, where it differs appreciably from the receipt basis, represents an increase in the accuracy of apportionment of income between different accounting periods, and the question as to which basis to use is partly one of how great a degree of refinement is warranted and partly one of how wide a deviation from common sense usage any given refinement requires.

---

[2] *National Income in the United States, 1929–1935* (Bureau of Foreign and Domestic Commerce, 1936) overlooks these accruals. It says, p. 1: "The National Income paid out may be defined as the sum of payments to or receipts by individuals as compensation for economic services rendered."

3 Bases of Valuation

Income estimates may be presented on any of several bases of valuation for the various constituent items. Three principal types of valuation bases may be suggested: (a) current prices; (b) stabilized prices; (c) valuations that attempt to correct existing data for various distortions they are assumed to involve.

a) Current prices and values. For most items in a social income estimate the application of current prices and values raises few problems. For two types of items, however, there is ambiguity involved in the application of this basis: (i) imputed or non-money items, and (ii) incomes accruing to the owners' proprietorship equities.

(i) Imputed items. When imputed items are included in an estimate of social income, what prices should be used? Thus, in estimating the value of farm produce consumed on home farms, should realization prices at farms or retail prices in adjacent communities be used? The latter alternative has the advantage of facilitating geographical comparisons of income.

Another important imputed item involving a difficult valuation question is that of net income derived from home ownership. Should the gross rental used for such an estimate be varied from year to year with the year-to-year fluctuation in rents? In general it would seem that this item should be more stable than rents.

(ii) Proprietorship equity items. The ambiguity in the case of incomes accruing to the owners of proprietorship equities may be illustrated for owners of common stock. The owner receives in addition to cash dividends an item represented by the increase in the value of his equity during the year or other period. The three bases chiefly used in determining this income are: the book value of the equity, assuming standard accounting procedure; the value of the equity on the security markets; and an adjusted book value of the equity, assuming that both opening and closing inventories are valued at an average price for the year and that a kind of replacement accounting is used instead of depreciation accounting. If security market value is used, the question arises whether to use the price at a particular instant or the average of several quotations. Even when an average is used, variations in market values are so eccentric as to lead to bizarre results. The use of the adjusted book value basis, in the writer's opinion, should properly be considered as a partial stabilization of prices of the general type considered under (b) below.

b) Stabilized prices. Variations from period to period in social income as measured in current prices reflect in part changes in the physical volume of production of the economic system (or else in the physical volume of the wealth and labor used in production) and in part changes in prices. For many purposes it is desirable to attempt to correct dollar volume variations in income measured at current prices in such a way that they shall reveal only variations in physical volumes. This may be accomplished by estimates of what social income would have been, had one fixed set of prices prevailed throughout the various periods to be compared.

Theoretically, similar corrections might be applied in making comparisons of social income between communities. Practically, differences in the physical items included in social income in different communities are likely to be greater than are the corresponding differences in any two nearby periods of time for the same community. Hence, such corrections for geographic comparisons offer difficulties so great that no comprehensive attempt to make them has yet been offered, to the writer's knowledge. Even corrections for time comparisons are in a very elementary stage, and one might rightly hesitate to describe as 'comprehensive' any existing attempt to make corrections for price changes in the estimates of the national income of any nation for any two years.

c) Corrected valuations. Conceivably a great variety of corrections of income estimates may be attempted through adjusting valuations in individual items. Actually it may be easier to agree upon the existence of difficulties in the individual income items than upon the corrections to apply to them. Thus, some prevalent accounting practices may be regarded as undesirable, and various efforts might be made to estimate what would have been shown by the records had better accounting practices been followed. Somewhat the same thing may be said with respect to corrections for the eccentricities of government fiscal policy. Again, existing prices may be felt to reflect monopoly conditions, the unequal distribution of wealth and income, the failure to outlaw certain socially undesirable practices, etc. Efforts might be made to make corrections upon the assumption that each of these conditions in turn is replaced by a condition deemed preferable. But such corrections are so fraught with difficulty and so likely to prove arbitrary that there is a strong presumption against making any of them.

III MAIN BREAKDOWNS OF SOCIAL INCOME

Five principal types of breakdown of social income may be considered: by type of payment, industry, area, income class, and object of expenditure.

1 By Type of Payment or Distributive Share

Total social income may be conceived as consisting of three main types of income—employee labor income, property income and entrepreneurial profits. These correspond roughly to the wages, interest and profits of classical economic theory. For present purposes pensions and certain other types of compensation may be included under employee labor income along with payrolls. And in addition to interest and accruals pertaining to the holding of bonds or other forms of indebtedness the income that accrues to owners of corporate proprietorship equities may be considered property income. Entrepreneurial profit is a hybrid type of share, including both labor and property income. These three broad classes of income—employee labor income, property income and profits—constitute the chief primary distributive shares in the national dividend.

Classical economic theory would add a fourth—rent. Actually it is better to consider rents and royalties as gross income, since in most cases depreciation and various expenses paid to other enterprises (taxes, repairs, etc.) must be deducted from rent and royalty incomes. Moreover, interest and wage payments, as well as payments to other enterprises, may be made out of gross rent and royalty incomes. The residual after these deductions is more aptly described as net entrepreneurial profit from the ownership and management of properties than as a fourth main type of distributive share.

In addition to the primary distributive shares various redistributions of social income and the ownership of wealth may be made. The chief of these are considered below.

2 By Industry

Social income may be broken down according to the industries from which primary distributive shares are derived. Such a breakdown can be made in more detail and on a clearer basis for payroll income than for some of the other distributive shares. Were dependable basic data for entrepreneurial profits available, a detailed industrial breakdown for this type of income could also be made fairly satisfactorily. Difficulties arise, however, in the industrial apportionment of property incomes, owing both to the vertical integration of the large enterprises from which much of this type of income is derived, and to the fact that property income, instead of going directly to individuals, may first pass through the hands of various equity 'holding' companies (including banks and insurance companies).

It should be emphasized that the income derived from an industry does not necessarily represent the industry's contribution to the aggregate social income. Nor can any distributive share derived from any industry be assumed necessarily to represent the contribution of the factor of production remunerated thereby to aggregate social income or aggregate social production. If we question whether the contribution of monopolies to aggregate social income is accurately measured by the income derived from them, we question also whether the contributions of employees and owners of and of investors in those monopolies are measured accurately by the incomes derived from them.

3 By Area

When social income is apportioned geographically, we need to distinguish between the income derived from an area and the income received or receivable in it. Thus we may speak of the national income derived from the wealth and people of the United States or the national income received or receivable by the people of the United States. Similarly, we may speak of the income derived from farms and persons working on them, or of the income received or receivable by the farm population. The former is sometimes referred to as the income derived from agriculture and the latter as the income of the farm population.

4 By Income Class

While existing data for the United States provide far from satisfactory information for the allocation of social income by income classes, the nature of this type of distribution is in some ways simpler than that of any of the three preceding types. Classes in the total population, or in families and single persons, or in income recipients may be set up either by establishing absolute class limits in terms of dollars of income per annum or by the use of the quartiles, deciles or percentiles in the frequency distribution, and total social income received or receivable may then be apportioned among the classes so set up.

5 By Object of Expenditure

The apportionment of social income by object of expenditure may, as Dr. Warburton points out, provide very illuminating information concerning cyclical variations in the operation of the economic system, particularly if the social income to be distributed is enlarged to represent what may be called the gross value product or the net value product plus depreciation and depletion. We would have then three main types of expenditure: (a) replacements of wealth, (b) savings invested in new wealth, (c) goods and service consumed by ultimate consumers.

It scarcely need be added that various crosses of the five types of breakdown discussed above are both possible and useful.

IV   CHIEF ITEMS OF ESTIMATE

As a guide in discussing some of the moot questions in the definition of national income it is helpful to have before us a statement of the main items of estimate, using the net value product method.

For this purpose we may use a form of income statement that can be applied somewhat generally to the various types of enterprise involved, including business corporations, farms, and conceivably even governments. For simplicity we neglect several possible debit and credit items arising in connection with the attempt to put the items here presented upon an accrual basis. We may distinguish six main credit or revenue items and ten main debit items which show either expenses or distributive shares. It is assumed, of course, that the sums of debits and of credits will balance so that by a rearrangement of these items we may obtain two estimates of the national income derived from the operation of the nation's economic system. The six credit items are:

(1) Gross revenues from operations not elsewhere specified. For enterprises other than banks and certain other financial institutions this item will consist chiefly of operating revenues. As noted above, all rents and royalties will be included here as the operating revenues of businesses devoted to the ownership and management of properties. So far as imputed or non-money income items are to be included in the national income estimates, they will presumably be included under this item unless they can be treated directly as distributive shares. For the government, taxes and other revenue receipts would be included under this item.

(2) Interest income. This includes all interest income. For banks and certain other financial institutions it will, of course, represent the main item of operating income.

(3) Cash dividends received. This item is self-explanatory.

(4) Increase in tangible assets during the period. Increases in tangible assets should be included as a credit item when they are due to expenditures noted below under items (10) pay-

rolls; (11) purchases of materials and supplies; (13) taxes, including special assessments. For short-lived assets that may be treated on an inventory basis item (4) will represent a figure which, when deducted from purchases of merchandise and materials and direct labor, will give the expense figure, 'cost of goods sold.' [3] Accountants hesitate to treat item (4) as a revenue item, preferring to treat it as a deduction from purchases in order to give a net expense item for the period, thus: purchases plus opening inventory minus closing inventory equals cost of goods sold. From the point of view of the economic system as a whole, however, it is important to recognize item (4) as a revenue item or addition to the gross value product of the industry. This is true of additions to the long-lived tangible assets as well as of additions to inventories. This item represents force-account additions as distinguished from additions of long-lived assets purchased complete from contractors or other separate enterprises.

(5) Subsidy revenues derived from government. This item is self-explanatory.

(6) Valuation readjustment gains from balance sheet items other than inventories. Such gains may be shown either (a) through the sale of an asset at a figure above its book value or the retirement of a liability at a figure below its book value, or (b) by virtue of a decision to make an adjustment in the book value other than that provided for by following the established arrangement for writing off an asset or a liability during its life through charges to depreciation or for the accumulation of bond discount, the amortization of a bond premium, etc.

The ten debit items are:

(10) Payrolls and other forms of employee labor income. In employee labor income should be included wages, salaries, bonuses, commissions, etc.; also, either the employers' con-

---

[3] It may be noted that item (4) may include income from appreciation of inventories; but such an item would exist if inventories were accumulating, even if prices remained constant. With declining inventories and falling prices this item would assume a negative value.

tribution to employees' pensions and other benefit funds or the pensions and other benefits paid from employer-contributed funds directly during the period. Compensation for damages should be excluded (see item (16) below).

(11) Purchases of merchandise, materials and supplies, and of the services of other enterprises. Purchases will include payments for a great variety of things—freight, communication, advertising, insurance premiums not elsewhere specified, legal and medical services, electricity, contract repairs, etc.

(12) Depletion and depreciation of tangible assets not treated as inventories. It is assumed that except for the short-lived tangible assets depreciation and depletion accounting procedure is followed. Item (12) may be thought of as the decrease in a previously established valuation of any piece of tangible wealth (other than the short-lived goods) due to its use during the years or to the passage of time. Downward readjustments in an established valuation, on the basis of which depreciation or depletion is computed, are included elsewhere (see item (18)).

(13) Taxes paid, including special assessments. This item may be thought of as a special case of item (11), but it raises peculiar problems which merit separate discussion below. The line between those taxes paid by individual entrepreneurs which are to be regarded as paid by enterprises and those which are to be regarded as paid directly by families and individuals will necessarily depend in part upon the national income estimator's decision as to what items of imputed income he will recognize. Thus, if gross rental value of owned homes is included above under (1), taxes on these homes may properly be included here as a business cost.

(14) Interest paid. This item and item (15) are self-explanatory.

(15) Corporate cash dividends paid.

(16) Damages to employees and others. Business compensation expense for damages to all persons should be included here either on an outlay basis or as public liability damage insurance premiums paid.

(17) Gifts and charitable contributions. Business contributions to charity and, in the case of the government, certain so-called transfer payments belong here.

(18) Valuation readjustment losses. This item is the converse of item (6). It may represent either actual realizations or adjustments in established book valuations. It may arise in connection with durable tangible assets, with receivables and investments, or with liabilities.

(19) Additions to corporate surplus and (for individual business enterprises) profits. For any enterprise this item should be equal to the balance remaining after deducting the above nine debit items from the total of the six credit items. For corporations this item plus item (18) minus item (6) corresponds to 'additions to surplus,' in Dr. Kuznets' usage.

The above list of items is not intended to be exhaustive but rather to indicate the main types of income statement item that may be used to estimate the net value product derived from any enterprise or industry group. The advantages of setting up, in accounting form, the net value product method of estimate, using such a list of items, include: first, the possibility where adequate data are available of making two estimates that should check with each other; second, the possibility of using different kinds of items for estimating the net value products of different industry groups; third, the avoidance of oversights of important considerations in making estimates for any industry group even where data are not adequate for a double estimate; fourth, the recognition of the full logical implication of making an assumption or decision respecting the handling of any one moot item. Thus, the bearing of the decision to include or exclude the rental value of owned homes upon the handling of taxes has just been noted. In the writer's opinion, it is not adequate to say that this accounting form has advantages. It is wise to recognize that failure to use such a double entry approach is almost certain to lead either to counting items twice or to important omissions, or both.

Since the net value products of all enterprises may by their very nature be added together to give us a consolidated picture for the entire economic system, we can rearrange the sixteen items discussed above in such a way as to show an outline of an estimate of national income:

(1) gross revenue from operations not elsewhere classified, plus (4) increase in inventories and force-account additions to durable goods,[4]

plus (5) subsidy revenues derived from government,

less (11) purchases of merchandise, materials, and supplies and services from other enterprises, and

less (13) taxes paid, equals

(20) The gross social value product derived from the economic system before taking into account valuation adjustments. Dr. Warburton has called this 'the gross national product' or 'value of final product.' Except for the fact that item (20) deducts 'taxes paid' and broadens the meaning of item (11), by analogy to Census parlance we might also call item (20) 'value added by the year's operations.' It represents a concept whose usefulness has hitherto, in the writer's opinion, received inadequate attention. It will be further discussed below. If from the gross social value product, item (20), we deduct item (12) depreciation and depletion of durable goods, we have

(21) The net social value product derived from the operation of the economic system before taking into account valuation readjustments. In the writer's opinion, this concept should be regarded as the basic national income concept. We have reached it by deducting two items from the increase in inventories and force-account additions to plant and equipment, plus the gross revenue from general operations and from subsidies—first, inter-enterprise purchases of goods and services, and second, the wealth used up by the year's operations. This may be called the credit or revenue net value product method of estimate.

We can also reach this total by the debit or distributive-share

---

[4] This formula does not involve any commitment on the question, raised by Dr. Kuznets, as to whether inventory appreciation should count as income.

The significance of items (1), (4) and (11) in the formula can be more easily visualized if we consider its application to a merchandizing enterprise where force-account additions to plant and equipment are zero: $(1) + (4) - (11) =$ gross profit. The accountant prefers to write this formula $(1) - [(11) - (4)] =$ gross profit.

net value product method of estimate. In other words, item (21), net social value product derived from the operations of the economic system during the year, equals the sum of the following items:

(10) payrolls, pensions, etc.,

plus (14) minus (2) interest paid less interest received, or 'interest originating in' each enterprise or industry group,

plus (15) minus (3) cash dividends paid less cash dividends received, or cash dividends originating in each enterprise or industry group,

plus (16) damages to employees and others,

plus (17) charitable contributions, transfer payments, etc.,

plus (19) minus the difference ((6) minus (18)) i.e., additions to corporate surplus and individual business profits before taking account of valuation readjustment gains and losses.

For the sake of simplicity we are assuming that a consolidated statement for the item $[(19) - \{(6) - (18)\}]$ can be accomplished by a simple summation. The questions raised by this assumption are too involved to discuss here. Their existence is particularly important for the income concept next considered, item (22).

If to item (21), the total of items just listed, or the social income derived from the year's operations, we add the difference (item (6) minus item (18)), the net gain from valuation readjustments, we have

(22) Total social income including net valuation readjustment gains. National income may be either larger or smaller according to this concept than is national income as represented by item (21) although in a sense this concept is the more inclusive one. It is suggested, however, that this total be given a place subordinate to total (21) for two reasons: first, because the net valuation readjustment gains and losses represent transactions that are not necessarily directly attributable to the year's operations; and second, because the amounts involved in these transactions are to a much greater degree matters of judgment, upon the part either of the estimator or of those responsible for the accounting records that constitute his basic

data, than are the amounts involved in other items included in the income total.

Since we have elected to treat total (21) as the basic concept for social income derived from the operations of an economic system, we shall use it rather than total (22) in computing the total national income received or receivable. Thus,

(21) total national income derived from the country before taking account of valuation readjustments,

plus (23) net income received from abroad, equals

(24) total national income received or receivable in the country.

V SUMMARY *

1. National income is a special case of social income.

2. Social income = the value of goods and services consumed by ultimate consumers plus savings (or plus the increase in social wealth).

3. Social wealth and social income are estimated by consolidating balance sheets and income statements of separate enterprises and/or of individuals. Social wealth and income are accounting concepts, the validity of which may be checked by accounting techniques.

4. The income derived from an enterprise or calling should not be interpreted as a measure of the contribution made by the enterprise or calling to social income (i.e., to the value of goods and services consumed plus the increase in social wealth). Such a view would consider legal high finance as socially productive.

5. Social income derived from a community (inaccurately called 'income produced' in it) plus the net social income derived from elsewhere by its population equals social income received or receivable in the community.

6. Social income may be valued either in current dollars or in dollars reckoned at a constant set of prices. Special valuation problems arise in connection with various items of income,

---

* The summary includes several points made in the section of the original paper entitled "Some Moot Questions" that is omitted here.

particularly additions to corporate surplus, individual profits, and imputed incomes.

7. There are five major types of breakdown of social income: by (a) type of payment or distributive share (payrolls, interest, etc.); (b) industries; (c) areas; (d) income classes; (e) objects of expenditure.

8. There are two 'net value product' methods of estimating social income: (a) revenue from sales, etc., less payments to other enterprises and less depreciation, etc.; (b) the sum of the net distributive shares.

9. The 'gross value product' of a community ('net value product' plus depreciation and depletion), if deflated, would give a broad production index number.

10. Estimates of additions to corporate surplus are no less dependable than some of the other items in the social net value product, though this view seems implied in treating as basic the questionable concept 'income paid out.' 'Income actually received by individuals' might be a useful concept—hitherto it has not been seriously attempted for this country.

11. Estimates of 'entrepreneurial withdrawals' and 'individual busines savings' are as subjective as are estimates of the value of housewives' services.

12. To treat banks and other holders of 'earning assets' as 'associations of individuals' and to neglect short term interest items is to substitute an arbitrary guess for the measurement of important income items. For estimating 'total social income received or receivable' the net value product formula should be rigidly adhered to, even though some enterprises show negative net value products.*

13. 'Social net income from abroad' includes other items in addition to net in-payments of interest and dividends; e.g., (a) immigrants' entrance capital, (b) immigrant remittances (a negative item), (c) additions to foreign corporate surpluses owned here.

14. Under present conditions government interest, in estimating the social net value product, should be conceived as imputed net income from government-owned tangible wealth.

* See following article.

15. No sharp line can be drawn between government pay-rolls, which are distributive shares to be added to other shares to give the social net value product, and those relief payments which are mere transfer payments and are not to be added in.

16. Consumed income should be 'deflated' by an index of the costs of consumer goods and services. Saved income in current dollars cannot be directly deflated. Instead the wealth on January 1 and the wealth on December 31 should be deflated by an appropriate index of the prices of items of wealth.

17. Scarcity appreciation should be included in income meas-ured in current dollars, because of its bearing on income dis-tribution and because it allows us to equate 'saved income' with the increase in wealth in current dollars. Mere scarcity appreciation does not affect the total of deflated social income.

· XII ·

Problems in the Theory of National Income Peculiar to Financial Enterprises*

(1932)

THE theoretical problems of estimating the total pay-roll income of the United States and of apportioning total pay-roll income either on an industrial or a geographical basis are relatively not of great difficulty. Much the same is true of entrepreneurial income. It is property income which gives rise to the really baffling complications; this is due to the interlocking property relationships among various groups of enterprises —to the holding by certain corporate enterprise groups of equities in other groups. These complications are becoming of greater importance as time passes.

Consolidation and other accounting procedures play a fundamental part in the empirical determination of national net-value-product, labor income, property income, consumption, and savings. It is the present thesis that accounting technique offers the key to some vexed questions in the theory of national income. But it should be noted that the point of view of na-

* Extracted from, "Some Problems in the Theory of National Income."

tional accountancy differs from that of private accountancy because of the consolidation of accounts. In Davenport's terminology, it may be denominated a *collectivist* viewpoint. Moreover, as will presently appear, while the technique of private accountancy offers the key to certain problems in the theory of national income, there are others for which its technique offers no useful precedent.

The net-value-product method of estimating the national income involves setting up an income statement for each group of enterprises, though the grouping of items for this purpose differs from that of the ordinary income statement. From gross revenue from operations must first be deducted two chief groups of items: (2) expenses for goods and services which give rise to revenue for other enterprises, and (3) depreciation and depletion of owned tangible assets. These two deductions represent "consumption of goods and services in the process of production." The resulting "net-value-product" of the industry represents value added by the industry over and above national wealth used up by the industry in the process of production. These resulting "net-value-products" of the several groups may be added to give a total value of consumption goods and savings clean of duplications. An illustrative income statement follows:

INCOME STATEMENT FOR MANUFACTURING

      Cr. (1) Gross revenue from sales
Less Dr. (2) Operating and maintenance expenses paid to other enterprises for materials, supplies, and services §
Less Dr. (3) Depletion and depreciation (or replacement) expense of owned tangible assets (including depreciation of inventories)
Gives Cr. (4) Net-value-product (which equals the net total of the following items):
      Dr. (5) Pay-roll and pensions †

§ Excludes "replacements" so far as included in (3).
† Technically, increase in pension reserve during the year should be added to pensions to put this item on an accrual basis; but the addition is not important—except, perhaps, in the case of the federal government. The addition is a form of business savings.

Plus   Dr.   (6) All interest paid (plus bond discount accumulated
           and/or less bond premium amortized)
Plus   Dr.   (7) Cash dividends paid plus "business savings"
Less   Cr.   (8) Interest and dividend income and profits on sale of
           equities in other enterprises, etc.

We may consider next certain problems of property income, peculiar to financial enterprises, taking the group of commercial and savings banks as illustrative. An attempt to recast the foregoing model income statement, which is applicable to most industry groups, encounters immediate difficulties here. Interest income corresponds in a sense to gross operating revenue. It is the predominant credit item. But it comes from equities in other enterprises; and if we calculate "net-value-product" of banking as interest income plus other income minus cost of supplies, light, heat, taxes, depreciation, etc., we will evidently be doing double counting, for interest income from bank loans, discounts, and investments is part of the value product of railroads, manufacturing, etc.

If we look further at the model income statement, we find another place for interest income, item (8). Indeed, in deducting intercorporate interest and dividend income from gross interest and dividend payments of the *receiving* enterprise in the case of manufacturing, it was expressly stipulated that this procedure should be followed consistently throughout, in order to get interest and dividend income received by "individuals" or ultimate income recipients. But if this procedure is consistently adhered to in the case of banking, the net-value-product of this industry group will evidently be a negative quantity.

How does King [1] get out of this dilemma? As he follows the debit-net-value-product method [2] exclusively in this case, he is not directly concerned with what corresponds to item (1), gross

---

[1] W. I. King, *Wealth and Income of the People of the United States* (1915), *National Income and Its Purchasing Power* (1930); and joint author of *Income in the United States* (1922).

[2] King's estimates of national income are for income received by "individuals," i.e., real persons or, in a useful phraseology, "ultimate income recipients," or laborers and holders of ultimate equities in the national wealth. For the most part he does not, however, deduct from gross property income earned by each industry group an item (I) "property income *paid out to* or accruing to the credit of other enterprises," though this would be one logical way to get "in-

operating revenue. Item (8) he treats, not as total property income received, but only as income received on corporate *stocks* and *bonds* held. Certain other elements of interest income of banks are deducted from the *paying* enterprise, not from the *receiving* bank. And while dividends to stockholders are treated according to the property-income-*received* deduction formula, interest to depositors is treated by the formula "Total interest paid less interest *paid* to other enterprises equals interest paid to 'individuals.'" Thus King has deducted property income received by enterprises from gross property income "produced" by the *receiving* enterprises in some cases, and in other cases from the gross property income "produced" by the *paying* enterprises. This procedure may be summarized as follows:

1. Some interest paid to banks is deducted from gross property income of *paying* enterprises (this includes interest paid to banks by government, agriculture, construction, and foreigners).

2. *Interest* and dividends paid to banks on corporate securities are deducted from *dividends* paid by *receiving* banks.[3]

---

come received by individuals." Instead, in most cases, as shown in our model statement for manufacturing, he deducts (II) "property income *received from* other enterprises." These two types of deduction, *if* each is followed *consistently* throughout, should yield exactly the same total national income. $\Sigma(I) = \Sigma(II)$. The deduction of (II) instead of (I) commends itself for two reasons. The income statement data for industry groups are amenable to this procedure and not to deducting (I). Moreover, as is clear from our model income statement, deduction (II) must be used if we are to get the industry "net-value-product." The advantage of (II), then, is partly due to the fact that the "net-value-product" method of estimating income is not single but double. For most industry groups it is possible to estimate the debits and credits independently so that we have two estimates of "net-value-product" to check against each other.

But although King uses the method of deduction (II) for the most part, he is unable to take advantage of the check of debits against credits. This is because his figure, "total income realized from an industry group" excludes business savings (except those that are included in part in agriculture). Hence he does not make both a debit and a credit estimate for each group, but follows what may be called the credit net-value-product method in some groups $(1 - 2 - 3)$ and the debit net-value-product method $(5 + 6 + 7 - 8)$ in others. In the writer's opinion the importance of this possible check of debits against credits has been inadequately appreciated.

[3] Because of this and certain other procedures, King's separate totals for interest and dividends do not precisely represent the actual distribution in form of realized property income as between interest and dividends, as these two types are received by individuals.

3. Interest paid to other enterprises by banks is deducted from interest *paid* by banks.

It will be argued that this compromise procedure neither gives an approximately correct figure for banking, nor does it portray the year-to-year changes satisfactorily, and, further, that it gives incorrect figures for certain property-income items of other industry groups.

The relationship of income statement and balance sheet affords a clue to certain puzzles of property income. Does it afford a clue to the banking-income dilemma? Following is an attempt at a consolidated banking system balance sheet for approximately June 29, 1929. Because the Treasury Department performs monetary functions, the monetary treasury items have been included. To use this balance sheet as a basis for defining property income will, therefore, have the effect of including certain government property income, although corresponding government labor income is not included; but this item would be almost negligible in the totals.

Most of the items on this balance sheet are self-explanatory— it represents a consolidation of the balance sheets for (*a*) "all reporting banks" (national and state banks, trust companies, savings banks, and private banks), (*b*) the Federal Reserve Banks, and (*c*) the monetary assets and liabilities of the United States Treasury. Inter-bank items are eliminated. Thus, from the gross total of earning assets, the following items have been deducted to give item 1: rediscounts, bills payable, and Federal Reserve Bank stock. Item 3 represents total outstanding "Treasury currency" less available collateral, including the bullion value of silver, item 6. Till money has been deducted to give the net item 13, and items in process of collection deducted to give the net item 12. Item 15 is the balance of due from and due to banks and miscellaneous assets and equities. Because definitions of such items as "due from banks" and "due to banks," and certain collection items, are not entirely standardized, and because of the fact that not all balance sheets are for June 29, the consolidation is not entirely accurate. This applies especially to errors of classification as between items 12 and 15, which are not of great importance for our present purpose.

CONSOLIDATED BALANCE SHEET OF THE UNITED STATES
BANKING SYSTEM, JUNE 29, 1929

(In Billions of Dollars)

1. Earning assets	58.26	11. Proprietorship equity		9.92
2. Non-banking real estate	.39			
3. Deficit in treasury collateral	.77	12. Individual deposits	..	51.79
4. Total	59.42	13. Circulation		3.86
5. Gold stock	4.32			
6. Silver stock	.34	14. Accrued interest, taxes, etc.		.14
7. Banking house and fixtures	1.81	15. Net of miscellaneous assets and equities		.18
8. Total	6.47			
9. Total assets	65.89	19. Total equities	..	65.89

To be consistent with the procedure for other industry groups, we should define property income from banking so that it will bear a relation to that part of the national wealth used in the business which is typical of the return on investments in this line of business. The peculiar problems which arise from banking are due to its capital-raising function. It acts as an agent, securing funds at one rate and letting them out at a certain "mark-up." The funds let out are indicated as "equities in other businesses." They include loans and discounts, investments, non-banking real estate, and "deficit in Treasury collateral" for currency. Whether this last is correctly classified may be questioned; but it is clearly not a part of the national wealth used in banking; and, since its backing is the taxing power, it is in the nature of a claim primarily on non-banking property (or labor). The national wealth owned and used in banking includes bullion value of monetary gold and silver, and book value of banking house and fixtures. Current bank accounting undoubtedly undervalues banking real estate, and consequently also the proprietorship equity (capital, surplus, and undivided profits of all reporting banks plus Federal Reserve Banks' surplus). Absence of a satisfactory basis of correction, and the relatively small effect on the income estimates, make it seem best not to attempt any adjustment in the balance sheet.

Perhaps the most interesting, and for our present problem certainly the most puzzling, feature of this balance sheet is that the proprietorship equity is distinctly larger than that part of the national wealth used in the business. Evidently a part of this equity represents an indirect equity in other businesses. The balance sheet suggests, if we conceive the banking system as a capital-raising agency or financial "middleman," that we may draw an analogy between gross merchandising profit, or "value added in manufacturing," and bank interest income minus property income accruing to indirect equities in other business. We may call this "value added in banking," and deduct it from the property incomes of other industry groups as the price of banking service.[4] This procedure should give us a reasonable figure for banking property income on the basis of "national wealth owned in banking." Will it give us a correct net total of property incomes accruing to "individuals"? We may answer this question affirmatively in tabular form, thus:

	Dr.	Cr.
Non-financial enterprises	(1) Gross property income accruing to equity holders	(11) Property incomes received
		(12) Value added in banking, etc. = (13) − (3)
Financial enterprises as illustrated by banking	(3) Gross property income accruing to indirect equity holders	(13) Gross property income received (interest income)
	(4) Value added in banking, etc. = (13) − (3)	
	(5) Property income accruing to holders of direct equities in national wealth in banking business	
Totals, less (4) = (12)	(6) Gross property income accruing to holders of business equities (1) + (3) + (5)	(16) Total property income received by businesses (11) + (13)

Item (6) — item (16) gives property income received by individuals; our net total of property income is correct, (13) —

---

[4] See item 8, in the model income statement for manufacturing, above.

(4) = (3). Thus, the banking system is considered as an agency collecting this amount of property income, (13) — (4), and turning it over to others, item (3). Further, the net property income for banking on its own account is item (5), which represents the return on national wealth in banking. Finally, item (12) (as well as item (11)) may fairly be deducted from item (1), if we consider it as the price of raising capital, although an alternative treatment of it is suggested below.

It is clear that this method of avoiding the dilemma of banking property incomes involves a specific allocation of banking equities against specific groups of assets. So also does the procedure employed by King. Indeed, some such specific allocation seems unavoidable for this type of enterprise. Two chief methods of allocation for determining "value added in banking" may be considered: (I) The non-interest-bearing equity, circulation (and the small miscellaneous item), may be assigned directly against the asset group, "equities in other enterprises." The income-bearing equities will then be lumped together and a proportion of their income equal to

$$\left(1 - \frac{\text{National wealth owned and used in banking}}{\text{Total income-bearing equities}}\right)$$

multiplied by 100 per cent of that income will be treated as item (3), "gross property income accruing to indirect equity holders." (II) Circulation, deposits, and miscellaneous equities may be assigned directly against equities in other businesses. The formula for item (3) will then be

$$\left(1 - \frac{\text{National wealth in banking}}{\text{Proprietorship equity}}\right)$$

multiplied by 100 per cent of proprietorship income, plus interest to depositors. Both because deposits fall fairly clearly into the class of indirect equities, the bank acting as agent for the employment of these funds, and because method (II) gives a more reasonable figure for return on banking wealth, method (II) appears to be the better one.

It will be desirable to see how this method works out for a period of years and to compare the results with King's estimates. In applying this method a somewhat different procedure has been employed from that of King. He uses *national* bank data on payrolls (*fiscal*-year basis, two-year moving average) and on corporate investments. He employs only the debit "net-value-product" method and does not include Federal Reserve Banks and Treasury. The present estimates employ *all member*-bank data (*calendar*-year basis), and both debit and credit methods are employed, thus affording a check on the accuracy of the results. The income statement is a consolidated account including the Federal Reserve Banks and, for property income on gold and silver, the Treasury. The debits and credits on the all-reporting-banks-estimated-income statement did not agree precisely and half the error was prorated on the debits and half on the credits. The correction in every case was less than 1 per cent. The effect of undervaluation of real estate upon these estimates is chiefly to change slightly the fraction of proprietorship income included in item (3). If the present realty figures were increased 50 per cent, it would involve a change of about 2 per cent in the fraction; and an arbitrary correction of 2 per cent was applied to each year.

In computing income *realized* from banking (as distinguished from *accrued* income) in order to get a figure fairly comparable with King's totals, business savings must be deducted from the net-value-product. This raises an interesting question regarding the measuring of realized income. A part of interest and dividend income from other enterprises realized by banks in their capacity as capital-raising agents is not passed on as realized income but is retained in banking surplus. Thus, to get a total for all industries of income realized by individuals we must deduct from banking property income (equals a fraction of bank dividends plus a *fraction* of additions to "surplus") the *total* of bank additions to surplus.[5] In comparing these estimates with King's

[5] The alternative would be to deduct part of bank additions to surplus from banking property income and the rest of bank additions to surplus from property incomes of other enterprises. King's procedure is more nearly equivalent to the one here used, viz., to deduct all bank additions to surplus from bank property income. [The article as originally published contained a table showing a consolidated income statement for the nation's banking system, arranged to show "value added in banking" and "net value product of banking," and for purposes of comparison "bank realized income."—EDITOR.]

it should, perhaps, be noted that, while rent is here classed as a payment to other enterprises and therefore not included in banking net-value-product, this does not invalidate the comparison because King includes no rent item in his banking estimates.

By way of summary it may be noted that from the viewpoint of national accounting the concept "net-value-product" of an industry group has a double significance: (1) On the one hand it represents an intermediate stage in the consolidation process. It represents gross revenues less certain debit items which it is assumed are canceled by credit items of other groups. (2) It partakes of a cost-accounting nature in that it purports to state that part of the total cost of national production attributable to the given industry group. Were it not for this independent significance of an industry's "net-value-product," there would be no "banking dilemma"—no objection to a negative "net-value-product" for banking, since this would give a correct total national income. But because "net-value-product" is a measure of the social cost attributable to the production of an industry group, we must find a solution for the "banking dilemma."

The relationship between property income and the consolidated balance sheet of an industry group makes possible a more precise definition of "net-value-product" for banking and government. Because of the peculiar theoretical problem of defining "net-value-product" for banking, this group has been singled out for illustrative study, and estimates have been made by both the debit and credit methods. The concept "value added in banking" offers a solution of the banking dilemma. It meets satisfactorily both (*a*) the necessity of insuring complete and accurate deduction of "property incomes received by producing enterprises" from gross property income, and (*b*) the requirement that the return on the national wealth owned in banking shall be representative of the current return in this kind of business. Both because of the checks, and because of the more satisfactory data used (calendar-year data, a larger sample, and the inclusion of the Federal Reserve System), it is believed that the results represent a material improvement in accuracy.

· XIII ·

The Income and Product Circuit and the Money Circuit in India and the United States

(1951)

IT is coming to be standard practice to present national income and product statistics in the form of a set of interlocking social accounts—the comprehensive national income and product account together with accounts that show purchases of product by various sectors, public, private, and foreign receipts of distributive shares, and the balancing savings and investment account. Most people, when they first encounter such an exhibit and grasp the interrelationships it entails, are left with the question. How does money fit into this picture? What is the role of money in these interrelationships?

I think we can get a good deal of light on this question by delving into the subject of comparative economy, by making a series of comparisons between two economies that differ markedly in degree of industrialization and in degree of development of pecuniary institutions, India and the United States. It is proposed to consider first some structural comparisons between these two economies, and then some functional comparisons.

The comparisons will necessarily be somewhat tentative because I have only begun to learn about the Indian economy and its history. Moreover, what can be done in the way of such comparisons today is limited by the boundaries of the information now available. But these considerations do not argue against an attempt on my part to do what I can with the materials at hand. And the attempt should be helpful in planning next steps in economic-statistical inquiry.

The usual answer to the question about the role of money in the social accounts is, it seems fair to say, not an explanation of that role, but the computation of a ratio. To be sure this ratio has a name. It is called the income velocity of money. But the name raises quite as many questions as it answers. In 1948–49 this ratio for India was 3.4: for the United States in 1949 it was 1.8.[1]

Does this mean that money circulates nearly twice as rapidly in India as in the United States? I think not; I pose this first comparison merely to underscore the need for a different approach.

The national income and product account of a country portrays more than an overall national balance between value of total national output and value of distributive shares and other claims charged against that total. It portrays an economic circuit. The National Income Committee of India says on this point,

In the circuit flow of economic activity the same total can be measured at the point of production, as the sum of net outputs arising in the several industrial sectors of the nation's productive system; at the point of flow of incomes, as the sum of all incomes in cash, in kind and retained by enterprises as net profit; at the point of final utilization, as the sum of consumer expenditure, government purchase of goods and services, and net outlay on capital goods. . . . Net outputs, income flows, and final expenditure . . . reflect the total operations of the nation's economy at the levels of the three basic

---

[1] The numerator in each case is national income. The denominator for India is what the Reserve Bank calls 'money supply' plus coin in circulation plus the cash balance of the Central Government, Mar. 31, 1949. For the U.S. it is all currency and deposit liabilities of banks and the monetary system except time deposits, June 30, 1949.

184   *Fact and Theory in Economics*

economic functions, viz. production, distribution, and expenditure or consumption.[2]

This national income and product circuit is a two sector circuit. The intermediate or productive sector produces and sells the national product and divides up the entire proceeds into wages, interest, profits, etc. The final or ultimate sector receives the wages, interest, profits, etc., and spends the total of these income flows on purchases of the national product. For each of the two sectors its total inflow equals its total outflow. The outflow of either sector equals the inflow of the other.

It will be observed that this circuit consists of final product transactions and the final primary distribution of the national value product. Sales to merchants for resale are not final sales, and costs of materials are not final factor costs. They do not appear in this circuit. Nor do sales of stocks and bonds, nor non *quid pro quo* transactions such as gifts to charity. But these omitted transactions are parts of another economic circular flow, the money circuit. We have to deal with two distinct circuits.

One takes a step towards distinguishing these two when one contracts the income velocity of money with its transaction velocity. But latterly with the spread of the practice of appending to the national income and product account articulating accounts for private income and expenditure, for government revenue and expenditure, for savings and investment, and for transactions with the rest of the world, there has been a tendency to treat the two circuits as if they were really one. I think this tendency has been particularly evident in highly industrialized countries like the United States, where most of production takes place inside the money circuit. While appended articulating accounts, properly interpreted, add valuable information about money flows, they should not be allowed to obscure the distinction between the two circuits. These circuits overlap, but neither lies wholly within the other.

Theoretically we might consider either the overlap of the two in payments of distributive shares etc., or the overlap in final product sales. It will be convenient to focus attention on

[2] *First Report*, April, 1951.

the latter. How much of the total gross national product passes through the market? [3]

For the United States I have elsewhere estimated the proportion at 95 to 97% of the total.[4] The National Income Committee did not think it wise to name a single figure for India, but to point up the contrast I venture to offer a broad range. I suggest that the corresponding proportion lies between 50 and 75%.[5]

Regarding this contrast we may note that the smaller proportion of GNP passing through the market in India goes a long way towards explaining why we got such a high income velocity computation. Unless we take imputed income out of the numerator we necessarily get a spurious result. Moreover it is not entirely obvious how a nonspurious income velocity computation should be defined. Present social accounting conventions would suggest one definition if national income in kind were to be eliminated from the numerator, a different definition if final product expenditure in kind were to be eliminated.

So much for the relation of final product sales to total final product. What of the relation of final product sales and final distribution payments, wages, interest etc., to other money circuit transactions? This is a somewhat more complicated question. To get totals of money circuit transactions we might attempt to estimate debits to nonbank demand deposit accounts in India from data on bank clearings, and then adjust the debit and other means of settlement. This would be a substantial task. But we can be reasonably sure, even without performing it, what the result would be. Debits to demand deposit accounts in the United States in 1949 exceeded $1100 billion: they were between 4 and 5 times final product sales.[6] If we estimate debits

[3] It is easier to deal with this question in terms of gross national product than in terms of national income.

[4] See my book published by the National Bureau of Economic Research, New York, *A Study of Moneyflows in the United States*. The estimates are for 1936–42.

[5] The Committee notes that in the case of rice some 72% of the output lies outside the money circuit, op. cit., p. 36.

[6] Debits for U.S. weekly reporting banks were $1087 billions; the annual turn-over rate was 21.7. In India deposits (average of the two year ends) were Rs. 8.78 billion. If we estimate debits in India using a turn-over rate of 21.7, a ratio of debits to final product sales of 3½ would put final product sales at Rs. 55 billion; a ratio of 2½ at Rs. 74 billion.

in India on the assumption that deposits turned over as rapidly as in the larger U.S. banks, we get a total of about Rs. 190 billion for 1948–49. This should fix an upper limit. Indian debits probably did not exceed 2½ to 3½ times final product sales. Financial transactions are known to be a major component of these debits. Evidently financial transactions bulk a good deal larger in relation to ordinary business transactions in the United States than in India.

Because financial transactions often seem to follow a law of their own; it is for many purposes advantageous to think of the money circuit as consisting of two parts, the main stream of general business activity and what have been called financial whirl-pools. This does not mean there are no financial transactions in the main stream, but it does count as whirl-pools a major part of these transactions. The main money circuit on this view may be taken to include all nonfinancial transactions plus the net flow of funds through financial channels from one sector of the economy to another. I have estimated that total main circuit transactions so defined were in the United States in 1942, almost twice the sum of final product sales plus final payments of wages, interest, dividends, etc.[7]

It would be difficult, at present, to make a comparable estimate for India, but I think we can get some inkling of the difference between the two economies by comparing composition of money stock. By money stock I mean the total currency and demand deposits liabilities of Banks and the Monetary System to the rest of the economy, excluding interbank items. In 1949 currency represented 59% of the money stock in India; 24% in the United States.[8]

Obviously the 24% figure seriously understates the importance of final income and product transactions in the United States. One factor tending to decrease this ratio is the fact that deposits are needed to conduct financial transactions. But this

[7] See *A Study of Moneyflows in the United States*, cited above, Tables 2 and 3. To state the relationship the other way around, the final income and product money transactions were some 52% of total main money circuit transactions.

[8] See Note 1 for the money stock: For the U.S. currency includes currency outside banks and Treasury cash. The ratio for India is as of March 31; for the U.S. as of June 30.

can only be a minor factor; a small fraction of total deposits is known to handle a very large volume of financial transactions. Surely the chief qualifications attaching to this comparison are those due to differences in payment habits and in the availability of banking facilities in the two countries. Transactions typically handled with currency in India are typically settled by cheque in the States. Also a larger proportion of currency receipts is banked in the latter country. And while most Americans live near enough to a bank to make use of one, in India in 1950 the cities and other places that had banking offices accounted for only about one-seventh of the total population.[9]

Despite all this it seems reasonable to attribute a significant part of the disparity between the two currency ratios to the greater proportion of ordinary business transactions other than final income and product transactions—the greater proportion of nonfinal purchases and sales, transfer payments, and net intersector financial flows—in the main money circuit of the United States.

Comparisons of overlap between the income and product circuit and the money circuit may be called structural comparisons. They give us a static picture, a sort of snapshot. Let us turn now to functional relationships. In attempting to make functional comparisons between India and the United States I propose to focus attention on the cyclical fluctuations in net financial flows and in final income and product transactions. The interrelations among these flows are particularly important. If I neglect transfer payments and the nonfinal transactions in the production sphere, it is not because they deserve to be neglected—they do not. It is merely for the sake of brevity.

Cyclical increases in production, distribution, and aggregate national expenditure—as also cyclical decreases—characterize not the whole of the income and product circuit but that part of it which overlaps the money circuit. This fact suggests the

---

[9] See Statistical Tables Relating to Banks in India, 1950, Reserve Bank of India, p. 21. The total population so accounted for was estimated at 48 million. The corresponding ratio for the United States would be substantially the ratio of urban to total population. But such a comparison of ratios greatly understates the contrast, because in the United States a considerable part of the rural population can easily drive to town.

need for a type of national income measurement that, for national income, estimators have done little to provide. How do
the year-to-year variations in the nonmoney part of national
product differ from the year-to-year variations in final product
sales? For India such national income measurements would be
especially instructive if they could be made by states or districts,
so that the local year-to-year variations in nonmoney product
would not be lost to view in the national aggregates.

But this is only part of the problem. There is migration back
and forth between the nonmoney part of the income and product circuit and the money part. A crop failure or other disaster
to local nonmoney product forces on many that are accustomed
to living for the most part outside the money circuit the need
to purchase food. Conversely a business depression tends to
push the unemployed back into the nonmoney sphere. If business depression unemployment is still a very minor part of the
unemployment problem in India, it is, in part at least, because
there is still a very large nonmoney sphere to go back to. Even
in the United States, where the nonmoney sphere is presumably
smaller proportionately than in any other country, there was a
substantial urban-to-rural migration during the major depression of the 30's. We have a measurement of this geographical
movement from cities to rural areas. But no serious attempt
has been made to portray in terms of social accounts the accompanying increase in nonmoney product. If social accountants are to live up to their claim of providing a balanced,
summary view of what goes on in an economy, they must find
some way to show in their accounts the back-and-forth migration between production inside the money sphere and production outside it.

The explanation of business booms and business depressions
is still a decidedly moot point in economic theory. But let me
propose two propositions that should today command a fairly
wide agreement: (1) What goes on in the nonmoney part of
the income and product circuit is relatively unimportant to the
explanation. (2) Some of what goes on in the money circuit outside the income and product part of it—something in the
financial portion of that circuit—is essential to the explanation.

The first of these propositions must not be construed to deny that a bumper crop or a crop failure has sometimes brought a turning point in the business cycle. Surely some turning points have so originated. No doubt, too, this kind of turning point has been particularly important in the less industrialized countries.

But there were good and bad crops long before there were business cycles; and there have been many cyclical turning points without such acts of God.

The second proposition has a clear corollary for the social accountant. He should seek to show those transactions in the financial part of the money circuit that are particularly significant for the explanation of business cycles and business depressions. A growing recognition of this need is mainly responsible for the development of the practice of supplementing the income and product account with several articulating accounts. Present convention makes the national gross savings and investment account one of these supplements.

When this system of articulating accounts consists of five in all, the national income and product account, the savings investment account and three others, two of these other three may report the operations of separate sectors of the economy, Government and the Rest of the World. The fifth, the private appropriation account, lumps together most household transactions and business transactions on capital account.

Let us call this system of five social accounts the S and I system. The five accounts articulate in that any one of them can be deduced by consolidating the other four.[10]

This property of the system makes it a very ingenious layout, but unfortunately there are highly significant facts it does not bring out. In the first place the S and I account, precisely because it is technically a consolidated resting account does not show the flow of funds through financial channels between

[10] See Table 7 in the *First Report of the National Income Committee* referred to above. Consolidation of any four accounts yields the fifth with debits and credits reversed. The present U.S. scheme is slightly more complicated than a five-account system but Government and the Rest of the World are separately shown, and proceeds retained by business and proceeds distributed to households are not fully segregated.

Households and Industries. It would be far more revealing to
replace the private appropriation account and the S and I account with an Industries account and a Households account.
This would mean four clean-cut sector accounts:—Government, Rest of the World, Industries, and Households. (I say
Industries rather than businesses because farms and some other
small-scale enterprises may in the case of India, for example,
have to be combined with Households.)

A second short-coming of the S and I five-account system is
that it tells us nothing about money. To bring money into the
picture it is advisable for one thing to identify at least five
economic sectors. We should distinguish in addition to Industries, Government, Households, and the Rest of the World,
a sector that includes all deposit banking institutions plus the
monetary system.

Let me sketch for you the money circuit, when we think of
the economy as divided into these five sectors. Some of the
sectors engage in production and in final product sales. They
distribute part of the proceeds of these sales to others and retain
the rest. For all five sectors together distributed proceeds plus
retained proceeds necessarily equal final product purchases, or
aggregate demand. But this proposition does not hold in general for any individual sector. Some sectors may spend more on
final product purchases than the proceeds they receive or retain: others may spend less. Some sectors may incur a cash
deficit; others enjoy a cash surplus.[11] I suggest it is here that
we can find a major part of the role of money in the money
circuit. In the first instance it is cash balances—i.e. money—
that offset these surpluses and deficits. However, to some extent
various other forms of credit have come to serve as money
substitutes in providing the offsets.

We began with the question, what place has money in the
scheme of social accounts? A summary of the answer here advanced may be in order. Money has no place in the national

[11] This implies no net transfer flows between sectors. The statement would be
more complicated if we took such flows into consideration. The statement also
assumes no change in trade receivables and payables; it should be elaborated to
take account of book credit.

income and product circuit as such. But the income and product circuit and the money circuit overlap. In the money circuit we have to reckon with cash surpluses and cash deficits. For all sectors of the economy together total cash surpluses equal total cash deficits. But some sectors may have cash deficits mainly because they spend more on final product purchases than they receive or retain in the way of final proceeds; others may have cash surpluses mainly because of the shortfall of final purchases below final proceeds received or retained. Money has an important part to play in offsetting these sector cash surpluses and cash deficits. But in a credit economy other forms of credit may in some measure serve as money substitutes in providing the offsets.

All this implies that there is need not only to identify a fifth sector, Banks and the Monetary System, but also to elaborate considerably the information that is only sketchily suggested in the S and I five account system. We need to know for each sector, for example, its cash balance, its trade receivables and portfolios, and its debts.

These comments on the nature of the money circuit imply something in regard to the way cyclical expansions and contractions come about. They imply that any sector can decrease its final product purchases below the level of the final proceeds it receives or retains, and to the extent it does so it will tend to have a cash surplus, also any sector can increase its demand for final product above the level of the final proceeds it receives or retains, to the extent that it can finance a cash deficit. By financing a cash deficit I mean principally drawing down its cash balance, liquidating its portfolios, or increasing its debts.

Let us take first the part played by the Rest of the World in the cycle. Our information is fullest for this sector.[12] The Rest of the World can bring about a turning point in the cycle, starting a business expansion by demanding more exports, or a contraction by demanding less. When a contraction so originates the domestic sectors of the economy, Government, In-

[12] The Rest of the World account is a condensation of the balance of payments statement. The original purpose of that statement was to provide precisely the kind of information needed here.

dustries, Households, and Banks and the Monetary System considered collectively, are likely to run a cash deficit with the Rest of the World. Such a deficit means a decrease of external credits or an increase of external debts, or both. Its initial impact is commonly on international cash balances.

Conversely, when a business expansion so originates, the Rest of the World is likely to run a cash deficit that must be financed by borrowing from the domestic sectors.

The significant difference here between the money circuit of India and that of the United States lies not so much in the nature of these processes as in the frequency of their occurrence. In the case of India most cyclical turning points in recent decades appear to have originated in the Rest of the World; in the case of the United States some have so originated, but —at least in the 20th century—not a clear majority. I shall pause to mention only two cases, two downturns that it is generally conceded originated in the domestic sectors of the United States, the sharp business decline of 1937–38 and the very mild one of 1949.

The beginnings of the former probably include United States Fiscal policy in late 1936 and early 1937. A marked decline in aggregate demand began in the third quarter 1937. During the last 4 months of that year there was a spectacular drop in industrial production, in which inventory liquidation played a leading role. But for our present purpose the decline in the U.S. demand for merchandise imports is especially important. During March 1937 imports totaled about $300 million. In a little over a year they dropped to around $150 million per month. Through this drop the U.S. recession was communicated to a large part of the Rest of the World.

The Rest of the World, in turn, decreased its demand for Indian merchandise. Prices in India, particularly the prices of cotton, cereals, and hides, declined. Mainly reflecting the fall in prices, the value of merchandise exports, between September 1937 and June 1938, showed a drop of some 25%.[13]

---

[13] *Report on Currency and Finance,* Reserve Bank of India, 1938–39, pp. 2 ff. These figures and other pre 1947 figures cited below refer to undivided British India excluding Burma.

In the case of cotton there was a marked drop in export physical volume, too, a drop that adversely affected railway earnings.[14] But this business recession in India was characterized by mixed trends. A tea restriction scheme had been set in operation; and the tea price rose during 1937. Industrial activity also apparently increased.

The 1949 U.S. recession [15] was too mild to become much of a worldwide recession. But there was a sufficient decline in the American external demand for goods, particularly from the sterling area, to put pressure on international cash balances. Thus this mild recession added to the growing dollar shortage that led to the September currency devaluations in which India followed the lead of the United Kingdom.

The fact that recent Indian cycles have started much more frequently abroad than at home may be due in part to the nature of her Rest of the World account. If so, the most pertinent aspect of this account is probably the composition of exports. Exports of free price commodities are a larger proportion of Indian exports and exports of administered price commodities, a larger proportion of exports from the United States. A given drop in the value of exports has wider repercussions in the case of free price commodities; to the extent of the price drop entailed a drop in internal incomes is directly induced by the decline in overseas demand.

But the major explanation of the difference we are considering between the two money circuits is presumably not this. Nor is it that the Rest of the World is more active in starting cycles in India than in the United States. Rather it is that the domestic sectors are more active in the United States than in India. India's industrial, commercial, and financial development has not yet 'progressed' to the point where the spontaneous generation of cycles in her domestic sectors is a frequent occurrence.

Theoretically, the process by which the domestic sectors of an economy can start a business upswing or downswing is quite

[14] *Idem*, 1937–38, pp. 2–3.
[15] Purchases of consumer durables and new construction in the U.S. declined in the fourth quarter of 1948.

similar to that described for the Rest of the World.[16] Thus Government can increase its purchases of the nation's product or Industries can increase private capital formation. In either case there will presumably be a cash deficit to finance. And the ability to make the added purchases will be contingent on the ability to finance them.

First, Is the Central Government in a position to finance that start of a peacetime boom in India? Wartime experience may throw a little light on the question. Let us begin our analysis of the war period with money.

In both India and the United States there was a substantial expansion in the money stock, i.e. in the currency and deposit liabilities of Banks and the Monetary System and in the cash balances of Industries, Households, etc. Of course banking assets expanded with banking liabilities. In the United States the added assets were primarily government obligations, in India primarily foreign balances and foreign securities held by the Reserve Bank. In both cases the increase in the money stock helped to finance increased purchases of national product. People put their money in banks—or to be more precise in banking obligations—and banks advanced the money to a sector that had a cash deficit to meet because of its increased purchases of product. In the United States the Federal Government met something approaching half its wartime deficit in this way. In India the process was more complicated. Central Government stepped up its purchases of national product as in the United States, but for a very large part of the added purchases it acted as an agent and received reimbursement from abroad, chiefly from the United Kingdom. Such recoverable expenditures for the six fiscal years ending 31st March 1946 totaled some Rs. 17 billion.[17] This amount plus other direct foreign expenditure left the Rest of the World with a cash deficit to be met in India. It was met mainly in two ways:— The sterling assets of the Reserve Bank increased by Rs. 16.6

[16] For brevity we will pass over Households.

[17] See *Report on Currency and Finance,* Reserve Bank of India, 1945–46, pp. 48 and 100; 1949–50, pp. 202–203.

billion, the Central Government's sterling debt decreased by Rs. 3.8 billion.

The two sterling items total to Rs. 20.4 billion. During the war India changed from a debtor to a creditor nation. We may take these items as a rough measure of the change; a precise measure is not available. Let us say that there was an increase in India's external credit of some Rs. 20 billion. How was all this money, advanced to the Rest of the World during these six fiscal years, raised in India? The answer is, Banks and the Monetary System obtained the money by an expansion of the money stock. That stock increased by Rs. 20 billion.[18]

Now the Central Government made war expenditure not only as an agent but also on its own account. And it had a substantial cash deficit of its own to finance. The increase in the Centre's net debt amounted to some Rs. 5.3 billion.[19] Most of these additional government obligations must have been purchased by Households and Industries.

I have dwelt on this phase of wartime experience partly because it seemed advisable to indicate the main significance of the expansions of the money stock. In both cases such expansion was a very convenient means of deficit financing. But to this a qualification should be added. Expansion of the money stock is a deficit financing device that can leave a legacy of subsequent problems. I shall merely mention the legacy of frozen external credits left to India, and the legacy of obstacles left for the American Federal Reserve System to overcome in order to regain its ability to restrain bank credit expansion.

What light does this wartime experience throw on the possibility of Government's financing the start of a boom in India? The implication is not clear, but it is suggestive. In the United States during World War II (though not during World War I) there was never any real question that it would be possible to finance the war production programme. It was recognised

---

[18] See *idem*, 1940–41, p. 70; 1945–46, p. 131; 1949–50, p. 241: The "money supply" increased by Rs. 14.8 billion; the Central Government's cash balance by Rs. 5.2 billion.

[19] *Idem*, 1949–50, pp. 202–203.

that the increase in the unspent proceeds received and retained by the rest of the economy, chiefly Households and Industries, would necessarily be equal to the cash deficit of the Federal Government. There were indeed financing problems relating to the restraint of civilian consumption and of the bidding up of prices but not relating to the feasibility of the overall step up in production. Still in spite of this, Federal deficit financing took the form—for an amount approaching half the wartime total—of an expansion of the money stock. On the other hand, in India, where capital is proverbially shy, the wartime deficit of the Central Government was financed largely without the aid of this device. It is true that the deficit for the six fiscal years ending with 1945–46 was only Rs. 5.3 billion; [20] while the Rest of the World had a deficit with India during this period of nearly four times this amount. Moreover capital is presumably less shy when business is already expanding and particularly so when investment helps to 'win the war.' Raising Rs. 5 billions in wartime is one thing; raising that much in peacetime is quite another. Still the proposition that when the Central Government has a cash deficit, the other sectors of the economy taken collectively must have an equal cash surplus is not confined to the United States and other pecuniarily advanced countries. It is a proposition in social accounting. Presumably it applies to the money circuit of India.

One is tempted to restate this proposition, paraphrasing Say's Law. Demand is supply; the demand for goods creates an equal supply of funds, funds that can be borrowed to finance the demand. This does not mean that the Central Government can borrow and spend at will, that the lender has no discretion over his lending. It does mean, in highly industrialized economies at any rate, the budgetary habits in other economic sectors are such that the funds are likely to be forth-coming, that potential lenders are likely to be actual lenders. Keynes seized upon this fact for Households and schematized the Households budget behaviour pattern in terms of the marginal propensity

[20] For this purpose the deficit is taken to equal the increase in outstanding interest-bearing obligations minus the increase in cash and interest-yielding assets.

to consume and the consumption function. I think he over-schematized the Household pattern and erred in neglecting the patterns on other sectors (business savings are important in the United States). But that is beside the question. He was right in emphasizing the role of the budget behaviour pattern in the money circuit of highly industrialized countries. The question is, are budget-habit patterns so different in India that funds for large deficit financed purchases of national product by the Central Government are likely to be unavailable in peacetime? Or, is extensive government deficit financing feasible in India? The wartime experience seems to suggest the latter possibility. But surely we need more information on this point.

If there is a question about the Centre's ability to finance purchases of national product, what is to be said of the possibility that a boom might originate in the Industries sector in India? The informational basis for dealing with this question is particularly deficient. The National Income Committee in its First Report did not offer an estimate for 1948–49 either of gross private capital formation or of the proceeds retained by private business. It is hoped that both estimates will be attempted in the near future. Other figures that would be helpful are data on business inventories, liquid assets,[21] and debts.

In the circumstances I shall offer only two brief comments on the Indian Industries sector as a possible originator of booms. (1) Many have doubted the feasibility—or else the advisability—of substantial government deficit financing at present. So far as these doubts relate to feasibility they imply something about budget habits that would make capital shy in an overall sense. Or it may not. In either case it seems probable that it is shy in a differential sense, i.e. shy of business ventures. The Industrial Finance Corporation of India and its state counterparts bear witness on this point. The differential shyness of capital tells definitely against the possibility of booms originating in the Industries sector.

(2) The second comment relates to the fraction of final product sales represented by private gross capital formation. In the

[21] Data on bank deposits are currently available in the Reserve Bank's survey of deposit ownership.

United States in 1949 this fraction was slightly over 13%.[22] In private capital formation, it suggests the part of it that is significant here is of the order of magnitude of 1% of total gross national product sold. It seems doubtful whether so small a tail can be expected cyclically to wag the whole (marketed) national product.

[22] The denominator here is gross national product minus imputed items. For India the fraction must be a good deal smaller. In the new First Five Year Plan the Planning Commission's proposals for capital outlay by private large scale industry are about Rs. 6/10 billion per year. This item does not cover all.

THEORY

· XIV ·

Communities of Economic Interest and the Price System *

(1924)

I. PRICE AND WELFARE

PROFESSOR Fisher tells us that compensating the dollar "would directly and indirectly accomplish more social justice and go farther in the solution of our industrial, commercial, and financial problems than almost any other reform proposed in the world today." This seems a far-reaching, almost an extravagant claim. And yet in a society where a pecuniary standard is employed to make the measurements by which the resources and agents of production are apportioned among the several industries and trades and by which the distribution of products and services is determined, any imperfections in that standard would necessarily have very serious consequences for economic welfare and justice. And admittedly our dollar yardstick works quite imperfectly: there are many wide discrepancies between the price measures that the market puts on things and the costs in human effort and suffering that have been required to make them, or their significance for consumers' welfare; there are many wide discrepancies between the net value in exchange received by a "producer" and his

* With one exception the rather extensive footnotes of reference and commentary that accompanied the original text are omitted here.

net addition to the serviceability of the product. If somehow we could eliminate these discrepancies, if in this broader sense we could "compensate the dollar," we should indeed work a mighty reform for economic welfare and justice.

Although our present concern is not directly with the problems of social reform, it does have to do with the introduction of corrections into our pecuniary measure which will make it a more satisfactory standard. There are clearly two questions, more or less capable of separate consideration: (1) What are economic justice and common welfare? By what standard shall we measure or otherwise determine the welfare or justice of a given situation? (2) When and insofar as the situation falls short of this standard, how can it be brought to agreement with it? We shall attempt to confine our attention to the first question, and to formulate in pecuniary terms a tentative statement of the direction in which the common economic interest lies.

Impressed by the numerous and far-reaching imperfections of the price measure, many economists have given it up and sought some other standard by which to appraise the current situation. Certain writers have even gone so far as to abandon the problem to other fields of thought. It will be a part of our task in this preliminary sketch (for it makes no claim to finality) to consider some of these views. But in the end we shall return again to pecuniary value, believing that it is worth preserving and improving upon as a standard of welfare and justice, in spite of its many short-comings, and that, even if we cannot rely on it exclusively, its advantages are such that where it is applicable we cannot afford to do without it. First of all, however, it will be desirable to make an analysis of the discrepancies in our pecuniary standard, in the hope of tracing these discrepancies to some phase or phases of the present institutional situation, for a knowledge of causes may be of assistance in making accurately—even if only hypothetically—the requisite corrections. What then is the relation between price and welfare in our present society?

II. SOME DISCREPANCIES IN THE
PECUNIARY STANDARD

Economists have often looked on the world and seen that it was good. Here was a vast, complicated society composed of highly specialized workers, a net-work of interdependent families and communities without any general manager. There are many functional foremen, of course, managers of particular organizations devoted to some specialized line of production, but no one coördinates all these independent enterprises. "Every individual . . . intends only his own gain." Yet somehow, "the study of his own advantage, naturally, or rather necessarily, leads him to prefer that employment which is most advantageous to the society"; somehow there is coördination of specialists. To Adam Smith it seemed, indeed, that "he is in this, as in many other cases, led by an invisible hand to promote an end which was no part of his intention." If we may make a substitution for the "unseen hand," we may say that certain economic institutions accomplish this leaderless coördination —exchange, price, and money. Each exchanges what he produces (production being conceived in a physical sense) for money, and then exchanges money for the goods and services of others. The price or rate of exchange is fixed at the point where supply and demand are equal, and competitive bidding insures fair play. Thus, according to the classical view, we have leaderless exchange coördination of specialists, and the common welfare coincides with the private interests of each individual under conditions of free competition.

Socialists have more frequently looked on the darker side of life and found waste of natural resources, chronic idleness of people and of industrial apparatus; non-living wages, insecurity of workers, wasteful use of their services and inhuman treatment; diversion of human effort into the production of armaments, luxuries, adulterated products and advertizing; ample incomes to non-workers; and autocratic control by a capitalistic minority whose title is hereditary. Some have laid most of these evils to the existence of money and of middlemen, and have been prone to overlook the merits of the present system. Marx, at least, accepted much of the classical view of exchange coördination, including the materialistic conception of production. But he did not accept the imputation of product to the capitalist. In general, value equalled cost of production, but for labor, value greatly exceeded cost of living—here alone was a *produit net,* a surplus value. In appropriating it, the capitalist exploited labor, and to exploitation Marx would trace our economic ills.

The voluminous arguments between the holders of these opposing views have usually convicted no one of a more serious charge than disagreement with his opponents' premises, at least so far as the main outlines of the system are concerned. The issue between them is, Does one produce who owns active industrial equipment? In some respects the Marxian view is the more realistic, but so long as we accept the classical formulation of the issue, the argument as to which way lies economic welfare and justice must always be a " 'Tis" and " 'Tain't" affair. Fortunately there has been made possible something of a synthesis, that will assist us in constructing standards of social appraisal.

The broad, general truth of the classical explanation of the coördination of specialists without any general manager, there is not disposition here to call in question. It appeals and persists because of its comparative simplicity as well as its approximate truth. But what is insisted on is that it is only an approximation, so rough and crude that it fails to account for any of the imperfections of coördination except as deviations from the theoretical norm. Business depressions have been construed as abnormal times, trusts as unnatural monopolies, non-living wages as true only for the short-run, and many social evils have been blamed on individuals and the inaccuracies of their felicific calculations. More frequently, perhaps, because the "pure theory" of exchange did not apply to these cases, they have been left to "applied theory."

Many of the necessary corrections in this analysis of leaderless exchange coördination have already been pointed out, but it may be well to recall the chief ones here, especially as their full significance for economic welfare is not yet generally ap-

preciated. Wealth and economic goods have usually been conceived as including scarce, desirable, material objects and perhaps human services. Producer's goods, being durable, are thus
for the most part regarded as exclusively material. Production,
as the creation of wealth or performance of service, is typically industrial-extraction, manufacture, transportation, storage.
Marketing is only a special kind of production, in which the
functions of the travelling salesman tend to become confused
with those of the delivery boy. Even the business enterpriser
is sometimes thought of as primarily a factory superintendent,
technologist, and efficiency engineer. But what is exchanged
is not physical objects and processes but legal rights, and the
measures which are applied by the undertakers of economic
activity, are not ultimately measures of weight or bulk but of
price. To be accurate we must make, not a productivity analysis but a profitivity analysis.

What difference does it make to distinguish "making goods
and making money"? And how does it affect the problem of
economic welfare? In the first place to put the analysis in technological and physical terms, rather than in legal and pecuniary
terms, may give economists the sensation of having an exact
science, modelled on Newtonian mechanics, but it eliminates
from value theory the consideration of the actual conflicts and
coincidences of human interests between classes in modern
society. Foot-pounds of labor, acres of land, and square feet of
factory floor-space require no reference to particular persons
or groups. But legal rights do require such reference, and are
perpetually in conflict. To own property is not simply "to
have and to hold" physically, particularly in the case of capital
goods. It is to have a bundle of legal rights, rights of alienation,
rights to income, rights of business management. Managerial
rights may conflict with the contract rights of others—the rights
to hire and fire with the right to organize. Or some property
rights may conflict with others—the right to build factories in
a residential district with the rights of residence owners. Some
of these conflicts are recognized at law; compensation is payable for torts. But in many cases the law does not appreciate
the economic significance of the conflicts—there are many de

facto torts. It should be the task of the economist to investigate the relation of these conflicts of rights and interests to price and exchange.

Moreover, when one confuses making profit with making product, the only ways an enterprise can increase the net return, namely (1) increasing gross revenue and (2) decreasing costs, become identified with (1) increasing output and (2) decreasing the amount of labor, materials, or industrial apparatus required in this or some antecedent process. The prices of these objects and processes are fixed by supply and demand, and all the manager can do on the business (as distinct from the industrial) side is to seek diligently for the best bids or offers. (The only exception allowable to this rule is in the case of monopoly, and too little is said on the score of including such partial monopolies as "good will" in this "abnormal" analysis.) The objective of an enterprise thus becomes to minimize the quantity of labor, materials, land, and plant required to produce a unit of product or service; or to maximize the product given the factors.

Thus the law of proportion of factors (together with the assumption of free competition) implies the full use of plant and equipment, which necessitates construing depressions as abnormal. But the chief significance of the shift from the pecuniary to the technological reckoning lies in the shift of viewpoints it involves: money income to the enterprise is thus confused with physical output of goods and services for consumption as the motive to production, and money outlay by the enterprise with the intake of labor-sacrifice undergone by its employees as an item to be economized. Not only does a productivity analysis make it easy for the theorist to overlook class conflicts, but it even helps him to identify the interests of the tradesman with those of his customers and the interests of the employer with those of his employees.

But there are many exceptions to a materialistic conception of economic goods besides personal services, and to a technological basis for profitivity besides those thus far listed. Property rights attach to other things besides physical objects and processes, to ideas, to bits of technological theory embodied in the

objects and processes—rights to employ the idea by manufacture, use, or sale; to names and symbols; to social situations
such as good business connections or a high reputation; to
incorporeal persons like corporations; to credit; to contracts.
And these items of property exchange, at least, as freely as
more tangible assets. They do not, however, fit so neatly into
the older theory of exchange coördination, and certain economists have tried to read them out of the market.[1] By way
of explanation it has been urged that these items would be
eliminated, if all property were held by a single owner; hence
they are not "social" wealth. But this is a curious defense for
those who insist that competition and multiple ownership are
"normal." For the present purpose it is important to remember
in this connection that the bulk of civil law is a set of precedents

[1] A. Marshall, *Principles of Economics*, 7th ed., 1916, 60–61, 76 ff. Marshall
classifies wealth and capital as individual and social or cosmopolitan. But "by
far the most important usage of the term Capital in general, i.e. *from the social
point of view*, is in the inquiry how the three agents of production . . . contribute to producing the national income . . . and how that income is *distributed* among the three agents" (78). (Italics are the present writer's.) Taussig
eliminates all gains by one enterprise at someone else's expense from the class
"productive activities" by asking "whether the labor adds to the sum of utilities" (yours being added to mine apparently). *Principles of Economics*, 1915,
Chap. II, secs. 3, 4. On capital he applies a cancellation of inter-individual
claims to distinguish individual from social. "For the purposes of economic
study, we shall disregard the individual's point of view. . . . In speaking of
capital we shall have in mind real things, and not the right to things . . . , the
community's apparatus of production" (83–84). But how can non-predacious labor and social capital be used to explain actual competitive prices? For Ely,
intangibles cancel from the social point of view. But good will, etc., must be
included in a pecuniary estimate even of social wealth, *Outlines of Economics*,
1917, 109–111. Some writers discuss only the elimination of inter-individual
debts. For this it is only necessary to conceive physical objects to which titles
attach as held unencumbered by debt. It is not clear what disposal is to be
made of the public debt. Fisher, *Elementary Principles of Economics*, 1912, 51 ff.,
especially 56; Fetter, *Economic Principles*, 1915, 265. (But see 282–3 on intangibles.) Seligman, *Principles of Economics*, 1905, 20.
  Comparing the present situation with "natural value" in an imaginary Crusoe
or collectivist economy is another way of eliminating intangibles and conflicts
of interests from consideration. Cf. H. J. Davenport, *Value and Distribution*,
358 ff. H. G. Brown appears to use this method, *Economic Science and Modern
Welfare*, 1923, II, 14–15. He recognizes immaterial and predatory capital (82–83)
as things which might be prohibited (167)—minor discrepancies in our organization—but adheres on the whole to a productivity rather than a profitivity
analysis.

delimiting the conflicting property and civil rights that enter into exchange. To assume that a formal legal change, such as transference of titles to the state, would eliminate not merely these intangible forms of property but also all the conflicts in the great complex fabric of human interests in our highly specialized society is to join hands with the state socialists. And yet it seems to be just this assumption that has enabled economic theorists to overlook the conflicts of interest that are the essence of modern economic problems and hypothesize for the pure science a pre-established harmony. That it is not merely a materialistic bias that is involved would seem to be attested by the omission from consideration of certain tangible goods as well—shyster lawyers' libraries, bill boards, adulterated products, etc.

If property rights attach to other things than physical objects and processes, so also pecuniary value attaches to property by virtue of other than technological performance. Making money is broader than making goods—it includes creating a market as well. One can adapt a man's desires to one's product as well as adapt the product to the man's desires; economic guidance is a part of "value production." Business includes much besides industry. It is important not only to use little and produce much, but to buy cheap and sell dear, especially under conditions of inadequate information, partial monopolies and trade ethics, economic friction in entering into alternative transactions, differences of skill in bargaining and persuasion, differences in ability to wait or to avoid the transaction altogether, in ability to take the matter to court and in the importance of the transaction as a precedent, variability of human tastes, overhead and joint costs. For making profit it is more important to bombard the consumer with an admixture of information and persuasion, establish advantageous business connections, make the most of the worker's weaknesses in bargaining, and hire lawyers to stretch one's legal rights for all they are worth, than to produce efficiently. It is a commonplace that the factors which play the major part in determining the policies of business management are exceptions to the (physical) productivity theory.

Thus far we have seen how the materialistic conception of economic goods and processes has led to an economic theory in which imperfections in the competitive functioning of leaderless exchange coördination are viewed as abnormal. A profitivity theory, as distinguished from such a productivity theory, accounts for coördination and coincidence of interests insofar as maximizing net profit involves as by-products both turning out goods for consumption and economizing on the materials, equipment, and labor-sacrifice required, and only insofar. It also accounts for conflicts of interests and rights, for one man's gaining a merely differential advantage at some one else's expense. Thus it reconciles the classical conflict between the economist's explanation of leaderless coördination and the socialist's desire to explain economic "illfare." But we have yet to inquire: Just what sorts of discrepancies in price as a measure of social welfare, as an incentive to and reward for productive services to others, as a distributor of the power to call on others for service, arise from these conflicts of interests? What sort of standard of welfare can we apply to these discrepancies, that will indicate the direction in which a remedy should lie?

It is clear that money, price, and exchange, while they accomplish a rough, approximate coördination of specialists, often lead people not only to profit at the expense of others, but also to get themselves into difficulties. Each, seeking his own greatest gain, helps to bring about a result which was no part of his intention. But that result is not always the common good of the self-seeking parties; it may be a common misfortune —cut-throat competition, a business depression, a war among the nations of which they are subjects, or waste of the national resources. Because there are imperfections in the pecuniary standard, because making money does not necessarily mean making goods nor making goods always mean making money, each seeking his own differential pecuniary advantage may help to get himself as well as everyone else into trouble.

If our property and other civil-economic rights were such that each person or organization, in entering or refraining from any transaction, had to bear all the costs and could reap all the gains of so doing, we should probably be safe in assuming the coincidence of individual interests and the common welfare. This would imply that each independent fiscal unit, family, business enterprise, state, municipality, etc., could increase the volume of services it received from others only by increasing its money payments to them, could decrease its money payments only by decreasing the burden on them, could increase its money receipts only by increasing the service rendered, and could decrease its service rendered only by suffering a fall in money receipts—save only for lending and borrowing. In other words money—and the commercial banking system—would be performing perfectly the function of keeping score in the great game of getting a living, the function of a social cost-accounting system. Under such circumstances consumer's demand might shape business policy rather than conversely, and technological efficiency might be the chief task of business management.

But it is obvious that things are far otherwise today. Thus, in spite of the pronouncements of economic theorists, under the present system of civil-economic rights, it pays differentially to make the work go around. Laborers "go slow," and business men are concerned to create as big a market as they can— to get as much business as possible. A "favorable balance of trade" helps to make the work go around, and differentially is advantageous, perhaps to everyone in the country—it helps to start the upward swing of the business cycle. There is more truth in Mercantilism than most economists have been prepared to admit, and hence it survives all their protests. For the proper functioning of exchange coördination in the country it is often important to "keep the dollar circulating at home." The classical refutation of the Mercantilist contentions, more explicitly than the contentions themselves, runs in terms of a long-time trend, and it confuses the common welfare with differential advantage. What is required is an investigation in the light of a differential profitivity theory of the bearing of the Mercantilist contentions on the cyclical deviations from the secular trend.

To recognize such imperfections in the functioning of exchange coördination is to recognize (1) that it pays differentially to do many things that are at best of doubtful advantage to the community and (2) that undertakings in the common interest do not necessarily pay any of the independent fiscal units acting in severalty. Frequently one is in a position to acquire or dispose of legal rights, when their exchange-value or exchange cost to him offers a sufficient pecuniary inducement, but when to do so conflicts with the economic interests of others who are unable under our present legal and economic institutions to command appropriate compensation. Or, one's legal rights may offer only an inadequate pecuniary inducement to perform a service for others, because existing law and practice does not enable one to collect from all of those who benefit by it.

But if we are to be able to get any general agreement as to how a case of differential advantage should be handled, we shall have to carry our analysis farther than this. In the first place we must be able to specify the parties whose interests are affected adversely or favorably, but do not affect the decision of the party to whose differential advantage it is to enter or refrain from a particular transaction—the party in discretion. We may designate those whose welfare is involved but not considered as the non-discretionary parties. In some cases they may be parties to the transaction which affects them for better or worse, in some cases they may be competing for the transaction, and again they may be only remotely related to the market in which it takes place. Another aspect of differential advantage, which is of importance by virtue of the limits which it imposes on precision, is the kind of interest of the non-discretionary parties affected. The cases which should be capable of a fairly accurate treatment are those in which the money income or outlays of the non-discretionary parties are affected, or perhaps the market value of their property. But it may be "human cost" or "psychic income" that is involved. The consideration which bears most directly on divergences between differential advantage and the common welfare is that which has to do with the character of the effect on the non-discretionary party. Is it favorable or unfavorable? The most complicated aspect of differential advantage, and perhaps the most important for an accurate analysis of many of our economic problems, is the variability in shape and uniformity of the cost items involved. What is meant by variation of cost shape may be illustrated by the case of that part of the cost of a product which falls on the manufacturer as an overhead charge but is converted into a direct cost to the purchaser. The conversion may run the other way—from direct to overhead—and we may also include capital-revenue charge conversions. Uniformity of cost is employed in the usual sense, referring to the equality of unit costs of competitors. We have, then, four principal considerations on the basis of which we may attempt a tentative classification of differential advantages:

A. Relation of non-discretionary party to discretionary party's transaction
   (1) A party to the transaction—vertical relationship
     (a) Buyer
     (b) Seller
   (2) Not a party to the transaction
     (a) Horizontal relationship
       (i) Competitor for the transaction
       (ii) In a complementary line to that of the discretionary party for purposes of this transaction
     (b) Oblique or more remote relationship
B. Kinds of interest of non-discretionary party affected
   (1) Cases involving purely pecuniary interests
   (2) Cases involving "human cost" and "psychic income" as well as pecuniary interests
C. Effect on non-discretionary party's economic welfare
   (1) Favorable—adds to his income
   (2) Unfavorable—adds to his costs
D. Variations in the shape and uniformity of costs involved
   (1) No variation in shape or uniformity involved
   (2) Overhead costs to non-discretionary party fall on discretionary party as direct costs, and conversely
   (3) Capital charges to non-discretionary party fall on discretionary party as revenue charges, and conversely
   (4) Non-uniform costs to producers fall on consumers as uniform costs

Any particular differential advantage should fall into some class under each of at least the first three principal heads—A, B, and C. Thus, to take a simple case, what has been called a de facto tort would involve: (A) frequently a remote relationship of the non-discretionary party to the transaction responsible for (C) an unfavorable effect on his economic welfare (B) only his pecuniary interests being affected, and (D) these without variation in shape or uniformity of costs.

With cases where there is a mixture of pecuniary interests with "human cost" and "psychic income," or more strictly cases of non-pecuniary advantages and burdens expressed in pecuniary terms by the necessity for choice and so combined with money gains and money losses, it is not possible to deal very satisfactorily by statistical and accounting methods. If they are less important in their bearing on our economic problems, it is not because of the difficulty of treating them objectively; but this combination of circumstances may serve as an excuse for slighting them in a preliminary formulation like the present. Where only pecuniary interests are involved it should be possible not only to identify the non-discretionary parties affected by any transaction that pays (or fails to pay) differentially, but also with proper investigation to state approximately the amount of adverse (or favorable) effect, and to point out what, if any, variations in shape and uniformity of costs have played a part in making the transaction differentially profitable (or unprofitable).

The way in which these differential advantages arise out of the conflicting civil rights that enter into exchange and the miscarriage of pecuniary incidence in certain types of decisions should now be easily followed. The type of differential advantage that has been longest recognized, perhaps in part because it involves no variations of shape, is that of monopoly on one side of a market—it pays differentially to manipulate the price by curtailing output (or intake) so as to add to the total net profit by increasing the gross profit per unit, and the non-discretionary party on the other side of the market foots the bill. Under conditions of uneven and scanty distribution of information and of economic friction, this type is highly pervasive in "partial" and "effective" forms.

But it should be clear that differential profits are to be derived under competitive as well as monopoly conditions. Thus it may pay differentially to advertize because there are legal rights in habitual customers and because one can legitimately acquire more of these rights from his competitors by advertizing or can keep them from acquiring some of his. Again, it frequently pays differentially, especially for a large business, to employ lawyers to discover how the line can be drawn between its legal rights and the rights of others, so as to fall farthest over upon what might otherwise be the domain of someone else, or to prevent others from legal encroachment on its own preserves. Finally we may take a case where only direct costs affect the profitivity of a transaction to the discretionary party, while the unfavorable effect on the pecuniary interests of the non-discretionary party is due to the fact that his account includes overhead costs as well. When one's overhead is already cared for by regular customers, it may pay differentially to offer goods to a competitor's customers at anything above the additional cost of producing these additional goods. And it may still pay differentially to extend such an offer even after the competitor has retaliated and enticed away a part of one's regular customers by similar tactics, leaving a part of one's own overhead uncompensated. In each case such an offer pays because only a part of the burden falls on the discretionary party— part falls on the competitor who suffers a larger decrement of revenue than of costs, because some of his costs are overhead and continue without direct relation to output. In a competitive market it pays differentially under conditions of overhead and fixed costs to engage in cut-throat competition, and hence in a variety of discriminatory practices between markets, lines of goods, etc. It is significant in this connection that in a régime of chronic underemployment of persons and plant, overhead costs affect the working of competition in nearly every market.

There can be no presumption, then, either in a competitive or a monopolistic market that making money is a proper norm by which to have productive organizations guided. Differential profitivity is unsuitable as a social policy, but what shall we put in its place?

It is not easy to specify the conditions under which differential advantage could be made to coincide with the common welfare. We cannot get very far by assuming a static society, with free competition and constant or increasing costs for each enterprise, for by so doing we rule out nearly all the factors to which imperfections in the functioning of exchange coördination are due. Unless we can (eventually) get a formula that will take in all these factors we have solved our problem by eliminating it. And if we were to succeed, would we not have prescribed the conditions, possible or only conceptual, that would constitute an ideal society, a utopia? Can we define the ideal situation with which mere differential advantage contrasts, except in terms of the millennium? Must we not conclude with Plato that ideal (economic) justice is to be found only in an ideal society?

Perhaps we shall have to be satisfied with something more tentative and more compromising, but it is clear that we must have some standard other than differential advantage. The very term, differential advantage, implies something with which it is to be contrasted. Before turning to investigate the merits of various theories as to what this contrasting term should be, it will be necessary to consider briefly the claim of this problem to receive the attention of economists.

III. SCIENCE AND WELFARE

With the growth of discrepancies between the classical theory of coincidence of individual interest with the common welfare on the one hand and the practices of the business world following in the wake of the industrial revolution on the other, the necessity for economists to take some stand on the issue has become of increasing importance. Most of those modern economists who are prepared to recognize the full extent of these discrepancies in their "theory" and a similar proportion of the much larger group who are not, have followed one of two courses: Either, disillusioned by the many short-comings of our price measure, they have set up some non-pecuniary standard of social appraisal; or, leaving the job to the ethicist, they have tried to confine their own attention more or less consistently to a purely colorless description of economic processes. It would be impossible in the limits of the present paper to consider adequately the line of division between economics and ethics as it bears on our problem, but it may be worth while to see briefly what some of the issues involved are, before turning to the question of non-pecuniary standards of appraisal.

Historically there is good ground for the position that economists had better leave appraisal alone, or at any rate that they had better leave certain kinds of appraisal alone. The use of such words as "natural" and "normal" has often been attended by results of very doubtful scientific value. When observed facts do not fit one's theory, instead of appraising the theory as untrue or inaccurate and setting to work to get a new theory that shall be a description more closely approximating the facts, one may keep the old theory and appraise the facts instead—regard them as "abnormal" or "unnatural." Perhaps the chief difficulty with such a procedure is that it is in the nature of the case impossible to tell how far a theory of what normally occurs is to be understood as a statement of what does occur, and how far as a proposal for what should occur. "What is" is inextricably mixed up with "what ought to be."

Traditionally the field of science has been divided into the positive and the normative sciences, and a distinction has been drawn between pure and applied science. The distinctions on which these divisions of the field of knowledge rest are as important today as they ever were; indeed it is probably more important today to separate carefully an impersonal account of what is taking place from a statement of one's private tastes and attitudes toward these occurrences, altho the problem of the social scientists may be peculiarly intricate here. But it is not so clear that the field of science either does or should divide along these traditional lines. One may recognize fully the importance of the distinctions, and still hold that the most efficient division of academic labor requires an apportionment of the field of thought along other lines.

The position of economics in this scheme of things has been anomalous from the start. Economists, with physics as their model of scientific procedure, have often held that economic science should confine itself to an objective description of such processes as production and exchange, that it was rightfully a pure, positive science. According to this view the problem of the common welfare has been relegated to "applied economics" and ethics. Philosophers, on the other hand, have been wont to class economics with ethics, logic, and esthetics, because like them it has to do with evaluation and appraisal, with human desires, tastes, and preferences. Nor can it be said that economics differs from these others in that it is its task merely to describe objectively the desires and preferences of other people, for there are also ethical and esthetic theorists who would take the same position, e.g., they might undertake to trace objectively the cultural evolution of canons of taste and conduct. But the point of chief significance for our present purpose is that this distinction, despite the extent to which it has been relied upon by "anti-welfare" economists, does not and cannot exclude our inquiry from the field of economics. If it is proper to describe other people's interests and preferences objectively, then by the same token it is proper to investigate the relations between them—their coincidences and conflicts of interest and the conditions that give rise to them—it is even proper to ask how a change of conditions would alter these relationships or what change in conditions an alteration of the coincidences and conflicts would involve.

All this raises another issue which Professor Perry has employed to preserve to ethics certain problems that have traditionally belonged to it and in particular the problem of social welfare and justice, with the economic phases of which we are here concerned. To him it has seemed that the economist should concern himself with the distribution that results from the pursuit by each individual of his own private interest, including thereunder such a prudent regard for the interests of his fellows as is calculated to give him the maximum gain in the long run. The question as to the result of each individual's considering the interests of his fellows on their own account is reserved to the ethicist. Perry thus clearly recognizes that the issue is not between description and appraisal, but between investigation of individual welfare on the one hand and of the

common welfare on the other. Apparently he would keep for
ethics the investigation of an "inter-subjective" view that embraces the conflicting interests of competing individuals. The
precise line is not clear, but its tendency is to make of economics an individual and of ethics a social science, for otherwise it would be open to the economist to concern himself with
any and all the relations between the (economic) interests of
different individuals, actual and possible.

Perhaps Perry and those whom he typifies are the more ready
to reserve to ethics such questions as, "What sorts of railroad
rates protect the interests of the investors and at the same time
those of the several shippers, without neglecting the interests of
any of them?" or "What policies are in the common interest in
dealing with the business cycle?"; because they are not institutionalists. At any rate he does not ask, "Are these conflicts
of individual interest due to the perversity of human nature or
are they to a considerable extent the result of human institutions?"; he appears to assume the former alternative as a matter
of course. To one who prefers the other view the problems of the
common economic welfare become, not questions adapted to the
tastes and training of the closet-philosopher, whose view, however broad, is wanting in contact with the present economic
institutions and classes involved; but problems which only a
trained economist is competent to undertake. According to this
view the investigation of the common welfare is alloted to
economics because, with the existing logical inter-relationships
of problems, only so can there be an efficient division of academic labor. Even Professor Perry does not prohibit this sphere
to the economist; he merely asks that he shall approach it not
as a mere economist but shall bear in mind some of the broader
ethical issues involved—surely not an unreasonable request. On
the other question as to whether this inquiry is a part of value
theory ("pure economic science") little need be said. It both is
a theory in the sense of an attempt at generalization and has to
do with value in exchange or price.

Assuming that the investigation of the conflicts and coincidences of interests of different individuals is quite as scientific
an undertaking as the study of the interests of any single in-

dividual, and that the economist is best equipped to investigate the common economic interest, one further question arises. To state objectively that the common interest is thus and so, should be precisely like any other impersonal description, commanding acceptance because it is a consistent and accurate generalization, or arousing disagreement because it is inaccurate or inconsistent. But the matter does not necessarily end there. Many of us incline, as a matter of taste, to lend our approval and support to such a course as the common interest is stated to require. In this, perhaps, we overstep the bounds of science, for it is not logic that requires us to take this step. In taking it we are not so much stepping out of economics and into ethics, as stepping according to an ethical rather than a logical canon of conduct. It is a moral act rather than the theorizing of a moralist. In what follows we shall attempt to confine ourselves to objective statements as to which way the common interest lies, leaving anyone free who so desires to take this further step for himself. And yet this mere description, like every scientific inquiry, betrays an appraisal in that it is undertaken in preference to some other inquiry. In this case the significance of investigating conditions of harmony of interests is that it yields us standards of comparison, standards to which many of us as non-scientists lend our approval. In this sense they are standards of appraisal.

IV. SOME STANDARDS CONSIDERED

Most of those who have been deeply impressed with the defects of the pecuniary standard as a measure of an individual's contribution to the welfare of his fellows or of theirs to his welfare, have felt it necessary to abandon the pecuniary standard altogether and set up some other measure of economic welfare. Professor Fetter has even gone so far as to advocate classifying economic theories as either "price economics" or "welfare economics." It is unfortunate that these non-pecuniary standards of welfare have seldom been fully and accurately described. Too often they have been in the nature of unformulated or partially formulated assumptions. It is difficult, therefore, to do justice to those who hold them.

It will be convenient for purposes of our discussion to consider examples of three principal types of theories—(1) physical or technological theories, (2) human and psychological theories, and (3) socio-organic and group-personality theories. Perhaps because their views are recalcitrant to classification in the categories of another outlook, perhaps because they are genuinely of a dual nature, certain writers find their way into more than one group.

The first group of theories are alike in that they designate as in the common interest certain technological or physical magnitudes which stand in contradistinction to pecuniary magnitudes, or that they attempt to exclude as contrary to the common interest certain pecuniary magnitudes which have no direct technological or physical significance. The more purely technological theories are seldom given explicit formulation, but it is often urged, particularly by socialist writers, that industry should be run to turn out products and services rather than to turn out profits, thus implying a technological standard of appraisal. So long as different physical quantities of the same product are in question, we may with some assurance assume that they measure different degrees of subservience to the common interest. But, as soon as it becomes necessary to compare one product with another or with the raw materials, hours of labor, and so forth, consumed in its manufacture, any purely technological theory breaks down. We must have some common measure, some standard of comparison. Under such circumstances there are but two alternatives. One will be discussed presently under the third group of theories—we may shift from heterogeneous physical magnitudes to some sort of "collective utility" as the common measure. The other involves the setting up of some set of exchange relationships between the different commodities, services, and so forth, with, presumably, some one as a "standard of value." In other words the theory thereby ceases to be a substitution of technological for pecuniary magnitudes and becomes one of correcting the price measure, of substituting one set of pecuniary magnitudes for another.

The more explicit and tenable technological theories recognize this difficulty and undertake to correct the actual pecuniary measures by eliminating income claims which have no technological or physical basis. Insofar as the normative aspects of a productivity theory can be separated from its descriptive aspects its confusion of productivity with profitivity may be said to make of normal price a correction of the existing pecuniary measure by a technological standard. A more clear-cut form of this position appears to underlie Veblen's distinction between pecuniary and industrial employments—the purely pecuniary or acquisitive activities of business men are not, like the industrial activities of engineers, foremen, and manual laborers, readily construed as subservient to the common interests, for the latter directly increase the physical volume of product, while the manipulations of the former serve only to acquire a larger share of the claims upon it. Another version of the distinction, more explicit on some points of present moment, appears in Davenport's theory of primary and secondary distributions. The primary claims to distributive shares are held by virtue of human labor and supervisory activity and the ownership of instrumental goods and loaned funds. The secondary distributive shares are due "to bad institutions of property rights and inheritance, to bad taxation, to class privileges, to stock exchange manipulation, political favor, legislative and administrative corruption . . . and every sort of vested right in iniquity." "Technological value-productivity" is contrasted with the "value-productivity" of good will, high finance, etc., and with claims not derived from enterprise—inheritance, indirect effects of taxation, etc. But the line between "a distribution by right of productive contribution" and one by some other right is not too easily drawn, for even the primary distribution "takes place" under "political and property institutions." The productive contribution of those who "live by owning" is sufficiently less obvious than the productive contribution of those who live by the sweat of their brow to leave ample room for dispute.

Nor is this the only defect of the distinction for our purposes. It is doubtless true that most of our industrial processes are advantageous to the consuming public, and it may even be that no purely acquisitive act can be construed as in the common interest. But, clearly there are some acts generally sup-

posed to be in the common interest which no more directly increase the physical volume of product than acquisition; and as
truly affect its distribution. Such are legislation, and administration and interpretation of laws, at least insofar as they are not
regarded as a part of the administration and direction of industry. So also adapting a man's desires to a product rather
than the product to his desires may in some cases be held, if
not in subservience to his desires, at least for what is commonly
held to be his welfare in a hygienic, intellectual, or moral sense
by altering and educating his desires or choosing for him in
questions where he is not competent to speak for himself. If
these do not fall in the acquisitive class, at least they are outside of the technological. And on the other hand some physical
products are definitely out of accord with the common interest
—poison gas, anarchist dynamite, impure foods, etc.

We may conclude, then, that technological magnitudes have
the advantage of being easily and objectively ascertainable, and
so, where it is only a question of the magnitude of a single
item, like barrels of flour, they may be very useful. Furthermore, to employ them may be a good, quick way to unmask the
intricacies of pecuniary and legal relationships, and to get at
least a suggestion as to how the land lies. But the distinction
between acquisitive and technological will be differently construed by people of differing class prejudices and is only roughly
coincident with what we are seeking as a measure of business
policy. It succeeds better in specifying policies which are dictated by purely differential advantage, than in offering a constructive standard of appraisal.

The human or psychological theories have in common that
they measure welfare in terms of some biological or psychological trait of man. Hobson has given perhaps the most complete
recent formulation of this type of theory, tracing in some detail
the discrepancies between the pecuniary costs of production and
the human costs and gains that the productive process entails on
the one hand and between the pecuniary value of the product
and the human gains and costs to which its consumption gives
rise on the other. Hobson recognizes that the principal discrepancies are not those between the different human costs and

Communities of Economic Interest 223

gains and their pecuniary expression where only one person is involved, but rather between the human costs and gains for several different persons and the pecuniary estimates put upon them. It is, therefore, necessary to find some standard which will enable us to express A's desires and preferences and B's desires and preferences in common units. To do this we may resort to a "price-system," or what comes to about the same thing, assign various weights, dispersions and skewnesses to the desires of the several persons. Or, as in the case of technological theories, we may shift to a socio-organic position, in which each man's interests are interests of the "collective personality." Hobson does both. In following the first method he criticizes the weights that price assigns today, and also the "every-man-to-count-as-one" theory and suggests that human cost of production varies inversely with worker's ability, while human gain from consumption varies directly with needs. But since his corrections are expressed in "psychological" magnitudes, it is difficult if not impossible to determine how large or how small the pecuniary corrections should be. Indeed, except in cases generally approved or generally condemned, it can be only a matter of opinion or taste whether to make the sign plus or minus.

A version, intermediate between the psychological and socio-organic types of theory, runs in terms of instincts. They are presumed to be the traits of individuals, but because their ground of survival can be understood in terms of the race as a unit, a judicious use of the concept of instinct-expression may make it possible to solve the difficulty of inter-individual conflicts. The use of instincts as a standard of socio-economic appraisal is suggested by several writers. But no two are agreed as to what instincts man possesses, still less as to what constitutes expression and what "balking"; and some hold a view of instincts which offers little basis for appraisal. Here too, then, we find that the psychological theories, however attractive in the abstract, are hopelessly ambiguous when it comes to any concrete application on which there is not already general agreement, and are lacking in the objectivity and definiteness to which science aspires. It may be that in some cases economists have no alternative but to attempt corrections of the pecuniary standard by estimating human costs and human gains; but in general it should hardly be their first resort.

Both in the case of the technological and in that of the psychological theories we found it possible to meet the need for an inter-commodity and inter-individual standard by resort to some sort of a group-personality, who should embrace within himself all desires for all goods and all dislikes for tasks and sacrifices, and somehow settle all their conflicts. This is the third type of theory in one of its extremer forms. The common point of all such socio-organic theories is that they regard certain groups of people as units, each unit bearing a greater or less resemblance to a living organism and that some of these resemblances give a basis of appraisal with respect to the group regarded as a unit. For those who do not hesitate to personify the group this basis is that the group personality has interests like the rest of us. The bearing of any development or situation upon the common welfare may be appraised in terms of its subservience to those interests.

But fortunately we do not have to choose between such a view and a complete denial of similarity on the part of any group of people to a single organism. The question is one of degree. We may attempt to specify a minimum limit of the organic character of a social group which we shall designate as "pecuniary society." In this group are included all parties currently and recurrently to exchange in any market throughout the world, and also the dependents of these parties. The following resemblances between pecuniary society and a typical metazoan organism may be listed: (1) Pecuniary society is a complex of more or less highly differentiated and specialized individuals, while a metazoan organism is a complex of differentiated cells. The individuals like the cells of the organism are dependent on each other for the continuance of their specialized life. (2) The group has certain characteristics and behaves in certain ways in a large measure independently of the constituent individuals involved, just as a metazoan may replace worn-out tissue and regenerate, within limits, its parts and still maintain its identity structurally and functionally. Pecuniary society goes through an industrial revolution and forward peoples exploit backward peoples without much reference to the rise of any single person to financial power or the death of any financier. (3) Certain sub-groups, or certain institutions (to analyze pecuniary society along somewhat different lines) can with as much propriety as bodily organs be construed as having special functions. And when we admit this resemblance, we have it open to us, following the lead of the pathologist, to ask "Does this group or this institution perform its function properly? And if not, how does it come to function as it does?" Thus a socio-organic view becomes the basis of appraisal. We are at present, indeed, investigating just these questions in regard to the functions of money, price, and exchange—coördination, apportionment, and distribution.

It may be the part of caution to set down here, by way of contrast, three of the distinguishing features of a biological organism which pecuniary society and (except possibly for part of the second) every other social group clearly lacks: (1) definiteness of size, and of structure or of location of parts (2) reproduction of like organisms at roughly regular intervals of a generation, and death as the end of a fairly definite life-cycle and (3) contiguity of organic parts. With less confidence we may add that the cells, tissues, and organs of a metazoan—particularly of a human—organism do not prey upon and conflict with each other in their functioning in a manner fairly analogous to the conflict and predation among individuals and groups that characterize society; the functioning of the parts of society displays less perfect coördination than is to be found in the individual organism, unless perhaps we wish to compare society to a pathological specimen.

To some it has seemed that by analyzing pecuniary society logically into the behavior of its constituent individuals they might somehow do away with pecuniary society. But surely logical analysis does not necessarily invalidate the concept analyzed; nor does it destroy the thing conceived. Having made the analysis, it still remains to see how the activities of the constituent individuals articulate in the functioning of pecuniary society so, for example, as to produce the rhythmical movement of the business cycle. And this would seem to be the job of an economic price theorist.

But how far ought we to go in the direction of endowing pecuniary society with the traits of a living organism or with those of that very special case, man? Has pecuniary society a mind? Has it interests, desires, preferences? If not, will the sort of appraisal that the concept "function" permits suffice to arbitrate between the conflicting interests of individuals? Hobson, at any rate, is among those who do not hesitate to go the whole way. And on the hypothesis of a group personality, whose interests are versatile enough to embrace the interests of all men, the investigation of the settlement of conflicts of individual interest becomes a study in volitional "social" psychology. The economist is likely to make this into a social felicific calculus, taking place perhaps in the social subconscious.

A somewhat similar effect is obtained by employing the situation in a "collective society" as the antithesis to what pays differentially today. Thus for Davenport, money as a record of and incentive to individual performance and as a claim against the social product is absent. And he has the society (personified?) "making comparison . . . according to considerations of utility—marginal utility, of a vague and average sort." His concept of a competitive economy logically implies such a regime. And yet, what has one whose "business is solely with the facts" to do with imagining a society so impossible as this collectivism? It is by no means clear that a society with labor as minutely divided as it is today could avoid exchange and price. And if it could, why study only the behavior of individuals in the one case and only the behavior of society (or its leader?) in the other? Why not espouse the "group mind" theory (or the heroistic interpretation of social process) in both cases or in neither? Are not separate individuals, each having his own interests and choosing accordingly, with their several interests and preferences in greater or less conflict, characteristic of any society?

But it would seem the part of caution, where pecuniary society obviously differs in many respects not only from man but from any living organism, not to employ animistic or anthropomorphic categories except where careful examination shows that they imply no incorrect assumption of resemblance. We shall do well to avoid speaking of "the interests or the welfare of society." Thus far we have used "the common interest" as being a term of fairly neutral cast. Hereafter we shall refer to a "community of interests" and never "the interests of a community." And the problem of the common welfare becomes one of harmony and coincidence of individual interests, of individual welfares. It will be our task to investigate what lines between the legal and effective rights of separate individuals give rise to conflicts and what to communities of interests.

The objection to socio-anthropomorphism in its extremer forms is not merely on the ground of accuracy. Interests and preferences cannot readily be assigned to the group personality on the basis of any objective criterion capable of inducing agreement among different economists; or at any rate, if such a criterion is found, then that and not the group personality is the essential point of the theory for our purposes. But more likely the tastes and preferences assigned will depend, so far as they are given concreteness, on the class and other preconceptions of the particular economist. Like the individual psychology theories, the group personality theories are chiefly useful in cases already settled.

But we have seen that the more guarded and presumably more accurate formulation of the socio-organic view allows of at least two types of scientific, economic investigation, which have to do with setting up standards of comparison and appraisal for the structure and functioning of a social group as a unit: (1) To speak of the function of this institution or that group raises the question, "To what extent does it perform the function?" In dealing with this question the ideal performance of the function becomes the standard by which the actual performance (or lack of it) may be appraised. (2) We may study the conditions which give rise to communities and conflicts of individual interests. Thus a hypothetical community of interests among a group of people becomes the standard with which the actual conflict of interests among the group under present institutions may be compared. To these we may now add a third:

(3) A community of interests is a particular sort of articulation of heterogeneous interests—each seeks "his own gain" which is presumably a different result from what every other seeks, at least in the persons affected. But there also may be groups, the members of which have certain identical interests, tastes, or ideals—certain notions of what things ought or ought not to be done by or to happen to a person. These ideals may offer us still another standard of comparison for what actually occurs. Where an event or condition is generally condemned, we may measure the extent of present deviation from the ideal by such tangible statistical items as the number of industrial accidents, windowless tenement rooms, etc. None of these three lines of inquiry requires us to personify pecuniary society or even to make of it a social organism, and only in the first does the economist himself venture overtly to appraise.

V. A REVISION OF THE PECUNIARY STANDARD

So much for non-pecuniary standards of appraisal. But do the many short-comings of price require us to abandon it altogether as a method of stating where common interests lie? Or may we not somehow doctor the pecuniary measure, "compensate the dollar," and so use price to compare with price and to specify the direction of a harmony of interest? If we may, the pecuniary measure has certain obvious advantages: It is a definite affair, capable of statistical and accounting treatment. It is sufficiently objective so that different observers should expect to get comparable results. Since price plays a central part in the incentives to economic performance and in the apportionment of men and the non-human factors among the several lines, to state a community of interests in pecuniary terms should throw a considerable light on the methods by which such a community might be achieved.

Many indications point towards a pecuniary standard. Price is continually becoming a more predominant factor in our lives as specialization proceeds and more of the phases of our household economy move out into the world of business. Some standard is desirable which will relate the variegated interests of a host of separate individuals, and apparently that means some sort of price-system. Both the technological and the psychological theories led either to a group personality or to some pecuniary theory. So also the classical value theory has set up a pecuniary norm with which the observed prices might be compared—what would occur under free competition. But if we are to set up a pecuniary standard, it must differ in at least two important respects from the classical normal value: (1) As has already been intimated, it must make no pretense of being in some subtle sense an "explanation" of actual prices, precisely because it is a standard with which to compare them. Our present concern is strictly and solely with the standard. (2) The pecuniary results of present competition are not acceptable as indicating the direction in which a community of interests may lie, and in some cases at least, this appears to be due, not so much to lack of perfect freedom as to the presence of competition under present legal rights: waste of natural resources like oil, cut-throat competition, business depressions, competitive armaments (insofar as competition induces producers to "develop" the state as a market and insofar as they are successful), child labor, bad working conditions, seasonal industry, etc. Enough has already been said to throw grave doubt on the accuracy of the assumption that each seeking his own gain under free competition tends to promote the common welfare. We shall, therefore, attempt to formulate a standard which shall be independent of the short-comings of both monopoly and competition.

The general character of the standard required has already been hinted at in the discussion of differential advantage. Given two or more persons, each acting independently in pursuit of his own differential advantage, under what circumstances might we find a community of interests among them? And why look for our community of interests among this particular group of two or more? The characteristic which led us to designate any personal gain as a differential advantage was that in some respect the costs fell differently on the discretionary party (or the gains accrued to him differently) from their incidence upon others. In other words, to refer to a gain as a differential advantage is to point out some particular discrepancy in the way in which money functions to keep the cost records of pecuniary society. And when we attempted to analyze differential advantage, we found that we could specify not only the discretionary party, but also the non-discretionary parties whose interests were directly involved, but whose gains and losses from the transaction in question were inaccurately reflected in the accounts of the party in discretion. Here, then, we have the group whose interests require to be integrated—in theory—into a community.

The outline of this process of pecuniary integration should now be clear. Given certain discretionary parties to whom, differentially, a certain course of action is a paying proposition, and given the non-discretionary parties and the effects of the course of action on their interests; what alterations would there be in costs and gains accruing from this action to the discretionary parties, if all the costs falling on non-discretionary parties could be passed on to the discretionary parties in the same "shape" and if all of the gains could similarly be passed on —including, if possible, items representing human costs and psychic income? And, reckoning in these further items attributable to the course of action in question, does it pay integrally? Or, if not, what course of action does the integral advantage of the discretionary parties dictate? This integral advantage should, if properly defined, be in harmony with the interests of the non-discretionary parties; and so together they constitute what has been called a community of economic interests—barring, of course, other differentials than the one just considered involving several of the same parties.

It may be easier to see just what is involved in this process of integration if we employ it separately on some of the special types of differential advantage.

In cases of horizontal and oblique relationships of the non-discretionary parties to the transaction in question we may frequently neglect any variations in the shape and uniformity of costs involved, and confine our attention to the effect on the non-discretionary parties' welfare. Is it favorable or unfavorable? And how large is it? The relation between differential and integral advantage here is comparatively simple. By way of illustration we may take a case where the pecuniary effect is unfavorable, what we have called a de facto tort. Integration here is only a question of adding the pecuniary costs inflicted on the non-discretionary parties to the costs which already fall on the discretionary party in case he decides to follow the course of action he has under consideration. In such a case it may well result that it would not pay him integrally to do what is differentially to his advantage. The case where the pecuniary effect is favorable to the non-discretionary parties is to be treated similarly. Here the additional money gains attributable to the undertaking of the discretionary party may make that undertaking pay integrally when differentially it is not worth while. Theoretically the problem need not be altered when the effect on the non-discretionary party is no longer on money income or outgo or on the market value of property, but is rather an advantage or disadvantage because of the particular interests and preferences of the party involved—a part of his "human costs" or "psychic income." But practically it is difficult to make such an integration, because of the vagueness and uncertainty of the pecuniary measures for these "psychic magnitudes."

Cases which involve differences in the shape and uniformity of the items are more complicated. These are usually characterized by a vertical relationship between the two sorts of parties—both are parties to the transaction, but not equally in discretion. There are several differences in the shape and uniformity of pecuniary items at different stages in the backward flow of income that accompanies the forward flow of goods, of which a theory of differential and integral profitivity must take account:

(1) Professor Clark has called attention to the importance, in this connection, of conversions between direct and overhead cost items and has worked out their integration in some detail. It may suffice here to consider briefly the special case where an overhead cost item at one stage in the channel of trade is converted to a direct cost item in the next succeeding stage. To the seller certain costs of rendering the service are overhead, continuing whether the then volume of service is rendered or

whether the volume is somewhat more or less. To the buyer these costs are direct, this being the custom in sales contracts. Under these circumstances it may pay him differentially, if business is not very good, to stop buying and thereby avoid entirely for the time the pecuniary burden of this service. But this burden is not thereby stopped for the seller, and if we are to integrate the pecuniary interests involved into a community we shall have to assume some alteration of the institutional situation that will make these costs overhead to the buyer as well as to the seller. Then it might pay the buyer integrally to keep on buying, because he could save very little by stopping. Certain interesting complications in the overhead cost analysis are raised by cases where the buyers considerably outnumber the sellers, but their consideration would unduly prolong a preliminary sketch like the present.

(2) Another difference of pecuniary shape is that between capital and revenue items, between investment costs and costs of doing current business. At one stage in a channel of trade the costs of a particular item of technological performance may be chargeable and the revenue derived therefrom creditable to the year's profit and loss account. But at the next stage these items may be chargeable to capital assets. The building contractor derives income, but the corresponding outgo is permanent investment, not current expense. Decisions to make or withdraw investments are made purely on the grounds of their pecuniary virtues or vices as paying investments, not at all with regard to their effects on the incomes of those who produce these producers' goods purchased for investment. Hence it may pay differentially to invest or to withdraw investment when integral advantage would dictate another course. Curiously, when we come to integrate this case, it turns out to be a special instance of the previous one, for a pooling of accounts would require us to make the contractor's profit and loss account an analysis of the cost of building account. Revenue debits and credits are converted to capital debits and credits, not conversely. And if the accounts of all producers of capital goods are thus integrated with those of their purchasers, the decisions of the purchasers will still be made on investment grounds. But

all the investment costs were previously directly attributable to particular investments—investment costs, that could be avoided by avoiding those investments. Integrally, however, the overhead of the producers of capital goods cannot be avoided by the investor-purchasers. They now have to carry these costs anyway.

In order, then, to find a differential advantage due to this change of shape as such, we should have to find contractors deciding on grounds of income and expense what integrally is a question of investment cost and ownership. But on this question contractors are not the chief discretionary parties. It would seem, therefore, that this shift of form from capital to revenue items does not give rise to any differential advantage on its own account. It is important, in the case we have just considered, as a combining element. So, also, it is of considerable consequence in differentials such as typical cases of corporate manipulation and high finance, cases where one man's capital is juggled to become another man's income. But these are de facto torts, requiring only addition in order to specify the integral advantage—the losses to stockholders are to be added to the expenses of "finance" in the individual accounts of the financier. Because of these interrelations, if not on its own account, the capital-revenue conversion of form requires attention.

(3) Beside these two variations in the shape of the cost items, we must list those frequent cases of variation in their uniformity where a number of enterprises or persons produce the same good or service at different costs per unit, but sell it in the same market at the same price. Under these circumstances the infra-marginal producer commands a differential income, sometimes at the expense of the consumer, sometimes in part at least at the expense of the higher-cost enterprises or persons. A number of factors are involved in the allocation of the burden as between purchaser and high-cost competitor: the market price, the terms of the sale contract, the conditions that give rise to non-uniform costs, etc. It is a nice problem in pecuniary incidence, to which considerable attention has been given. We shall, therefore, content ourselves with having listed it here.

Before proceeding to a more detailed illustration of the relation between differential and integral pecuniary advantage, it may be well to present certain qualifications of the integration process. In the first place, integration is not a mere pooling of pecuniary interests. It does imply pooling in a certain sense. A gain for one party should represent a clear addition to the gains of the group as a whole, and should never be at the expense of some other party to the integration. Furthermore the "shape" of costs and other items should be uniform throughout, the standard of shape being that which would result from a consolidation of the accounts. But integration does not imply any loss of the lines of demarcation between the several parties. Unlike pooling, each party still seeks independently to maximize his own private gains, reckoning the costs and yields to himself. Integration does not mean combination of several independent fiscal units into a single independent fiscal unit. It means only that the pecuniary situation is so altered that the alternatives open to one of these fiscal units require it to carry all the costs it imposes on the other parties, without any change of shape, and allow it to realize all their gains which are attributable to its action. It is a community or harmonization of individual pecuniary interests, rather than a consolidation into a single discretionary and accounting unit that obliterates the individuality of the constituent parties.

In this connection it may be well to recall our investigation of the group personality theories led us to confine the use of such terms as "interest" and "advantage" to individuals, avoiding such socio-anthropomorphic conceptions as "the interests of a group." When some or all the pecuniary interests of several persons are added together—the incomes pooled—at some stage of the distributive process, we may perhaps be pardoned for allowing the phrase, "the interests of the group," as an abbreviation for "the sum of the (pecuniary) interests of the members of the group." But we should never lose sight of the reference of interests or advantages to individuals. Hence, in formulating a term to contrast with differential advantage it seems desirable that it should be just as precise in its reference of advantage to individuals as the given differential allows, that it should preserve intact each of the independent fiscal and

accounting units with which we start. In some cases, as we shall
see, it may even be necessary to break up a given pool or combination of interests into its constituent parts because the pooling has brought about a very imperfect integration, because
some of the parts can gain differentially at the expense of
others. But even here it will still be true that integral advantage
always means advantage to the same discretionary party as that
whose differential advantage is under investigation—whether
this be an individual, or less accurately a group, whose advantages are pooled, whose incomes are summed.

Yet the analogy to consolidation and pooling may be pushed
farther if one cares to do so. So viewed, the independent fiscal
unit, participating in a community of interests, becomes a
managerial and cost-accounting unit in a larger organization,
whose limits tend to spread and become coextensive with those
of pecuniary society. So viewed, too, the economist appears as
something of a social cost accountant when he studies the conflicts and harmonies of pecuniary interest, and points out places
where costs are not borne or gains realized by those responsible
for them, or describes the alterations in the pecuniary situation
which would bring about a more accurate allocation of costs
and gains according to responsibility. Indeed, the whole present
conception of differential and integral advantage is an elaboration of the cost-accounting "mores" that each should pay in full
for all he gets, according to its cost of production, and should
be fully paid for all that others get from him.

It requires perhaps to be pointed out again that a statement
of what integral advantage is, is only a statement of a standard
with which the existing (differential) situation may be compared. It is in no sense a remedy or a method of reform to be
applied to the situation, although this formulation of the
standard, this statement of the direction in which a community
of interest lies, may condition the choice of methods (by those
concerned with problems of method). The course by which
such a community of pecuniary interests may be achieved, may
be a change of titles, or of the property rights attaching to certain titles, special taxation, new contract forms, a more centralized control of separate enterprises and trades, or any of a

variety of other remedies. Our present concern is not with these ways and means, but only to specify wherein a community of interests consists, only to formulate an ideal standard of comparison.

One further qualification seems called for. Integral advantage is admittedly, only a proximate standard. It always has specific reference to some contrasting differential advantage. The community of interests in which it finds a place is necessarily a limited community, falling short of embracing all the interests of pecuniary society. Any community of interests, were it to be actually achieved, would involve readjustments and alterations ramifying throughout the entire fabric of the system of prices, to say nothing of the accompanying technological changes. Under these circumstances it is impossible, even if we were to perform all our integrations at once, to regard the result as one all-inclusive community of interests, for that result would necessarily be built upon such derivatives of current differential advantage as the present distribution of income. We shall have, therefore, to be content with the more proximate standards of specific integrals, admitting that these integrals may turn out to be differentials with respect to some larger group. We can claim only that certain differential advantages have been integrated, subjecting others, as rapidly as they appear to the same treatment. As already intimated, complete integration is possible only in an ideal society, and could throw little light on immediate economic problems, if we attained it.

As a corollary of this specific reference of integral advantage we may note that the theory is limited in its applicability by the nature of the available data. Because a statement in terms of integral profitivity is a more accurate formulation of the nature of communities of economic interest than one in terms of productivity under free competition, it necessarily requires a more complete and specific observational basis. While statistics at present available should be adequate in many—perhaps in most—important cases for a rough determination as to whether present conditions are in accord with the integral advantages of the parties concerned, a precise application of the theory must wait upon accounting publicity and uniformity. Without such information there can be no accurate ground for holding either that the status quo does or that it does not give rise to a harmonious coincidence of pecuniary interests. Except on the basis of reliable statistics such an objective social appraisal of the functioning of exchange coördination as that here contemplated is impossible. Economic condemnation, and likewise and to the same extent economic approval, are otherwise very nearly certain to be mere matters of private taste and prejudice. Accuracy and objectivity require an observational basis.

By way of summary it may be advantageous to compare the present position with that of Davenport. According to the latter view, our competitive economy is contrasted with a collective economy. Conflicts and divergences of interest appear to be due chiefly to multiple ownership and discretion, to the fact that each may choose for himself. According to the former, multiple legal rights are well-nigh inevitable under modern technology and multiple discretion is the essence of any social group, but drawing legal or pecuniary lines differently may transform conflicts of interest into communities, and the contrast is between these two, both competitive and both in pecuniary terms—between a situation giving rise to differential and one giving rise to integral advantage. Unlike the Davenportian position, such a contrast is always specific, indicating the nondiscretionary parties whose interests are affected and the pecuniary alterations in the institutional situation which would change the differential into an integral advantage, that carried all its own costs in their original shape and reaped all its own gains. Being institutional, it finds competition and legal rights vastly more flexible, and since only minor differences in these institutions are involved in the contrast, the actual and the hypothetical situations are enough alike so that one may shed considerable light upon the other.

By way of making the theory of differential and integral pecuniary advantage more concrete, and of insuring that the relation shall be clear between the generalized formulation of the contrast of the common welfare with private special interests on the one hand and certain more specific contrasts—some of them commonplace and widely accepted—on the other, we may now set forth in bare outline a few important applications of the theory. Properly these illustrations should make the effort to specify the pecuniary magnitudes involved, where adequate information is available, since such a specification is an essential part of our contention; but the attempt would inevitably raise questions of statistical technique that would carry the discussion far beyond the appointed limits of the present paper.

I. Technological improvements and certain related developments present a number of contrasts between differential and integral advantage. Differentially it has often paid to introduce a new technological process because a large part of the costs fell on somebody else—the costs of depreciation through obsolescence. Pigou calls regarding this as a case of differential advantage a "specious fallacy," advancing as his reason that curious classicism, "Whatever loss the old producers suffer through a reduction in the price of their products is balanced by the gain which the reduction confers upon the purchasers of these products." But that hardly meets the point that one man suffers damages that another may gain; or that the technological change often involves, on the integral reckoning, an increase in the interest, depreciation, and maintenance charges in connection with the investment in new equipment that exceeds the saving in operating costs—a net integral loss. Knauth's reasoning would seem more agreeable to the present view. Indeed, he draws almost precisely the present distinction between what pays differentially, disregarding the annual costs which someone else has contracted for a few years in advance in order to be equipped to operate the old process, and what pays integrally, when one carries all the costs involved. In order to make an accurate estimate of the net integral profit or loss on such a transaction, it would seem necessary to have access to the books of enterprises in the industry, but a rough estimate could doubtless often be made with the generally available information.

Two analogies may be suggested from the status of the laborer: (1) One type of cost which has not, until recently, fallen on the employer in its true form, is that of depreciation through senescence. Differentially it has paid him to lay off old employees without provision for further maintenance, and in the extreme, to overwork them to a premature old age. (2) The differential profitivity of importing immigrants in part derives from the fact that employers do not have to carry the depreciation of earning power of those with a higher standard of living.

But differential advantage is not always on the side of technological change. Standardization and interchangeability of parts among the products of competing and complementary enterprises might well enable them to supply the most utility to the consumer at the lowest cost. Integrally, therefore (including in the community these enterprises and the customer), it should pay each enterprise so to act that this result would be brought about. But, differentially, such an innovation not only does not pay, but it is even profitable to invent needless diversity so as to market duplicate parts that fit only one brand of apparatus and so help make the work go around. The combined integral loss involved in such a situation should be measured approximately by the additional costs of producing these unnecessary duplicates, less whatever increased costs are involved in producing standardized products. Integrally, too (including the coal industry and its consumers in the community), it would seem a very wasteful technology that carries raw bituminous coal to hundreds of thousands of small consumers, lets them burn valuable by-products in amateur fires and pollute the air, and carries the ashes away again. Integrally it should pay to refine the coal, save the by-products, carry the energy by wire as electric current, or by pipe line as gas or benzol, or perhaps by rail or truck as artificial anthracite. Differentially such a technological revolution does not appeal strongly to any single enterprise in the coal industry because no single enterprise could undertake it. Nor is it likely in the immediate future to appeal differentially to the investment banker, the ownership of the industry being so minutely divided, and the legal restraints on combination and integration being what they are. An attempt to estimate the amount of the total integral loss annually incurred under the present technology has been made by Gilbert and Pogue.

II. Rhythmical unemployment of persons and industrial apparatus is of two chief types, seasonal and business-cyclical. We shall consider only those cases of seasonal unemployment where the effect of the seasons is not so direct as to be nearly inevitable. Here, and in the case of cyclical unemployment, there is a clear difference between what pays differentially and what pays integrally. Differentially each enterprise may count the interest on its investment as overhead, continuing regardless of operation or shut-down. So also it may reckon depreciation and some maintenance, salaries of most managers, and so forth. But practically all of wages, materials, and supplies will be direct, avoidable costs. Differentially, therefore, there is a considerable difference between the cost of full-time operation and part-time operation or complete shut-down. And if the season is dull or prices low, or if the market is dull or likely to be so owing to an unfavorable turn of the business cycle, it will pay differentially in most cases to lay off employees and stop buying, entirely or in part. But in a period of industrial crisis this is what many other firms are doing, and as unemployment increases consumers have less to spend. Thus it pays differentially in dull markets so to act that markets will be duller—no single firm can afford to do otherwise. But integrally, Professor Clark finds that the direct costs of full operation with respect to the business cycle are almost nothing, since nearly all of wages (as covering the cost of living) as well as interest on property investment, are overhead. Hence only a nominal revenue should be sufficient to make full operation pay. Much the same would appear to be true of seasonal industries in trades like clothing and coal.

Another curious discrepancy between differential and integral profitivity in connection with the business cycle appears in the fluctuating activity of those trades which produce relatively durable goods, notably the construction industries. Integrally considered (including in our community of interests (1) the enterprises in these trades, (2) those in others to which their employees or equipment might be transferred, and (3) the customers of both) it would seem that these trades might serve as levelers of the industrial load. Since the product is durable, the need for continuous production is less pressing. In boom times, with a general shortage of men and equipment, with building costs soaring like the rest, it should pay integrally for investors in plant and so forth, considered as a unit, to postpone further construction and release the employees and equipment as far as possible for more immediately pressing tasks. Then, when times are dull and unemployment rife, when construction costs are at their lowest, it should pay them integrally to build for the future. But differentially it pays to do exactly the reverse—the flattest industries in time of depression are usually those connected with construction, and the busiest ones when the boom is on are these same producers of durable goods. Differentially it pays to withdraw investment during depression by deferring maintenance and depleting inventories, and to increase investment during prosperity by making up back maintenance, stocking up, and purchasing new plant and equipment. In part this differential advantage derives from the combined direct-overhead and capital-revenue conversion already discussed. In part also it derives from the shifting identity and uncertain commercial status of small separate enterprises. Differentially, it may not pay a firm to build in off-peak times, because it is too near bankruptcy or because it is not yet organized. And again, differential advantage is a matter of estimating the future, and estimates have often been made with inadequate information and understanding of the business cycle.

A well-worn illustration from the business cycle is afforded by the old banking system, under which it paid each bank differentially to call in its deposits with other banks in a financial crisis, in order to increase its own cash reserve at the expense of some other bank's reserve. Assuming it succeeded, it would have gained nothing integrally, unless the new distribution of reserves happened to be more in accord with the requirements of the financial situation—a gain which is difficult to measure in pecuniary terms.

III. Our natural resources are held under property rights which give rise to important discrepancies between differential and integral profitivity. Integrally, it would pay only as many owners of bituminous coal lands to open mines as could in the present market maintain fairly uninterrupted operation. Differentially, it pays not only to provide the extra capacity required by bad seasonal or cyclical load factors, but also to add a very considerable excess above the requirements of the peak load. The direct results of excess capacity are cut-throat competition, fluctuating prices and part-time operation. The indirect results include the necessity for cutting (differential) overhead and investment costs to a minimum, and so discourage the hiring of competent foremen and technologists and the adoption of machinery and methods involving a large original outlay like the long wall system. Again, cut-throat prices and poor technology encourage incomplete extraction; and the pillar and stall method enhances risks. Once differential advantage has led to over-development, the complications continue indefinitely. To estimate the combined integral loss to which over-development gives rise would be indeed a baffling problem.

With petroleum the case is far worse. Integrally it would seem that one well should be enough to sink into one prospect, at least until oil is struck. Not so, differentially. Under existing property rights it may pay the owner best to lease his property in quarter-sections to competing prospectors. Nor can one prospector afford to await the findings of a competitor—the first to tap the common source gets the lion's share of the oil. The cost of sinking these unnecessary wells would give some idea of the total integral loss involved, though it takes no account of the accompanying wasteful and incomplete extraction of petroleum.

In the case of forests there are yet other complications. Only a part of the costs of deforestation fall on the forest-owner. As a consequence of his decision the neighboring territory may have a regular water supply replaced by spring floods and fall droughts, and fertile farm lands may be wasted away in spring mud. Estimates of damages from such de facto torts would probably vary widely, but there is no question that their total annual amount for the country has often been a large item.

With water-power the case is reversed. Mineral deposits stand nearly still awaiting exploitation, but the energy of a waterfall is constantly wasting away. Yet differentially it does

not pay under divided ownership to develop our hydraulic
energy resources to anything like the full, without the assistance of special legislation. Thus riparian rights to drainage of
property upstream interfere with necessary storage for evening
the flow, and their owner can (acting differentially) exact
monopoly tribute, unless the power-development project can
exercise the right of eminent domain. In the larger streams there
are also complications of navigation rights and often of sover-
eign jurisdiction.

IV. The incentive problem in business organization illustrates another aspect of the theory. Differential advantage is not
always a matter of relations between separate business enterprises. And, if integration is not a mere pooling but preserves
the identity of the separate parties, it may sometimes be required to disentangle the parties to a pool or a consolidation.
In a sense we may think of the several departments or branches
of an enterprise as elements of a consolidated whole. And the
question arises, What are the incentives of department managers? Or what does it pay each differentially to do or neglect?
How widely does a manager's differential advantage diverge
from what would pay him integrally, from what would pay him
if he could gain only by adding to the company's profits and if
any increase in profits for which he was responsible was reflected
in a loss to him? To answer this question the enterprise must be
split up into separate cost-accounting units, according to managerial responsibility, and records kept of individual managerial
pecuniary performance. The question is then, How accurately
does his pay vary with his value to the enterprise? The Law of
Size of Firm has usually contemplated profits as the type of incentive payment and one such accounting unit per firm. The
gradual development of separate cost-accounting units within
each firm and of managerial and other bonus-systems now in
process offers interesting possibilities for the significance of this
law. In combination with the competition for place and promotion, we may find here something that may some day be
designated intra-corporate competitive profits.

VI. CONCLUSION

In a specialized and inter-dependent society as complex as our own it is little wonder that there are many far-reaching conflicts of interest, little wonder that pecuniary values, resting, as they do, upon an elaborate code of legal precedents entrusted to the keeping of a specialized cult, should fail frequently to check exactly with one another, owing to the difficulty in so intricate a situation of tracing the responsibility for each cost and gain, and should in failing give rise to differential advantages to one man at the expense of another—differential advantages that pervade and distort the whole fabric of the price-system. The wonder is, indeed, that communities of interest should be as many and as inclusive as they are; and yet economists, impressed by that great community of specialized servants of their fellows who are also generalized consumers of their fellows' services—"the great coöperation"—have too often left no place in their "theory" for anything but harmony. So pervasive, indeed, are these differential advantages and so inextricably are their various distortions intertwined that when one attempts to introduce corrections into the process of social cost accounting which money, price, and exchange perform, he is compelled to confine himself to a single, somewhat narrowly defined, community of interest. Integral advantage stands always in contrast to some particular differential advantage, having reference to the same party to whose discretion the differential advantage makes appeal, and being, like it, stated in pecuniary terms. It differs from differential advantage in that the discretionary party counts all the costs and all the gains without change of shape, which his action imposes on the pecuniary interests of others. But, being thus a resultant of more accurate social cost accounting, its definiteness of reference and of pecuniary statement make it a peculiarly significant form of specifying the direction in which a community of interests lies.

It is not intended to suggest that all communities of interest can thus definitely be formulated. As we have seen, in cases where the effect on non-discretionary parties is in terms of real cost or psychic income, a definite statement of integral advantage cannot be made with any great assurance. And these are but the borderland of cases that the economist is likely to slight, cases in which pecuniary value does not enter at all. We may, quite properly, look forward with Professor Cooley to a progressive assimilation of these non-pecuniary realms of human appraisal by price. And as rapidly as this "progress in pecuniary values" takes place, they will be brought within the scope of our analysis. But the limits of the analysis are not less real nor less important because they happen to be changing.

Nor should it be thought an implication of the present position that conflicts of pecuniary interest can ever be completely and permanently eliminated, either in theory or in fact. In a changing society such as ours, established legal rights and precedents are perpetually getting out of adjustment with technology and social organization; new conflicts of interests arise as rapidly as older conflicts are eliminated. Conflicts are the inevitable accompaniment of institutional evolution.

It is not expected that the statement of integral pecuniary advantage should be the only standard of comparison employed even by the economist, or the only method of expressing divergences of the actual situation from the common interest. It may be desirable to make other revisions of the pecuniary standard, such as estimates of the effect on prices of more adequate market information more evenly distributed. In certain cases, statistics in physical units may be very useful, as already indicated—man-days of unemployment, calories of wasted fuel-energy, and so forth. And so the technological processes underlying a confusion of differential pecuniary gains and interlocking legal claims may prove a handy short-cut to the integration analysis. Again, the mores and conventional codes of welfare—including the opinion typical of specialized groups, such as physicians—may well supplement the pecuniary standard. Statistics of industrial accidents stand fairly on their own merits. And it may well be that the economist will find it worth his while to investigate communities of non-pecuniary interests. Finally, we may list the notion of function which has recently gained currency in economic thought, and which, though open to grave abuses, should prove a valuable way of conceiving the behavior of groups and institutions.

To one who is willing to follow the statement of integral pecuniary advantage as a formulation of the direction in which a harmony of interests lies, it may very well seem an easy step to lend his approval to such a situation as is thus depicted and to offer his support for any proposal that promises to bring it about. But the acceptance of this pecuniary formulation of an ideal tends to condition the method employed in its realization —it suggests that the method of social reform employed, whatever other features it may embody, should be in the nature of an attempt to preserve and improve upon the various pecuniary incentives which now function imperfectly in exchange coördination. Property rights, contract forms, social organization, and so forth, should be altered so as to make individual gain more closely reflect service rendered. In so proceeding we should preserve a fundamental teaching of laissez-faire, reliance on the pursuit of one's private pecuniary gain as an incentive to the performance of service to others. In proportion as the integrations attempted were realized in practice, it would come to be more nearly true of everyone that "the study of his own advantage . . . leads him to prefer that employment which is most advantageous to the society," or more strictly, most advantageous to his fellows.

· XV ·

Monopolistic Competition

A

The Theory of Monopolistic Competition *

(1934)

CHAMBERLIN'S *Theory of Monopolistic Competition* [1] deserves to rank as one of the major contributions to the theory of
value and distribution in recent years. Holding constant most of
the other assumptions of neo-classical economics that have been
especially subjected to criticism of late, he proceeds to vary the
assumption that each market approximates either perfect competition or absolute monopoly. He postulates an imperfectly
competitive market consisting of a number of smaller markets,
each being characterized by a seller's monopoly imperfectly
isolated from the others. He studies this imperfect market
(which we will designate the genus market) through one of the
constituent (species) markets and through two demand curves
for it, which we will call the species curve and the average
genus curve. The species demand curve represents changes in
the purchases of a species when the price of that species alone is
varied. The average genus demand curve represents changes in
the purchases of a species when the prices of all other species in
the genus also vary so as to remain "identical" [2] with that of the

* Somewhat condensed.

[1] Edward Chamberlin, *The Theory of Monopolistic Competition* (Cambridge:
Harvard University Press, 1933). Pp. x + 213. $2.50.

[2] Chamberlin does not investigate what he means by "identical." If his theory
is to be broad enough to include the case where the different species

species under consideration. The extent of divergence of these two demand curves is a reflection of the effectiveness of competition, perfect competition appearing as a limiting case in which the species demand curve is horizontal. In the other limiting case, absolute monopoly so far as the genus under consideration is concerned, the two curves coincide.[3] When selling costs are introduced, two types of cost curves are found necessary, too, analogous to the two demand curves. Thus for a given price, the species selling-cost-per-unit curve assumes the selling costs of the competing monopolies constant; the average genus selling-cost-per-unit curve assumes the same sales cost by each seller in the genus market.

The (reviewer's) words, "genus" and "species," suggest quality differences in the good dealt in. Chamberlin's theory is intended to embrace geographical differences and differences in terms of sale as well. Most of his theory, except the appendix on pure spatial competition, proceeds on the assumption that each species competes equally closely with every other, but he deals briefly with the case of near and remote competitors under the caption of "oligopoly." In the reviewer's opinion this case is the rule, and merits more extended treatment.

While Chamberlin has by no means exhausted the possibilities of varying the assumption regarding monopoly and competition, his conclusions are instructive. Under the usual neo-classical assumptions including perfect competition, each enterpriser pursuing his own maximum profit (and each consumer-laborer-saver pursuing his own maximum utility) so acts as to maximize the physical volume of national income. Clearly Chamberlin's modification of neo-classical assumptions introduces one important—though not the only important—qualification on the validity of this view that private profit is

---

represent, e.g., different but competing freight hauls, "identical" appears to be the wrong word.

[3] In addition to offering us a generalized theory under which both perfect (price) competition and absolute monopoly are subsumed as limiting cases, Chamberlin's analysis implies that logically neo-classical theory should include a theory of pure quality competition, which by analogy to the conventional treatment of pure price competition in the "law of supply and demand" might lead to a "law of single quality."

a good index of public policy. He offers us a theory the implications of which definitely depart from laissez faire and move toward what is variously called "social control," "public regulation," "economic planning."

It is the virtue of Chamberlin's treatment [4] that he offers us a theory not of a single enterprise but of a *market* consisting on one side of competing monopolies. He does not, however, carry the analysis to its final stage—the economic system as a whole.[5] The reviewer suspects that, if it were carried to this final stage, there would be interesting and fundamentally important implications (1) for Say's Law; [6] (2) for the theory of the business cycle; (3) for the theory of the level of prices; (4) for the determinacy of the equilibrium point on the assumptions made.

The theory of monopolistic competition clearly opens new vistas for what has been called pure, abstract, or deductive economics. But its novelty is necessarily precarious. For most economists have long recognized, in mental compartments separate from what they call "theory," markets with the characteristics on which Chamberlin insists. Thus few students of railroad rate theory have sought to force the market for railroad service either into the perfect monopoly or into the perfect competition category. Hence it should be easy to read Chamberlin's *Theory* (as many appear to have read Clark's *Overhead Costs*) without recognizing its real novelty.

Nonetheless, it may be suggested that Chamberlin offers

[4] Contrast Robinson's *Economics of Imperfect Competition*, London, 1933.

[5] In discussing sales effort he says: "In the analysis to follow, we shall not go beyond the adjustments within the single group. It will be evident that a method similar to that applied as between the individuals in one group could be extended to systems of interdependent groups and even to the all-inclusive problem of the whole economic system."

[6] Chamberlin claims to offer an explanation of permanent excess capacity of plants (Chap. v, Sec. 5). The reviewer is still unconvinced that his market theory (as distinguished from a theory for the entire economic system) explains more than a negligible amount of permanent excess capacity. His position seems to imply (1) that the size of the enterprise at equilibrium is less than the most efficient size of plant, and (2) that it will pay the enterprise in the long run to employ a plant of such size that it would be capable of an appreciably larger continuing output without increasing the average production cost per unit.

It should be added, however, that he has explained chronic excess capacity for one factor—entrepreneurship.

us in addition to his specific theoretical novelty important light upon the vexed question of the relative merits of induction and deduction. Neo-classical economic theory has often been criticized as being "purely deductive." In the sense in which it is "purely deductive" Chamberlin is "purely deductive" too. But he has changed one of the premises. The real criticism of neo-classical theory implied in characterizing it as "purely deductive" is that it has clung so steadfastly to a single set of premises, never really probing the logical implications of alternative assumptions.

In lesser degree this criticism applies to Chamberlin. Particularly is it to be regretted that he has accepted the usual neo-classical oversimplifications of time relationships.[7] Thus his theory gives no recognition to the competitive relationship between a present monopolistic buyer or seller and his own future self—a relationship particularly important for differences in bargaining power. Again his cost curves are all premised upon the assumption that every cost is *directly* assignable to some accounting period, that there are no overhead costs in Clark's sense. Further, although the convergence between the species and the average genus demand curve may be an adequate measure of resistance to shifting from one species market to another for the neo-classical assumptions as to time (even here to make the species curve approximately a straight line is arbitrary), it fails to take account of the time-shape of such resistance. Thus his two-dimensional diagrams do not show the relation between the cost of establishing and the cost of maintaining a business. And they do not portray the problem of fixing a single price for successive periods in which the demand schedule is expected to vary from one to another. Nor do the curves portray the relative profitableness of such a policy of price maintenance as compared to alternative policies.

All of which is to say that Chamberlin is a pioneer. If he has missed some of the paths that others have found, and if many interesting by-paths have escaped him, he has nevertheless gone

[7] "The curve of selling costs has been defined without reference to the period of time and to the distinction between short-time and long-time results" (p. 139). Chamberlin even follows the classical tradition here to the extent of omitting capitalization doctrine.

far into new and promising territory—much farther than anyone else who has come to the reviewer's attention. And with
few exceptions, he has traveled this new territory with an
accuracy of thought that has too seldom been equaled even
in the well-worn paths of value theory.

B

A Comment on Advertising *

(1925)

The very existence of advertising evidences the absence of the
conditions necessary for a perfect market. Manufacturers who
advertise are monopolies of competing brands. Each brand is a
distinct commodity which consumers can substitute for the
others if the difference in their prices offers sufficient inducement. Branding is thus one method of dividing the market,
fairly analogous in limiting the freedom of competition to a
division along territorial lines. Price is higher than marginal
or direct cost. There is nothing in division of the market by
branding to insure the manufacturer a 'reasonable return on
a fair valuation'—no more and no less.

C

Competing Products and Monopolistic Competition

(1940)

This paper will attempt a supplement to a part of Chamberlin's *Theory of Monopolistic Competition*.[1] Chamberlin distinguishes three [2] main types of competition: (a) price competition, (b) sales effort competition, and (c) product or quality
competition. Attention will be devoted principally to the third
type, quality competition. This will be conceived in a broad

---

* Extracted and condensed from "The Economics of Advertising" (Discussion),
American Economic Review, March 1925 (Supplement), pp. 38–41.

[1] Edward Chamberlin, *The Theory of Monopolistic Competition*, 3d Edition,
Cambridge, 1938. The writer gratefully acknowledges the helpful criticism and
suggestions received from Professor Chamberlin.

[2] It is not intended here to imply that this three-fold classification is exhaustive.

sense, which includes spatial competition, brand competition, competition in the specifications of a product, and competition in terms of sale.

In addition to this question of quality competition, two other aspects of Chamberlin's theory will be touched on:

(a) Chamberlin has occasion to make certain assumptions regarding the structure of monopolistic-competitive markets and regarding conditions of entry into them. We shall be concerned to investigate both the conditions of entry into and the structure of monopolistic-competitive markets.

(b) Chamberlin distinguishes two types of demand curve. We have elsewhere suggested * that these curves may be referred to, respectively, as the apportioned genus demand curve and the species demand curve,[3] and this usage will be followed here. Chamberlin makes certain assumptions regarding the relations between these two demand curves which will be investigated.

In general, the discussion that follows employs the definitions and assumptions employed by Chamberlin. In certain respects, noted below, modifications have been introduced.

We shall first consider a case of pure spatial competition. Subsequently, we shall investigate the frequently noted analogy between brand and specification competition, on the one hand, and spatial competition on the other. This analogy is implicit in such phrases as "near competitors" and "remote competitors." It is proposed here to make the most of it.

The method which will be followed is frankly that of pure theory. Lest we forget that this method involves a considerable measure of oversimplification of actual conditions, we shall assume an Imaginary Economic State to which our simplified assumptions fully apply. The conclusions which follow logically from these assumptions should, of course, also apply

* See part A above.

[3] *Journal of Political Economy*, Vol. XLII, p. 531. Chamberlin does not name the curves. He refers to the species demand curve as showing the demand for one seller, the prices and specification for other sellers being constant. He refers to the apportioned genus demand for one seller as "a fractional part of the demand . . . for the general class of product," and as the result of a "concurrent movement of all prices" of the various near competitors.

to this Imaginary Economic State. In the interest of brevity we shall consider only incidentally how our conclusions would be affected by the complications to be found in any actual historical situation. It will be convenient to begin our analysis with two special cases.

Case I. *Spatial competition in one dimension.* Let us assume that the map of our Imaginary Economic State is a single straight line, and that distances along this line represent transportation costs measured in Imaginary dollars and cents. Let us further assume that the buyers are distributed along this line at equal intervals; that their locations are fixed; that they are far more numerous than sellers; that each buyer's demand price, at the point at which he is located, is $1.50 for one unit of product; and that he will take no more goods, whatever the price. Let us assume that each seller produces a product having physical specifications identical with the product of each other seller; that sellers have fixed locations at equal intervals along the line; that each sale is for cash, f.o.b. point of sale; and that there are no price differentials and no conditional sales. Let us assume that the pecuniary distance between each pair of adjacent sellers is $1.00 in Imaginary currency, and that between each pair of adjacent buyers is $.001. Let us neglect the situation which exists at the ends of the "map." [4]

It is submitted that a consideration of this situation leads to the conclusion that each seller will be operating under monopolistic-competitive conditions. Let us think of a species market as located at the point where the seller is located, and determine whether there is a relation between the species demand curve and the apportioned genus demand curve of the type called for by Chamberlin's theory—i.e. whether we find for the goods sold by a given seller, when the prices of his near competitors are fixed, a demand curve of finite elasticity, and for goods sold by our given seller, when his price and the prices of his near

---

[4] These assumptions are similar to those of A. P. Lerner and H. W. Singer, *Journal of Political Economy*, Vol. XLV, pp. 149 ff. However, they are concerned largely with the ends of the "map." And while they assume buyers to have fixed locations, sellers are taken to be perfectly mobile. Moreover, the seller's location is varied for different points on the species demand curve; and the apportioned genus demand curve is neglected.

competitors move together, a somewhat less elastic demand curve. If there is, we have monopolistic competition.

In order to determine the demand curves in each seller's market (neglecting those at the ends of the map), we must convert the local demand of each buyer into an effective demand at the point of sale. His effective demand price at this point will be his actual local demand price less delivery cost. Let A, B, C, D, etc. be consecutive points at which sellers are located, and let us examine the species market located at B. The effective demand price for a buyer located at any near-by point X will be $1.50 minus XB, if XB represents not only the distance from X to B but also the unit transportation cost. Now Chamberlin's theory calls for an investigation of the demand at B under two sets of conditions; first, when the prices at the nearest selling points A and C are held constant and equal while the price at B varies (in which case we will refer to the price at A or C as the base price); and second, when the prices at A, B, and C vary together and are always identical.[5] The first set of conditions yields a species demand curve (one for each pair of equal base prices), the second set, the apportioned genus demand curve. If every species demand curve is horizontal, we have a perfect competitive market. If each species demand curve were to coincide with the apportioned genus demand curve throughout, we would have absolute monopoly.[6] If the species demand curve lies between these two limits, we have monopolistic competition.

Under the conditions we have assumed, there are 1,000 buyers who are nearer to B than to A or C or any other seller. So long as the prices at A, B, C, etc. are equal, all these buyers will prefer to buy at B. But as the prices at A, B, and C rise,

[5] Chamberlin's general theory is unfortunately stated in terms which limit its applicability to spatial competition. Thus, he defines the apportioned genus demand schedule as "the demand for the product of any one seller at various prices on the assumption that his competitors' prices are always identical with his," op. cit., p. 90. What "identical prices" mean as applied to cases where A, B, and C represent different specification, brands, or terms of sale, Chamberlin does not explain.

[6] If all near competitors in a qualitative sense are included in our investigation, this limiting case is presumably never fully realized.

a level is presently reached at which buyers begin to be excluded from the market. Evidently, the apportioned genus demand curve starts as a vertical straight line rising from the horizontal axis at 1,000 units. When the price level reaches $1.00, a buyer located halfway between A and B can just afford to buy, for his transportation cost $XB = 50$ cents. Thus, the apportioned genus demand at B will start to decrease when the price becomes $1.00 and will become zero at $1.50. See Figure 1.

Now let us consider the species demand curve, i.e. the demand at B as price varies, the prices at A and C being held constant. Let us assume that the base price at A and at C, or b, equals 50 cents. Now if the price at B, or $b + \Delta b$, equals 80 cents, a buyer located at a point Y, 35 cents from B and 65 cents from C, will be able to buy and will buy indifferently

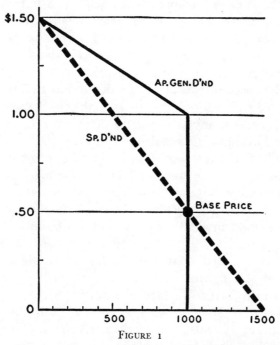

FIGURE 1

Figure 1 assumes the distance between sellers to be $1.00 and between buyers to be $.001. The local demand price of each buyer is assumed to be $1.50.

at *B* or *C*. It will be convenient to refer to *BY* as the market radius. Between *B* and *Y*, buyers will prefer to buy at *B;* between *Y* and *C,* they will prefer to buy at *C.* However, if the price at *B* plus the transportation cost to *Y* is greater than the buyer's demand price, he will, of course, not buy at all. The species demand thus depends partly upon the price differential Δb, which shortens or lengthens the market radius for the seller at *B,* and partly upon the price level, $b + \Delta b$, plus the transportation cost, which may exclude some buyers entirely. It will be convenient to designate the maximum distance a buyer who has a given demand price can be away from *B,* and still buy at the given price, as the buying range for that price. If the price at *B* were zero, the market radius would extend for 75 cents on either side of *B,* and the demand would be 1,500. When $\Delta b = 0$, or $b + \Delta b = 50$ cents, the species demand will be the same as the apportioned genus demand, viz., 1,000. When $b + \Delta b$ reaches \$1.50, the market radius becomes zero and consequently the species demand is zero also. In this case, the price level plus the transportation cost does not begin to exclude buyers entirely until the price of \$1.50 is reached. Hence the species demand can be discovered by investigating the market radius alone in this special case. In general, the species demand at any price will be determined by the market radius or buying range, whichever is less.

Figure 1 shows the species and apportioned genus demand curves for the case we have just been considering. The assumption that, except for transportation costs, all buyers' demand prices are the same, gives an odd shape to the apportioned genus demand curve. A slight variation of our assumptions will give a more usual result. Let us suppose that $AB = BC = 50$ cents and that there are 100 buyers evenly distributed between *A* and *B,* 100 between *B* and *C,* etc. Let us suppose also that each buyer will take one unit at \$1.50; a second at \$1.25; a third at \$1.00; a fourth at 75 cents; a fifth at 50 cents; and a sixth at 25 cents. The resulting species and apportioned genus demand curves are shown in Figure 2.

We may take the situation represented by Figure 2 (to which we shall refer as Case I) as illustrating spatial competition in

general. Let us assume that sellers in a two-dimensional community are evenly distributed in a pattern that marks out
equilateral triangles, and that the more numerous buyers are
distributed in a similar pattern. When equal prices are charged
by all sellers, the market radii will indicate equal hexagonal
markets.[7] If other sellers hold their prices fixed, and seller *B*
varies his, his market radius will extend as his price falls and
shorten as his price rises, just as it did in the one-dimensional
community. But now he will have six nearest competitors instead of two. The apportioned genus demand curve will repre-

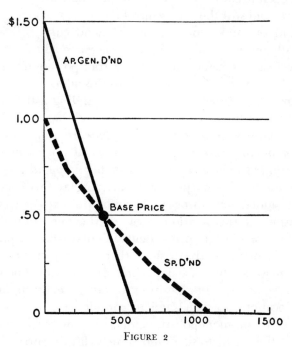

FIGURE 2

This figure assumes that the distance between sellers
is $.50, that the distance between buyers is $.005 and
that each buyer will take one unit of good at $1.50,
two units at $1.25, three units at $1.00, four units at
75 cents, five units at 50 cents, and six units at 25 cents.

[7] Cf. August Lösch, *Southern Economic Journal*, July, 1938, pp. 72–3. This
arrangement assumes that buyers and sellers may trespass freely, and that no
specialized space devoted to highways is necessary.

sent the buyers located in an area marked out by a market radius which assumes equal prices. The spread between this curve and the species demand curve, in the vicinity of their intersection, will still depend upon the density of demand, i.e. upon the number of new units of demand which will come in with a given extension of market area.

This situation may be further complicated by substituting the earth's surface for an Euclidean plane, by recognizing that highways occupy space, and by assuming transportation costs which are not proportional to distance. Still the apportioned genus demand curve will represent the demand from a constant area, and still the divergence between any species demand curve and the apportioned genus demand curve will depend principally on two factors, (1) the market area added by a given price decrease, as determined by the transportation cost structure, and (2) the density of demand in this added area.

We may now briefly generalize our findings: *When sellers are selling unbranded goods of identical specifications on identical terms, transportation costs alone are sufficient to give rise to monopolistic competition, provided buyers and sellers are distributed somewhat evenly over the map and buyers outnumber sellers.* In the process of arriving at this conclusion, we have added something to Chamberlin's analysis, viz., an explanation of the relation between the apportioned genus demand curve and the species demand curve. This explanation will enable us presently to show that the two curves may be related in ways which Chamberlin's diagrams do not suggest. Further, we are now in a position to waive the assumption that sellers' locations are fixed and to consider a central aspect of the problem of monopolistic-competitive market structure—the conditions which surround a new firm's entry into the market.

Chamberlin deals with two main types of market structure, (a) oligopoly, where competitors are few and access to the genus market is restricted, and (b) what may be called a perfect monopolistic-competitive market, a genus market in which the number of near competitors is large and entry into which is free. The situation in Case I is evidently oligopolistic, in that there are few near competitors—two in our one-dimensional community and possibly six in a two-dimensional one. However, we need assume no restrictions upon access by new competitors to the genus market, except that positions already occupied are not freely open to them, and except that the costs of moving must be met.[8]

Let us assume that, prior to entry by a new competitor, the existing sellers have distributed themselves evenly. If moving were costless, this would be the most profitable arrangement, although in view of moving costs and the number of moves needed to reach an even distribution, such an arrangement might never be fully realized in fact. However, assuming that such a distribution is at least roughly approximated, it is clear that it might not pay an additional seller to enter the genus market until a price situation is reached which will attract a number of new competitors all at one time. Until this situation is reached, old sellers will realize excess profits.

Suppose, for example, in our one-dimensional Case I, that we have reached a situation in which it pays a new seller to enter between each two adjacent old sellers. The most profitable locations will be at the mid-points, halfway between *A* and *B,* halfway between *B* and *C,* etc. In this type of case, the effect of a doubled number of sellers will, in general, be to cut the abscissae of each apportioned genus demand curve approximately in half. In this type of case, also, the spread between the species demand curve and the apportioned genus demand curve will, in general, not be greatly affected, because the spread depends chiefly upon the demand in the "area" which is shifted within the market radius or outside the market radius of seller *B* by a given price differential, and because the shifted "area," which consists of two segments of the line *ABC,* is, in the vicinity of the intersection of the two demand curves, independent of the distance between sellers. The two demand curves, after the number of competitors has been doubled, are shown in Figure 3.

---

[8] Assuming that moving is costly, we shall get more stable conditions than Lerner and Singer do. But the tendency of their sellers to play tag is due in part also to their assumption of a single demand price at each location.

The spread between the species demand and the apportioned genus demand at a price which is Δb above or below the base price cannot exceed the total local demand lying within the area shifted from one species market [9] to another by the price increment Δb. Thus, since the area shifted from one seller to another is the same if Δb is small, the spread between the two demand curves in Figure 3 and in Figure 2 is the same.

Farther from the intersection of the two demand curves we may note two effects of a doubling of the number of sellers: (a) a doubling of the number of sellers decreases the price differential above the base price at which demand becomes zero; (b) a doubling of the number of sellers decreases the price

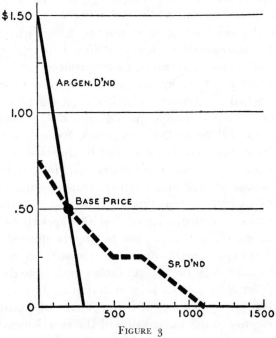

FIGURE 3

This figure assumes that the distance between sellers is $.25, that the distance between buyers is $.005 and that each buyer will take one unit of good at $1.50, two units at $1.25, three units at $1.00, four units at 75 cents, five units at 50 cents, and six units at 25 cents.

[9] The spread may be less than this, even near the intersection, if some of the demand is outside of the buying range.

differential below the base price at which new market areas come within the market radius of seller *B*. Thus, in Figure 3, $AB = BC = 25$ cents. Hence, when the price reaches 25 cents, $\Delta b = 25$ cents, and the market radius suddenly increases from 25 cents (since a buyer at *C* can now just afford to buy from *B*) to $37\frac{1}{2}$ cents (since a buyer halfway from *C* to *D* can also just afford to buy of *B*).

Special significance attaches to a species demand curve in the vicinity of its intersection with the apportioned genus demand curve, because equilibrium occurs at such an intersection. Although the spread between the two curves may be increased by a doubling of the number of sellers, there is a definite limit to this increase in the vicnity of their intersection: viz., the local demand to be found on a segment of our linear map, having a length of $2\Delta b$. The species demand in the vicinity of the base price is thus tied to the apportioned genus demand. Accordingly, the "slope" of the species demand curve, in our one-dimensional case, cannot differ from the slope of the apportioned genus demand curve by more than the fixed spread permits. In two (or more) dimensions the two curves are similarly tied together.

Now, with a slope for the species demand curve at any price so tied, it is true, as Kaldor contends, "that elasticities increase as the number of firms gets larger." [10] But the increased elasticity of species demand will not "necessarily reduce the degree of market imperfection," [11] if by "market imperfection" is meant the characteristics of a genus market in which the

[10] *Quarterly Journal of Economics*, Vol. LII, p. 519. Incidentally, we may concur in Kaldor's conclusion that "unless . . . the diseconomies of small scale production . . . or 'institutional monopolies' " prevent, the tendency toward an increasing number of firms and progressive parcelation of the market will continue "until producers equate price with marginal costs," and market imperfection is eliminated. But be it noted that this conclusion is purely tautologous. It is no answer to the question as to "Whether and, if so, how far is the tendency to parcelation operative?", i.e. to the question, "Are the conditions necessary and sufficient for monopolistic competition present in any given case?"

[11] It is proposed shortly to argue (a) that the tendency toward a progressive parcelation of the market may, under some circumstances, exist independently of Kaldor's condition that *production* costs are constant or increasing, may even be aided by a condition of decreasing *production* costs; and (b) that *sales* costs are of a type such that they impose a limit on the operation of the tendency to progressive parcelation. See below, p. 277.

elasticity of every species demand curve at the point of its intersection with the apportioned genus demand curve is finite.
An increased elasticity of species demand at the point of intersection between the two demand curves will diminish the
difference between the price under monopolistic competitive
conditions, and the price under appropriately defined, analogous perfect competitive conditions. But so long as there is a
finite and appreciable difference between these two prices, we
shall need to take account of the various separate species markets in a genus market, and of separate species demand curves
in each species market. We shall need to take account also of
differences in location of different buyers and sellers. And, if
sellers can influence buyer locations or distances between buyer
locations, we must take account of sales effort also. The difference between monopolistic competition and perfect competition
may rest at bottom upon a *difference in degree* of slope of
species demand curves; but the difference between monopolistic
competition and perfect competition may still properly be
called a *difference in kind*.

Case II. *Brand and specification competition in one dimension.* Let us assume that we have, in general, conditions similar
to those in Case I—sellers 50 cents apart and a number of buyers
for each seller. But suppose now that all buyers are concentrated
at the points of sale, 500 buyers at each such point. Let us suppose also that each buyer takes only one unit of the good, and
that buyers' demand prices vary from zero to $1.50, the buyers
being evenly distributed over this range. Under these conditions, the apportioned genus demand curve will be a straight
line from zero at $1.50 to 500 at a price of zero, as in Figure 4.
The essential difference between this case (which we will call
Case II) and Case I is that buyers are concentrated at the points
of sale, instead of being evenly distributed through space.

It will be convenient to assume a base price of 75 cents. With
this base price, the species demand curve will coincide with the
apportioned genus demand curve throughout the interval, 25
cents to $1.25. At $1.25, the species demand curve will move
horizontally to zero; at 25 cents it will move horizontally to the
right until the demand at that price is more than doubled, and

then start to slope downward again. Thus, while in general under monopolistic competition the species demand curve tends to lie between the apportioned genus demand curve and a horizontal line crossing it at the base price, the apportioned genus demand curve represents a limit which the species demand curve in such a case as Case II may actually reach in the vicinity of the base price. The two curves coincide for an interval in Case II because of the concentration of buyers at point *B*. The price differential does not shift a buyer from one species market to another until it equals the transportation cost from *B* to *C*. When the price at *B* exceeds $1.25 (is more than 50 cents above the price at *A* and *C*), all the buyers at *B* will shift to these two markets. Conversely, if the price at *B* falls

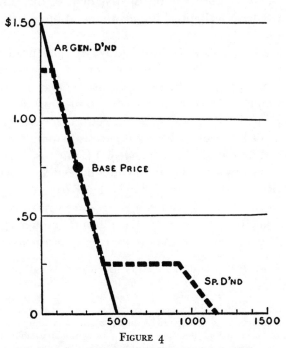

FIGURE 4

Figure 4 assumes the distance between adjacent sellers to be 50 cents. Five hundred buyers are assumed to be clustered about each seller. Each buyer will take a single unit of good, the demand prices of buyers varying upward from zero to $1.50.

to 25 cents, buyers at *A* and *C* who are willing to pay 75 cents can deal with *B* as well as with their local sellers. With prices below 25 cents, they will prefer to buy of *B*.

Case I we took to represent the problems of spatial competition on the assumption that, in our Imaginary Economic State, transportation costs are directly proportional to distance. By contrast, the conditions we have assumed for Case II may be taken to represent specification and brand competition with different positions on the one-dimensional map now representing different brands and specifications, the "positions" being so arranged that "near competitors" are near each other on this "map" of different commodity specifications. In order to eliminate for the moment the complications of spatial competition, we shall assume that the spatial map of our Imaginary Economic State is a single point, at which all buyers and sellers are located.

If we are to use Case II in this way, we shall need to oversimplify reality still further than we did in our portrayal of spatial competition. We shall need to assume that in our Imaginary Economic State all buyers at any point *B* on the specification "map" will shift to any adjacent point *C* on the same price differential of *C* under *B*. We shall need to assume further that this price differential is independent of the base price from which it is measured, and that an equal price differential in the opposite direction will shift all buyers away from *C*.[12]

With these assumptions we may treat the nearness of one species of good to, or its remoteness from, another species of good as quantitative, and may represent it on a map.[13] In this

[12] In the actual world, we should have to reckon with deviations from all of these assumptions. Some buyers might shift from one point to another on one price inducement, others on another; or one buyer might shift one part of his demand on one price inducement, and another part only on a larger price inducement. Moreover, the price inducement might be different at different base prices, and a different inducement might be required to shift all buyers' demand in one direction from that required to shift it in the opposite direction. In spite of the oversimplifications involved in the quantitative treatment here offered of qualitative differences in competing species of commodities, it is submitted that useful conclusions may be drawn from the analysis.

[13] We can, of course, make no direct measurement of the resistance or economic friction involved in shifting from point *A* to point *B*, for there is nothing

case, however, we cannot define our apportioned genus demand curve as we did in Case I by assuming identical prices at *A, B,* and *C.* We do not know in advance what price for a drink of Green River would be equal to any given price, say ten cents, for a drink of Coca Cola. We can, however, make an assumption which is equivalent to that of identical prices but is a little more devious. Having discovered the price differential, Δb, which is necessary to shift demand from *A* to *B,* we may, instead of speaking of the prices at *A* and *B* as identical, speak of a price at *B* which is always Δb Imaginary Dollars below the price at which demand would shift from *B* to *A.*

Restating the assumptions of Case II in this way, we may determine the apportioned genus demand curve and the species demand curve as shown in Figure 4. This diagram portrays a situation in which demand is assumed to concentrate itself on existing specifications and brands, i.e. buyers are located in clusters at the points of sale. The result of successfully establishing a new brand or specification of a commodity would then be the relocation of buyers at a point on the map representing the new brand and specifications.

If, under Case II, a new seller locates halfway between each existing pair of sellers, the apportioned genus demand curve at zero will be moved 250 units to the left, as in Figure 5. The species demand curve will still coincide with the apportioned genus demand curve in the vicinity of the base price.[14] But the range of this coincidence will be narrowed to the interval from 50 cents to $1.00 per unit. At $1.00 per unit, the species demand curve will move horizontally to the left to zero and at 50 cents per unit, it will move horizontally to the right.

These changes in the demand for the product of the seller we have under consideration are premised on the assumption that the entry of a new seller between each existing pair of sellers will, with the aid of sales effort, have the effect of re-

which corresponds directly to transportation cost in spatial competition. However, the effect is the same as if such a cause were present, and we can measure this effect as the price differential necessary to shift demand from one market to another.

[14] Thus in this case the elasticity of species demand at the base price is not increased by the increased number of sellers.

locating 25 per cent of the buyers now located at B, at a point in "quality space" halfway between A and B, and 25 per cent of these buyers at a point halfway between B and C. Similar relocations of buyers now located at points A and C are also assumed.

New sellers will find it most profitable to locate at the halfway points under the conditions of Case II, provided (1) the brand monopolies held by sellers A, B, C, etc. are such as to make close imitation difficult, and (2) the buyers at A, B, C, etc. are not too difficult to move by sales effort. With buyers who are hard to move or sellers whose products are easy to imitate, the new sellers may locate at A, B, C, etc. and competition between the two dealers at each point will be purely on a price basis. Where this type of location is possible and profitable, an increase in density of sellers in a market area

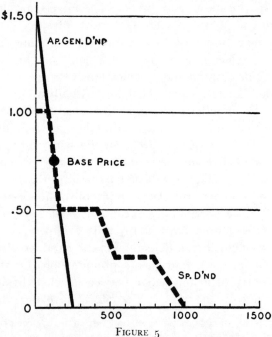

FIGURE 5

Figure 5 assumes the distance between adjacent sellers to be 25 cents and two hundred and fifty buyers to be clustered about each seller.

will indeed involve a closer approach to the conditions necessary to perfect competition. But if the locations of sellers *A*, *B*, *C*, etc. are protected by brands or other legal monopolies, there will be a compromise solution; the new seller will locate as near to the old as the law allows, and possibly sell his "substitute" at a slight discount. Such a location gives a result of the same general monopolistic-competitive type as the halfway location, if a group of buyers become habituated to the "substitute" and so become "relocated." For both *B* and his new very close competitor the apportioned genus demand curve and the species demand curve will coincide in the immediate vicinity of the base price, though the range about the base price within which these two curves coincide will be considerably narrowed. In such a case, the law of brands will prevent a further narrowing of the range of coincidence of the two demand curves. Indeed, we should not overlook the possibility that this range may be widened again. It is at least conceivable that sales effort may operate not by relocating buyers, but by increasing the "distance" between locations, i.e. by increasing the resistance to be overcome before a buyer located at *B* will buy at *A*.

Although we have assumed that buyers tend to cluster about sellers so that, at least approximately, the two demand curves coincide in the vicinity of the base price, nonetheless we need not deny that there are buyer-clusters located at points where there are no sellers—we need not deny that there are demands which no existing commodities satisfy. A part of quality competition aims at acquiring such unoccupied locations. A part of it aims also, through sales effort, to move buyers so as to make new clusters, new advantageous locations. Thus a potential new seller, in considering where to locate, will have to consider not only the number of buyers who might be moved to a prospective location but also the ease or difficulty of moving them, as compared with other possible locations at which the number of potential buyers is the same. It will be most profitable to encourage that relocation of buyers which is easiest to bring about, regardless of whether the location is hygienically, morally, aesthetically, or otherwise a good or a bad location. It is most profitable to develop the easiest tastes to develop, whatever they may be.

We have implied above that brand and specification competition is not precisely analogous to spatial competition. We may restate at this point several differences between these two types of quality or product competition. (a) If, in order to compete spatially, seller *B* would produce a commodity like his own in specification but located at *A,* his cost will be his ordinary product cost plus the cost of transport. The cost of transport is a last item in the sense that the "place utilities" may be added after the "form utilities" are complete. In the case of brand and specification competition, however, determination of specifications cannot ordinarily be put off until after other processes are completed. Moreover, it has been assumed that the producer located at *B* cannot legally reproduce the article sold by *A,* whatever his cost outlay. We may state this contrast differently. Either buyer or seller may move from one market to another in geographical space, but in the quasispace which represents specification and brand differences, only buyers may move about without changing the locations to which they are attached. (b) The seller is presumed to have no effect directly upon the location of the buyer in geographical space. On the other hand, the seller is presumed to exercise some influence over the buyer's location in "quality space." Indeed, sales effort outlays may be thought of as directed toward such a relocation of buyers through changes in their tastes and in the information at their disposal. (c) Buyers' locations tend to be somewhat evenly distributed in geographical space. Buyers tend to cluster [15] in "quality space." (d) The number of species along a line representing "quality-space" is limited to known points. Much of "quality space" is, and perhaps will continue to be, unexplored, in spite of invention and discovery. But the number of species in geographical space is, we may assume, no longer limited to any great extent by lack of exploration.

Quality competition in four dimensions. Thus far, we have made only incidental reference to the type of situation which exists when we deal with the nearness or remoteness of com-

[15] But see below, pp. 271–272, 276, 282.

petitors in more than one dimension. Actual spatial competition may be approximated by two Euclidean dimensions. Brand and specification competition involves a number of additional dimensions, the number depending upon the complexity of detail which we want to portray. If for the moment we neglect terms of sale, two specification dimensions will suffice to portray a wide variety of problems. One of these two specification dimensions may be taken to represent grade or class, i.e. differences between goods that appeal to the wealthy and those that appeal to the masses. Only a small finite segment of this dimension is likely to be significant. The other quality dimension may be employed to represent different types of commodities at different locations. On this scale, hats, shoes, bread, milk, etc. will each have an appropriate location nearest, of course, to its nearest competitor. As a minimum case, then, we might think in terms of four Euclidean dimensions, a north-south dimension, an east-west dimension, a grade or class dimension, and a species-proper dimension.

In Case I and Case II we have considered the competition between one species of product and other species of the same genus which are near competitors. Our analysis has run largely in terms of two types of demand curve—the species demand curve and the apportioned genus demand curve. The concepts of genus and species are thus basic to the whole analysis. The concept of a species market is presumably sufficiently sharply defined. In four dimensions it includes all sales, at a given latitude and longitude, of goods of certain definite specifications both as to general type (type of food, clothing, aut cet.) and as to grade, and under the same brand name. But the concept of genus is anything but sharp. The two space dimensions include remote as well as near points of our Imaginary Economic State. Does the genus market include the entire State or only one city or locality? And an analogous question must be faced regarding the brand and specification dimensions. If the genus market does not include all species markets of the entire economic system of our Imaginary Economic State, how is the genus market defined?

The question as to what is meant by the genus market involves two related questions: (1) what is the structure of the (genus) market? and (2) how does a new competitor enter the (genus) market or an old seller leave? Chamberlin's treatment of the theory of monopolistic competition touches only incidentally on the structure of the (genus) market. This is due in part to the assumption of perfect mobility of sellers, and in part to the fact that he begins his development of the theory of monopolistic competition with "the heroic assumption that both demand and cost curves for all the 'products' are uniform throughout the" [16] genus. In the discussion of this uniform situation his references to entry into the (genus) market and exit from it, in general, make no mention of any special location within the (genus) market. Thus, he speaks of additional sellers being attracted into the field of the genus market,[17] and the elimination of firms from the genus market,[18] without indicating whether firms are entering the genus market at its edge or its middle, or whether the departing firms are those located at the edge or at the middle.

The present approach to the theory of monopolistic competition differs from Chamberlin's in that it has assumed mobility of sellers [19] to be limited (a) by costs of moving [20] and of changing models, and (b) by ownership of sites and of brands. But we agree that the assumption of uniform demand and cost, however heroic, is a useful one as a starting point. Chamberlin appears to interpret it, however, to mean that if the supply in the genus market is increased by small successive doses (each dose presumably representing one or more new sellers), it will continue to be true, after, as well as before, each dose, that the demand and cost curves for all species of "products" are uniform throughout the genus. If this be a correct interpretation of his position, a challenge should be entered against it. In

---

[16] Op. cit., p. 82.   [17] For example, ibid., pp. 84, 92.

[18] Ibid., p. 93.

[19] Chamberlin does not make the same assumption for buyers. Restricted buyer mobility is an essential condition for monopolistic competition.

[20] It would be inconsistent to assume a considerable unit cost of transport for a commodity and at the same time to assume the cost of moving a dealer's entire stock of the commodity to be zero.

general, under monopolistic competition and in the absence of perfect seller mobility, the addition of a small dose to the supply in the genus market by the entry of a new seller will make the demand schedules in the various species markets of the genus non-uniform, if before the entry of the new seller they were uniform. Moreover, the conditions necessary to a free rearrangement of sellers, so as to re-establish uniformity after the entry of a new competitor, are rigorous. Granting that relocation is costless, sites may be owned by sellers in other genus markets than the one under examination. And if buyers are clustered as in Case II, or if the analysis is restricted to a limited region of economic space, uniformity may be impossible to attain.

While, in general, entry of a new competitor into a genus market has different effects upon the various older sellers, if they retain their locations in the genus market, there are certain conditions [21] under which all competitors will be equally affected. If all sellers (and all buyers) were to be located at a single point in economic space, the entry of a new seller into this genus market (i.e. location of the new seller at this one point) would affect all of the old sellers equally. This location-at-one-point assumption is the implicit assumption of neo-classical theory. If a sufficient number, both of buyers and of sellers, are located at a single point in economic space, we have a perfect competitive market.[22] In general, in discussing entry into or exit from a genus market, we shall do well to specify the position which the seller involved takes up or leaves, so that we may see which other sellers are most affected. In general, we may fairly suppose, too, that sellers and buyers are distributed throughout economic space in such a way that the perfect-competitive location-at-one-point assumption is not even approximately true.

Buyers and sellers are not to be thought of as grouped into separate genus markets, each a clearly defined cluster of species

---

[21] The possibility, except for the case of perfect competition, is so limited that we may pass it by.

[22] Assuming also that a suitable market information service is provided. Cf. Erich Schneider, *Schmollers Jahrbuch*, 1934, p. 258.

markets separated from all other species markets by vacant regions. Rather we should think of genus markets as frequently overlapping. Such an arrangement implies what may be called a relativistic definition of genus, as including all species within a specified distance of the species under consideration. If in the one-dimensional case we have species C under consideration, and are concerned with a price range of less than BC about the base price, we should include B and D, but not A. If we are studying B, we should include A and C, but not D.[23] With four dimensions the situation is more complicated, but the relativistic conception of a genus market still holds. The size of the slice of economic space which we shall need to include in our genus will depend upon the range of price variation on either side of the base price which we desire to investigate and on the arrangement of buyers and sellers in the vicinity of the central seller.

In Case I and Case II we have assumed that sellers at the outset were equally spaced. If we assume also that the number and distribution of buyers within a given distance of any two sellers are the same, the demand will be uniform for the various sellers. With uniform demand and uniform cost, sellers will not be attracted into a genus market in small doses; rather, a considerable increase in the base price might be necessary to attract a new seller, and a price increase sufficient to attract one will be sufficient to attract a number all at one time. But with absence of uniformity, either in respect to cost or in respect to demand, sellers will tend to enter and leave the genus market one at a time. With demand uniformly distributed throughout the genus market, and sellers unequally spaced, the first new seller will enter at the point which represents the largest species market he can find.

Consideration of quality or product competition in four dimensions does not lead us to alter the general conclusions of Case I and Case II. A seller will now be in competition with sellers who are near both geographically and in respect to

---

[23] If 50 cents $= AB = BC = CD$ etc., and if there are sellers at A, B, C, E, F, etc., but no seller at D, then B and E will both be in the genus market about C for a price range 50 cents, but A will not.

product specifications. But the apportioned genus demand curve will still represent the demand of buyers located nearer to *B* geographically and in their specification requirements than to any of *B*'s competitors, and the species demand curve will still deviate from the apportioned genus demand curve to an extent limited by the extent to which buyers shift from *B* to his competitors or to *B* from his competitors with a given (specification and geographical) price differential.

Absorption of delivery charges. Thus far we have assumed that each seller charges all buyers the same price, deals in a single brand and specification of product, and has a single point of sale. As we now proceed to modify these assumptions, several familiar features of our actual economy will appear in our Imaginary Economic State as the logical consequences of the theory of monopolistic competition, features which would have no logical place in our Imaginary Economic State, were we to assume perfect competitive markets.

Let us assume, first, that the seller absorbs delivery charges, that is to say, that for a specified area he has a blanket price. Sales at the edges of the area are thus made under conditions which may be described as concealed dumping. But this degree of price discrimination, it may be assumed, does not encounter any prejudice against price discrimination in our Imaginary Economic State.

Buyers in the immediate vicinity of *B* need little inducement to buy at *B* rather than at *A* or *C*. Buyers halfway or more to *A* can only be enticed to buy at *B* if the price impediment to buying elsewhere than from the nearest seller is removed and if they are within the buying range. A blanket price may pay, for one reason, because it widens the geographical market area in which sales effort can operate.

There is an important corollary of the introduction of blanket price policies into our Imaginary Economic State which bears on our previous analysis of the structure of the market and of entry into it. Under the one-price and one-product assumption, a space which is not very near any existing seller may not be occupied by a new seller, because it will not offer a large enough market to support a new firm. But with a blanket price policy on the part of sellers, there is a tendency to cover the whole field with a patchwork of abutting blanket areas. If there were an area lying between two blanket price territories and unoccupied, it would pay a seller to extend the blanket price territory in which he is located, if he is near enough so that direct production cost plus delivery cost is less than the price. On the other hand, if no seller is as near the unblanketed area as this, there should be a substantial area, including parts of present blanket price territories, which will offer a profitable market opening for one or more new sellers.

When sellers follow the one-price system strictly, and buyers are well distributed, sellers will, as we have seen, tend to distribute themselves; and a new seller will find it advantageous in general to locate "halfway" between two existing sellers. On the other hand, when sellers absorb delivery charges (if they do not assume also the transportation costs involved in the display of wares to prospective customers), the result is quite different from that under a strict one-price system. The tendency is for sellers, instead of distributing themselves, to congregate at points where prospective buyers are most likely to pass. A similar tendency will appear if the transportation cost of a customer and his purchases from the market to his "home" is but slightly more than the transportation cost of the customer alone. Hence, in retailing, we find in our Imaginary Economic State the development of a "downtown area" and subsidiary shopping centers in the larger cities.

Two limits to the tendency of sellers to congregate may be noted: (a) if the sellers' blanket price policy applies to a limited area, the tendency to congregate applies only within the blanketed area; (b) our present assumption involves the abandonment of the one-price policy with respect to the north-south dimension and the east-west dimension only. We shall assume that there can be no price policy in respect to the specification dimensions which corresponds to the absorption of delivery charges.[24] Consequently, the tendency for sellers to congregate does not hold with respect to the non-spatial dimensions.

[24] A contrary assumption might imply that one seller could reproduce the brand and specification of another.

If the seller, in addition to absorbing delivery costs, absorbs also the transportation costs involved in display of goods (for example, through traveling salesmen), or if this cost is inconsequential (as in the case of highly standardized commodities), sellers need not tend to congregate. If they are located at different positions in the same selling area, the result of absorbing delivery costs will be cross-haulage of goods. Hence, we shall find cross-haulage at wholesale in the case of numerous manufactured commodities in our Imaginary Economic State,[25] and an analogous situation in the retail field in the case of milk delivery.

The four-dimensional theory of monopolistic competition, in spite of its oversimplification of actual conditions, explains one other characteristic of our Imaginary Economic State which is a familiar feature also in the United States—the difference between plant and enterprise. Sales effort of the advertising type, particularly, calls for the use of media which serve a large number of sellers of different types of products. Such media may cover either local areas or the entire Imaginary Economic State. When the seller with a single plant and widening market reaches the point where advertising through a national medium is cheaper than advertising through the number of local media needed to dispose of his product, he reaches the point where it is advantageous to operate two or more plants as parts of a single enterprise. While this development of sales effort is doubtless not the only factor giving rise to chained plants in actual society, it is clearly sufficient alone to bring about this type of enterprise. Thus the enterprise ceases to be confined to one location in geographical space.

Price differentials and product diversification. Abandonment of the one-price system suggests the possibility of charging higher prices to those buyers who are able to pay. Such a scheme of price differentials ordinarily involves differences in brand and at least nominal differences in the specifications of the product.

Let us consider first a case in which seller *B* establishes him-

---

[25] Cf., for example, Vernon A. Mund, " 'Freight Allowed' Method of Price Quotation," *Quarterly Journal of Economics,* Vol. LIV, p. 239.

self at only two points on the grade or class dimension and has all possible grades of this type of commodity to himself. Let us assume also that we may neglect differences in cost as between the two grades, so that the output of both grades may be shown on the same cost curve, and that this curve is made up by adding a constant amount of direct cost per unit to the average "fixed" cost per unit. Under these conditions the margin between sales price and direct cost for the "honorific" brand may be far wider than is necessary to cover its share of the overhead. On the other hand, the "humilific" brand will, in general, be cheaper than a single brand would be.

Under the conditions assumed, there is, in a market of sufficient size, an advantage in dividing the market for any species proper into two grades, one appealing to the wealthier buyers and the other to the less wealthy market.[26] Our special case is

[26] The problem here involved may be called one of dividing the market vertically. It differs from the problem discussed in Joan Robinson's *Economics of Imperfect Competition,* London, 1934, Chapter XV. Mrs. Robinson's problem is that of allocating output between two markets between which buyers are assumed not to move ("the demand curve in each separate market is independent of the prices charged in the other," p. 181), although the seller is assumed to move between them perfectly freely. Analytically the equilibrium or maximum profit conditions for her problem are two simultaneous equations. If $y =$ price and $x =$ amount, if c, the marginal cost, is constant, and if the demand curves are $y_1 = f_1(x_1)$ and $y_2 = f_2(x_2)$, these equations are (1) $x_1\frac{dy_1}{dx_1} + y_1 = c$ and (2) $x_2\frac{dy_2}{dx_2} + y_2 = c$. In each species market "marginal revenue is equal to the marginal cost of the whole output," p. 182.

In the problem of dividing the market vertically the two species demand curves are overlapping segments of the combined demand curve $y = f(x)$, if buyer classification is perfect. It is easily shown that the condition of maximum profit for the dearer brand then is (1a) $x_1\frac{dy_1}{dx_1} + y_1 = y_2$. Marginal revenue is equated, not with marginal cost, but with the revenue from the cheaper brand which is foregone as x_1 increases. The other equilibrium condition is similar to (2) above, but since demand for the cheaper brand is now $(x_2 - x_1)$ this expression is substituted for x_2 and we have (2a) $(x_2 - x_1)\frac{dy_2}{dx_2} + y_2 = c$. If $\frac{dy}{dx} < 0$ through-out, evidently $y_1 > y_2$ and $x_2 > x_1$.

References to "higher class" and "high quality" brands (pp. 186 and 189n.) and to rich and poor (pp. 202 and 204) suggest that Mrs. Robinson would apply her analysis to the problem of dividing the market vertically. But her hypothesis that demand in one species market is independent of price in the others is

one of decreasing cost throughout, but the advantage in dividing the market is present, no matter whether the output of either brand alone would be subject to increasing or to decreasing cost of production and delivery. If two grades are, in general, more profitable than one, are three more profitable than two? And how far does the tendency to parcelation of the market go? Why not an indefinitely large number of grades? The answer to this question appears to be chiefly that each added grade means an added cost of sales effort.[27] The number of grades is limited because the added sales cost of one more grade may exceed the added revenue due to the capture of more consumers' rent.

Let us now inquire for our special case of fixed and direct cost, "Will the humilific grade or the honorific grade yield more profit, if we mean by 'profit yielded' the excess of the revenue from either grade over the direct cost (or added cost) of production for which it is responsible?" The answer to this question depends upon the nature of the demand curve and its relation to the cost curve. The shape of the demand curve depends, in turn, upon the distribution of buyers over the grade or class dimension. Our earlier discussion of Case II assumed the buyers to be concentrated at points of existing commodity specifications, but this assumption should not be applied to the grade or class dimension—buyers are presumably distributed continuously over this dimension, though throughout most of the significant range of grades the density of population increases as we descend the scale. If the demand curve has a long tail to the right and but a slight rise to the left, the humilific grade will be especially profitable, provided the long tail does not lie below the cost curve. If the tail is short and the rise to the left considerable, then more profit will be derived from the honorific grade. If the different classes of buyers show a distribution like the distribution of income, the tail on the de-

---

hard to reconcile with the nature of the problem of dividing the market vertically. And for a straight line demand curve her analysis yields the absurd conclusion that output would not be increased by dividing the market vertically.

[27] Some production costs will be increased also. Moreover, there is a problem of keeping the wealthy buyer from switching to the humilific brand.

mand curve will often be long enough to make the humilific grade distinctly the more profitable, provided the tail does not lie below the cost curve. The likelihood that for many goods the demand curve will have a long tail to the right suggests that large profits are often to be gained, if a grade can be designed with a low enough unit cost to sell at a price that will appeal to the masses and yield but a slight margin of profit.

A further consideration of the relative effectiveness of sales effort at different buyer levels tends to reinforce this conclusion. Sales effort is, presumably, mainly concerned with moving buyers at one level along the species-proper dimension. Buyers do not move up from a cheaper to a more luxurious article of the same type easily. It does not ordinarily pay to move them down the scale; and, in any case, they tend to move down without sales effort because of the price differential. The question then is, Will sales effort be more effective at shifting wealthy buyers from the honorific grade of one type of article to the honorific grade of another, or more effective at shifting customers in the lower income brackets from a cheaper grade of the first type of article to a cheaper grade of the second? The much greater density of population in the lower income brackets would seem to indicate that it often pays better to apply sales effort on a cheaper grade of product. Large profits await the seller if he can produce, at even a very narrow margin of profit, a cheap enough grade of product so that he can direct his sales appeal to the great mass of buyers.

All this suggests a lower level of prices than does Chamberlin's statement of the theory of monopolistic competition without class price discrimination. It would be difficult, however, to establish definitely which set of assumptions would lead to a lower general level of prices.

Price discrimination makes possible and profitable diversification of products in the grade or class dimension. It is by no means necessary to product diversification in the species proper dimension. Thus such product diversification results, in part, because established firms have many advantages over new ones in discovering new openings in related lines. Hence existing sellers tend to diversify, rather than new one-product firms to develop.

It is also true, however, that price discrimination encourages product diversification in the species proper dimension. Somewhat as the blanket price policy enabled seller B to enter geographical openings too small to support a whole new one-product firm and too far from B to be attractive to buyers without such price discrimination, so in the species proper dimension, under decreasing costs, price discrimination may make it profitable for seller B to enter an opening too small to make the establishment of a new firm profitable, provided the new line of goods covers its direct cost.

The individual seller is further urged to diversify his product in the species proper dimension by the peculiar nature of a brand-monopoly. A brand-monopoly protects the owner (let us say B) against competing sellers of this type of product anywhere in the two geographical dimensions, but at only one point in the grade dimension. Buyers are presumably located at various levels in the grade dimension. Therefore, a competing seller may profitably enter at some level other than that protected by the brand-monopoly. There is still clearly a limit to the size of opening on which a special line of sales effort can be made to pay; too minute a parcelation of consumer demand into separate species markets is unprofitable. But, nonetheless, the nature of the brand-monopoly encourages diversification of products in the species proper dimension.

The introduction of price discrimination and product diversification suggests some amendment of Chamberlin's view that the scale of output is curtailed to a point where production costs are decreasing and where the curve representing the species demand curve is tangent to production costs per unit plus sales cost per unit (total sales cost being regarded as fixed). With the introduction of price discrimination and diversification of product in the broad sense, including grade differentiation, the handling by one enterprise of different species of goods and the operation of different establishments (including extension of the market area through widening the area to

which the blanket price applies or otherwise meeting competitors' prices in remote places), there is introduced a tendency to increase the scale of production. A firm operating
initially at the scale of production which would represent
equilibrium, if it were confined to a one-product and a one-
price policy, would, with product-diversification and price discrimination allowed, tend to go on entering new species markets
or entering new territory until the added cost of the last added
line of goods or added locality served (including sales and
delivery cost) almost equals the added revenue.

Price discrimination and product diversification are thus
important offsets to what at first appeared to us as a severe
limitation of the effectiveness of monopolistic competition in
regulating profits; namely, the need for any unoccupied "in-
between" location to embrace a large area before a new firm
can afford to establish itself. Because with price discrimination and product diversification the scale of production tends
to expand, we may conclude that monopolistic competition
will, in the absence of restrictions other than those of site and
brand ownership and the costs of changing locations, prevent
most sellers from earning extensive monopoly profits continuously for any considerable period of time.

The perfect competitive market. It will now be convenient
to return to the set of assumptions which constituted the starting point of our consideration of Cases I and II. In part, these
assumptions provide concrete detail by way of illustration; in
part, they specify features or characteristics of a market region
which are essential if we are to have monopolistic competition.

The essentials of these assumptions as applied now to our
four-dimensional economic space may be formulated in three
propositions as follows: (1) that buyers are relatively more
numerous than sellers; (2) that buyers and sellers are both so
distributed that for most buyers there will be one seller materially nearer to each buyer than any other, and that for each
seller there will be a substantial number of buyers for whom he
is the nearest seller; and (3) that property rights protect the
various seller locations. To give further precision to the first of
these three propositions we may say that the number of buyers

for whom any seller *B* is the nearest seller shall be sufficient to avoid oligopsony.

It is not our present purpose to investigate monopsonistic competition. However, it seems appropriate to point out that if we had conditions corresponding to those set forth above, excepting that the statements applicable to buyers were made applicable to sellers and conversely, we might reasonably expect to have, not monopolistic competition, but monopsonistic competition. The growth of specialization and the development of technology and large scale production tend to make for a decided preponderance either of buyers or of sellers in most markets. If we assume a modern state of the arts in our Imaginary Economic State, we may expect to find that in most market regions we have either a sufficient preponderance of buyers for monopolistic competition or a sufficient preponderance of sellers (including those who let their labor) for monopsonistic competition.

The second condition stated above, namely, that the buyers and sellers are somewhat scattered over the region, is responsible for the introduction of friction into what we may call the region or, alternatively, the genus market. The friction introduced by this scattering of buyers and sellers isolates each seller and the buyers for whom he is the nearest seller from other sellers and buyers, although the isolation may be overcome by an appropriate price differential. It may be suggested that with buyers more numerous than sellers in a region, a part of which is relatively unoccupied, the friction will be increased by a more even distribution of buyers and sellers. It may further be suggested that such a distribution is advantageous to the sellers. They will tend to distribute themselves and to encourage the distribution of the buyers over the region, so that the distance of each species market from its nearest neighbors is about equal to the distance between any other pair of near neighbors; provided, of course, that the cost of relocation to the seller is not so great as to outweigh the monopoly advantage to be so gained. If sellers outnumber buyers, we may have a corresponding incentive to buyers to see that buyers and sellers are so distributed as to give each buyer a monopsonistic advantage.

We have, then, two tendencies in our Imaginary Economic State: (1) for the number of buyers and the number of sellers in most regions to be somewhat unequal, and (2) for buyers and sellers, when their numbers are unequal, to be scattered throughout the region, so that there will be either monopolistic competition or monopsonistic competition. The older type of economic theory not infrequently assumed the perfect competitive market to be a natural state of affairs, to which things would tend to revert if monopoly features were prohibited. Our consideration of the assumptions giving rise to monopolistic competition does not tend to confirm this view. On the contrary, there appear to be definite tendencies toward the development of either monopolistic or monopsonistic competition.

We have examined the type of market structure which has developed in our Imaginary Economic State, assuming that throughout a wide range of its four-dimensional economic space buyers outnumber sellers, that they are somewhat evenly distributed over the two geographical dimensions, and that in consumer goods markets they are distributed over the grade or class dimension somewhat on the pattern of the distribution of income, and, in the species proper dimension are clustered around established sellers. Various familiar features of the economic system of the United States have been disclosed in our Imaginary Economic State, features which are not compatible with the assumption of perfect competitive markets—absorption of delivery charges, cross-haulage, class price discrimination, national advertising, chain plants, diversified lines of goods produced by one concern.

Economists have frequently contrasted actual situations involving monopoly elements with what the situation would have been, if perfect competition had prevailed. Accordingly, it will be in order to inquire into the conditions which would need to be realized, possibly through legislative action, in order to establish a perfect competitive market in any region in our four-dimensional Imaginary Economic State, where buyers outnumber sellers. It will be appropriate also to comment upon contrasts between monopoly and perfect competitive situations in the light of our answer to the question, What is involved in establishing a perfect competitive market?

Now, if we are to have a perfect competitive market, we must have *inter alia* (1) no quality competition within the genus—no spatial competition, no brand and specification competition, no competition in terms of sale; and (2) a sufficient number of (identical) "species" within the genus to avoid a suspicion of oligopoly. Quality competition as between two related genera is not ruled out, but if it appears within either, that market ceases to be perfectly competitive.

If it is possible to require a sufficient number of near-competing sellers to occupy the same point in four-dimensional economic space, by prohibiting the surrounding area to all of them, both of the above conditions for establishing a perfect competitive market in our Imaginary Economic State will be realized. The procedure of forcing a number of sellers to locate at the same point by prohibiting a surrounding area suggests no difficulty as regards the grade and species-proper dimensions, for here the restraint on joint occupation of the same position is clearly legal in nature. Even as regards the geographical dimensions, the restraint (if any) which deters two bodies from occupying the same space in an economic sense is legal rather than physical. All that is needed to make various sellers and buyers occupy the same point *B* is to establish *B* at the genus basing-point and prohibit anyone from trading in an appropriate geographical area in the vicinity of *B*, except at a "*B*-plus" schedule of prices. Likewise, we must select, in the grade and the species-proper dimensions, and appropriate area of brands, specifications, and terms of sale which are closely competitive with the brand, specifications, and terms represented by the point *B*, and must prohibit sales of all such brands and specifications on all such terms—except, of course, the brand and terms at point *B*. The region so selected and proscribed in our four-dimensional economic space (geographical area and grade and species area) must be large enough to give a "thick" market at *B*; and the market at *B* must be thick enough to avoid oligopoly. A legal restriction on competition within such a region to sales at the point *B*, together with the usually specified condition of full market information, will establish a perfect competitive market in our Imaginary Economic State.

We have not, however, fully stated the possibilities of establishing a perfect competitive market. Instead of prescribing a "*B*-plus" schedule of prices in the selected geographical area, we might prescribe a blanket-price arrangement. Again, we might introduce into the "*B*-plus" scheme a number of arbitrary differentials for deliveries at arbitrarily selected destinations, and still, as long as all sellers are required to conform to the same scheme of differentials, we might have a perfect competitive market.[28] In a situation where buyers outnumber sellers, and where the distribution of buyers and sellers tends toward monopolistic competition, the possibilities of establishing a perfect competitive market may be stated as follows: (1) Throughout an appropriately selected genus market, a fixed scheme of price differentials as among the various species must be established and maintained. (2) The scheme of price differentials must be simple and easy to carry in mind. (3) The area included in the genus market may be selected in any of several ways, provided it is large enough to produce a market of the requisite thickness to avoid oligopoly. (4) There must be an adequate system of market information. Under these conditions, quality or product competition and sales effort will be eliminated and competition will be on a price basis. We ought perhaps to add one further condition, for a seller organization might impose at least three of these four conditions

---

[28] Nor does this fully exhaust the logically possible methods of establishing a perfect competitive market. If the assumptions which enabled us to represent grade and species differences in two Euclidean dimensions were not oversimplifications of reality, we might also produce a perfect competitive market in which two or more closely competing grades or types of article would be sold at prescribed differentials. Logically, in our Imaginary Economic State we could establish a perfect competitive market with a fixed schedule of grade and type-of-commodity differentials to give the market "thickness." But even if the simplification involved in our spatial portrayal of product specifications were not a serious drawback for such a possibility, the number of such arbitrary differentials which would be compatible with a perfect competitive market would be limited by the number of arbitrary differentials that buyers could carry actively in their minds.

and exercise monopoly powers at the same time. Although price differentials are fixed, the level of prices in the genus market must remain free. If we have a perfect competitive market, the level of genus prices may be expected to change with each change in the conditions of supply and demand.

With this consideration of the possibility of establishing a perfect competitive market in our Imaginary Economic State, we may attempt, in general terms, to contrast perfect competition with monopolistic competition:

(1) We must note, first, that the contrast must be general, because neither term in the contrast is uniquely defined. There has been wide recognition of the need for indicating what kind of monopoly is meant before a detailed contrast can be made. We have just shown that the same necessity exists with respect to perfect competition. Before we could make a detailed comparison, we should need to know what kind of perfect competition we are talking about, i.e. what region has been selected and what price policy prescribed for it.

(2) Reference has been made to the assumption sometimes made that a perfect competitive market is a natural state, to which a market will revert if monopolistic restraints are prohibited. It is true that monopolistic competition, as we have outlined it, involves restraints on the entry of a new competitor into a market and on seller mobility; but in a very real sense the establishment of a perfect competitive market may involve not so much the removal of these restraints as the imposition of more severe restrictions. If our two assumptions regarding the distribution of buyers and sellers and the preponderance of one group or the other apply, a perfect competitive market can only be established by definite economic planning.

(3) Prices to some buyers will be higher under monopolistic competition than under perfect competition; prices to other buyers will be lower. Without further consideration as to both types of competitive situations, we cannot say which way the advantage will lie in respect to prices; but we shall probably be safe in concluding that there will be a larger concealed transportation cost element in prices under perfect competition, and that under monopolistic competition prices will cover some

sales effort costs. We also know that under perfect competition there will be no class price discrimination to permit catering to the lower income brackets.

(4) With the greater variety of product specifications under monopolistic competition, consumers' tastes should be more fully satisfied. (5) Monopoly profit will be found here and there under monopolistic competition. Excess profits of favorably situated sellers will be found under perfect competition. In which situation total excess profits will be greater, we cannot say without further details about both types of competitive situations. (6) The volume of production will certainly be larger for some producers in one situation and for other producers in the other situation. We are a long way from being able to say with assurance on which side the preponderance will lie.[29] The absence of adequate market information under monopolistic competition,[30] and the presence of sales effort, will mean that the cheapest and most profitable buyers' tastes to develop will be developed most. (8) There may be cross-haulage of goods in both cases.

This comparison does not suggest a clear case either for or against perfect competition as compared with monopolistic competition. It suggests, however, that the case against laissez-faire is conclusive—not that we have shown any particular restraints on competition to be sound public policy, but rather that the possibility of avoiding restraints altogether is not open to us.

By way of conclusion, it may be appropriate to suggest some of the implications of the theory of monopolistic competition which remain to be explored.

(a) The possibilities of a theory of monopsonistic competition have already been touched upon. The need for the fuller development of such a theory, in view of the demonstrated significance of the theory of monopolistic competition, should be clear.

(b) The above comments on the theory of monopolistic competition, like Chamberlin's own theory, deal only with partial equilibria, i.e. they do not seek a simultaneous equilibrium adjustment in all species markets at one time. They do not deal with the economic system as a whole. In reviewing Chamberlin's theory, the writer ventured to suggest "that if it were carried to this final stage, there would be interesting and fundamentally important implications (1) for Say's Law, (2) for the theory of the business cycle, (3) for the theory of the level of prices, (4) for the determinacy of the equilibrium point on the assumptions made." [31] The suggestion still seems appropriate that an investigation of the general equilibrium (if it be determinate under monopolistic competitive assumptions [32]) would yield interesting and valuable results.

(c) The above comments on the theory of monopolistic competition, like Chamberlin's own theory, obviously run in "static" terms. In suggesting the need for developing the "dynamic" aspects of the theory of monopolistic competition, it is intended here to call attention to the need for a theory of monopolistic competition that will deal with the time-shape of price and the time-shape of the volume of goods marketed. List prices, price maintenance, and credit terms would necessarily be investigated. Such a theory also would involve consideration of capital outlays, including capital outlays on good will. It would find a larger place for inventories than economic theory has usually found. Such a theory would proceed on the basis of two simultaneous heterodox assumptions—the assumption of monopolistic competition and the assumption of overhead costs (i.e. costs previously incurred and often arbitrarily assigned by contract or by accounting convention to a given current accounting period). The time-shape, even of economic friction, would be looked into, for the difference between the cost of establishing and the cost of maintaining a business has important effects. Finally, the significance of these various matters for the relative bargaining power of buyers and sellers would be considered by such a dynamic theory of monopolistic competition.

[31] *Journal of Political Economy*, Vol. XLII, p. 534. [See p. 249 above.]
[32] One basis for questioning the concept of general equilibrium is given by Wolfgang F. Stolper, *Quarterly Journal of Economics*, Vol. LIV, p. 525.

· XVI ·

A Social Appraisal of
Differential Pricing

(1942)

THE remarks that follow will be addressed to the questions: When is it sound public policy to have two different prices for the same or similar goods or services? When is a price differential between the sales of the same goods or services, or between the sales of two similar goods or services, contrary to public policy? The expression "similar goods or services" in these questions is intended to apply to cases in which each product or service may be thought of as consisting of an identical component, A, plus a differentiated component, B, and in which the cost of the differentiated component, B, is much less than the cost of component A. We shall inquire what economic theory can contribute by way of answer to these questions.

The subject of price differentials is a broad one and it is proposed to limit the problem before us by several somewhat arbitrary exclusions.

Price differentials may arise as between two organized markets in each of which there is effective competition both among buyers and among sellers. Price differentials may also represent seller policy in cases where the seller's situation may fairly be described as one of monopolistic competition. Again, price differentials may represent buyer policy where the buyer's position is one of monopsonistic competition. We shall confine our attention largely to the second of these three situations, viz. to price differentials which represent seller policy.

The subject before us may be still further limited by excluding from any but incidental consideration seller price differentials of certain types. It is proposed to exclude, first, cases where the price differential represents a substantial difference geographically in the points at which delivery takes place. Second, it is proposed to exclude price differentials as between transactions separated in time, i.e., time differentials and price changes. Third, it is proposed to exclude price differentials in cases where the particular sale is tied in some way to other transactions between the buyer and seller as, for example, in the case of an exclusive dealer arrangement. Fourth, it is proposed to exclude price differentials as between different sellers.

Even with these limitations the problem remains a broad one. In order to indicate its scope, we may list certain of the bases of price differentials, thus,

(1) Terms cash, as against various credit terms
(2) Undelivered, or delivered within a specified limited area
(3) Brand or label differences
(4) Minor differences in physical specifications
(5) Differences in the container or differences in the obligation to return it
(6) Differences in the quantity sold, also for indefinite quantity contracts, differences in the period covered
(7) Differences between customers
(8) Differences in arrangements for incidental services such as free installation, free repairs, or return guarantee to a consumer, or free demonstrations and other free sales effort to a distributor
(9) Differences in the point of sale or in the method of receipt of the order

For convenience we shall refer to price differentials which rest on one of these nine bases or on some combination of two or more of these bases as enumerated price differentials. We shall confine our discussion largely but not entirely to enumerated differentials. These differentials will be considered without prejudice because of their legal status.

The mere enumeration of the aspects of the subject before us makes it clear that it is an extremely broad one. So broad a question may fairly be given a broad answer, viz., that enumerated price differentials are socially desirable if and when they lead on the whole to socially desirable results, and that they are socially undesirable if and when they lead to socially undesirable results. This answer is of greater consequence than appears at first blush. It clearly implies that neither blanket prices nor price differentials have any claim to virtue in and of themselves. There has been some disposition to regard a price differential as a form of discrimination contrary to the public interest, unless it is clearly based upon a substantial difference in the nature of the good or service or some special extenuating circumstance. The present contention is that a price differential or the absence of such a differential is to be judged without prejudice solely in terms of its social results.

It will be convenient in considering the theory of enumerated price differentials to have in mind a number of special cases. In some of these cases price differentials have been commonly held to be in the public interest. In others, price differentials have been commonly held to be contrary to the public interest. Nine main cases are offered for consideration.

Case I—The price in transaction "A" is lower than the price in transaction "B." Transaction "A" is in competition with some actual or potential transaction "C" in which a different seller is involved. Transaction "A" would be impossible at a higher price. Transaction "B" is not directly in competition with transaction "C." Under these circumstances it has frequently been alleged that a lower price for transaction "A" is in the public interest because it promotes competition by permitting our seller to enter a market or to remain in a market. We may note that there may be need to take into account other aspects of the situation in determining whether such a price differential is in the public interest. Competition is not necessarily an end in itself. In any event the case for such a differential would be doubtful if it could be established that the price proposed for transaction "A" would be less than the cost directly attributable to the transaction. This case will be referred to as "The Case Where Competition Is Promoted."

Case II—The need for further qualification will be clearer if we consider another case. Let us suppose that the circumstances are similar to those in Case I but more complicated. Transaction "A" of seller No. 1 is in competition with transaction "C" of seller No. 2. Transaction "B" of seller No. 1 is in competition with transaction "D" seller No. 2. Seller No. 1 makes a price concession on transaction "A" because of the competition with transaction "C." Seller No. 2 is induced thereby to make a concession on transaction "D" to meet competition with transaction "B." Cut-throat competition ensues. It is frequently thought that this type of price cutting is contrary to the public interest. It may not be if it has the effect of reducing prices from a level which is too high because of a monopolistic situation. This case will be referred to as "The Case of Cut-throat Competition."

Case III—Let us assume again a situation similar to Case I but more complicated. Transaction "A" of seller No. 1 illustrates a class of transactions which are in competition with transactions of class "C" of seller No. 2. Transactions of class "B" of seller No. 1 are not. The effect of a low price on transactions of Class "A" is to drive seller No. 2 out of business; and when the competitive reason for the price differential is eliminated, the differential ceases. It is generally considered that such a differential is contrary to the public interest. This case will be referred to as "The Case of Competition to Establish a Monopoly."

Case IV—Transaction "A" represents a class of transactions with business buyers who have come to depend upon this general type of good or service. A materially higher price would inflict upon these buyers a substantial loss of investment. Transaction "B" represents a class of transactions in the same or a similar good or service with buyers whose investments are not so situated. It has frequently been held that under such circumstances the continuation of a differential in favor of class "A" buyers, for a time at least, is in the public interest. This case will be referred to as "The Case of a Differential to Protect Vested Interests."

Case V—Transaction "A" represents a class of transactions with potential buyers. It is hoped that the charging of a special low price to these buyers for a limited period of time will encourage them to use a good or service that they had not previously been accustomed to use, and thus promote the fuller use of available resources. Transaction "B" represents a class of transactions with buyers already accustomed to the use of the good or service. It has frequently been held that this type of differential is in the public interest. This case will be referred to as "The Promotion of Use Case."

Case VI—Transaction "A" represents a class of transactions with buyers able to pay only a limited price. Transaction "B" represents a class of transactions with buyers who are able to pay more. The price proposed for transaction "A" is established to be sufficient to cover the costs directly traceable to this class of transactions. Under these circumstances it has frequently been held that a price differential of the sort assumed will encourage fuller use of resources and will be in the public interest, provided the price charged for "B" does not yield excessive profits. This case will be referred to as "The Fuller Use of Resources Case."

Case VII—Transaction "A" represents a class of transactions with a group of buyers that are able to pay only a low price. It is considered that making the good or service involved available to these buyers at the price proposed will aid in maintaining a minimum standard of life which is regarded as in the public interest. In such a case it may be held that a differential below other transactions is warranted, if adequate financing can be found for it, even though the differential does not mean a fuller use of resources. This case will be referred to as "The Minimum Standard of Life Case."

Case VIII—Transaction "B" involves the sale of a good or service, the use of which it is deemed in the public interest to discourage; while transaction "A" involves the sale of a good or service not held similarly open to objection. Under these circumstances it is clearly in the public interest to discourage

the use of the undesirable good or service through the use of a
higher price if, for any reason, adequate means of discouragement are not otherwise available. This case will be referred to
as "The Discouragement of Use Case."

Case IX—The buyer in Transaction "B" is able to pay more
than the buyer in Transaction "A." A differential based on
what the traffic will bear enables the seller to derive a larger
(monopoly) profit than would be possible with a single price.
Such a differential has been generally held to be against the
public interest. This case will be referred to as "The Charging
What the Traffic Will Bear Case."

It is not intended to suggest that these nine cases in any
sense exhaust the possibilities, or are even a representative
sample of the universe of the possible cases. On the contrary, it
is probably the usual assumption, in stating such cases as these,
that broadly speaking we should expect price differentials to
be based on differences in cost, but that in some cases special
circumstances may be such that a non-cost differential is in the
public interest; also that other special circumstances may make
a non-cost differential peculiarly obnoxious from the point of
view of the public interest.

In six of the nine cases a price differential is widely held to
be in the public interest:

Case I—The case where competition is promoted
Case IV—The case to protect vested interests (in this instance
the differential is justified only temporarily)
Case V—The promotion of use case (in this case the justifica-
tion is temporary also)
Case VI—The fuller use of resources case
Case VII—The minimum standard of life case
Case VIII—The discouragement of use case

In each of these except the case to promote competition the
seller is assumed to be a monopoly in a field in which there are
no close substitutes or else the differential is presumed to be
employed simultaneously by the several competing sellers. It is
believed that these six cases embrace those instances in which
an enumerated price differential is most widely recognized to

be in the public interest, independently of differences in cost.

It should be noted that the nine cases outlined above are not sharply marked off one from another and are not mutually exclusive. The same concrete situation might quite conceivably illustrate two or more of the cases. Attention has been called to the shadowy line between the Case Where Competition Is Promoted and the Cut-throat Competition Case. The line between the Fuller Use of Resources Case and the Charging What the Traffic Will Bear Case is equally shadowy. In practice it is difficult to tell on which side of the line of public interest a particular situation falls.

The language employed in stating these cases has been purposely broad. Any of the various bases for price differentials may be employed, brand differences, specification differences, etc. The seller in any case may conceivably be a railroad, a public utility, a manufacturer, a merchant, a farmers' cooperative, a professional practitioner or the government. The seller could not, however, be an employee or a farmer, since neither the individual employee nor the individual farmer handles a sufficiently large volume to permit him to fix enumerated price differentials. The language employed with respect to buyers is in two of the cases more specific than it is in respect to sellers. In the Protection of Vested Interests Case it is usually assumed that the buyer is a business enterprise. In the Minimum Standard of Life Case it is assumed that the buyer is an ultimate consumer. In the seven remaining cases the buyer may be either a business enterprise or an ultimate consumer.

Without attempting to take sides on the issue as to whether certain other cases are in the public interest, it seems desirable to call attention to them. They illustrate cases in which from the point of view of the individual business enterprise price differentials may prove advantageous. For a variety of reasons cut prices may be employed for the liquidation of stocks, e.g., bankruptcy,[1] speeding up a slow turnover, and style and model changes. Again, cut prices may represent sales effort, as in bargain sales, free samples, and loss-leaders. The distinction between these sales effort cases and the Promotion of Use Case

[1] Strictly speaking this is not an enumerated differential.

rests primarily on the monopolistic position of the seller in the Promotion of Use Case, or on a concurrent effort by several sellers to reach a new set of buyers—i.e., the sales effort in the case generally regarded as in the public interest is essentially non-competitive.

It has been noted above that many economists have held a presumption that a price differential is in the public interest when it represents a difference in cost and a presumption against a price differential which does not represent such a difference in cost. It is here contended that this position calls for substantial qualification. It seems to assume that differences in cost are objectively ascertainable. As sometimes stated, it also assumes that costs as recorded in the accounts of business enterprises accurately reflect costs from the point of view of society as a whole.

On the first of these points the most that can be said is that we may hope, as cost accounting methods develop and improve, to attain a fair degree of objectivity in measuring cost differences, so far as directly traceable costs go. When we come to consider the large element of indirect costs, we must candidly admit that allocation of overhead is highly subjective. With respect to the second point, the difference between private and social conceptions of cost, we may note that a larger proportion of cost is indirect from the social point of view than from the point of view of business accounts. The lack of objectivity in cost allocation is correspondingly larger. There is a wide area in which the view that price differentials should be based on differences in cost affords us little help in determining what price differentials accord with the public interest.

Even if the problem of overhead costs involved no difficulties, we would need sharply to distinguish two propositions—(1) that price differentials representing cost differences are, in specified areas desirable, and (2) that in specified areas we should by statute prohibit price differentials which do not correspond to cost differentials. Surely we may make use of cost concepts and may analyze cost data in arriving at general statements of social policy, even though it proves unwise to use such concepts and data for effectuating social policy in detail.

By way of illustration of the difference between the use of cost concepts and data in arriving at general policy statements and the use of such concepts and data in effectuating policy in detail, special reference may be made to the Robinson-Patman Act.

In general, if a rule is to be incorporated in a statute, it is desirable that there should be a strong probability in each individual case that its application will be in the public interest. Where the "probable error" of a broad rule if enacted into law would be high, it is generally thought better to state the desired objectives as general policies in the statute and to leave their detailed effectuation to administrative discretion.

The Robinson-Patman Act, although a broad rule, does make exceptions. Thus it does take account of the Case to Promote Competition. However, it does not take account of some of the other cases enumerated above. Thus insofar as it has ramifications which reach to the consumer level, it does not take account of the Fuller Use of Resources Case. Nor does it attempt to draw a very satisfactory line between forms of competition which function effectively in the public interest such as those to be assumed in the Case which Promotes Competition and forms of competition which do not, such as that in the Cut-throat Competition Case. Even if the attempt were made to take account of all nine of our cases, the Robinson-Patman Act would still be an extremely broad rule in a highly complicated situation. It might be compared to the attempt to fit a straight line to an intricate time series.

The nine cases we have considered suggest that when the effects sought to be obtained are effects upon business buyers and when the cause is some broad class of price differentials (or the absence of such differentials) the probable error of a statutory rule is almost certain to be high. These nine cases, together with the liquidation and sales effort cases give a minimum indication of the variety of possible social effects flowing from a given class of price differentials or from the absence of price differentials of a given type. The variety of social effects is particularly great when the buyers involved are business enterprises, because there may be differential effects in various directions on the physical methods of processing and handling goods, on the forms of business organization, and on market practices and structures. The variety of social effects clearly increases as we include more differentials. Hence as the language of a given statutory provision for or against enumerated price differentials becomes broader, the more difficult it becomes to say whether on the whole the effects of the statutory provision will be good or bad. The Long-and-short-haul Clause in its 1920 form, although relatively narrow in scope by comparison with the Robinson-Patman Act, has proven to involve serious difficulties because of the high "probable error" in applying so broad a provision under different circumstances.

Considerations affecting the flexibility of accounting definitions in the absence of a detailed regulation of accounts raise a further question regarding the Robinson-Patman Act. If one desires to frame a rule that can be enforced equitably and effectively in order to change men's ways of doing things, it is essential in wording such a rule to use language which has a firmly established meaning. When conformity to a rule can be accomplished by modification of the meaning of the words of the rule as applied in any particular case, the rule is unlikely greatly to change the ways in which men are accustomed to act. An analogy is instructive. If we wish to lift a heavy object with a lever and fulcrum, we must be sure that the fulcrum is more firmly fixed than the object to be moved. Whatever might have been the case, had we first succeeded in the intricate and difficult task of prescribing in detail cost-accounting methods for the businesses affected by the Robinson-Patman Act, and then sought to use such records as a basis for regulating business price policies; certainly it should have been clear from the start that with unregulated accounts we would have a highly unstable fulcrum on which to rest a legal lever.

It has been urged that because of the instability of cost measurements and because of the multiplicity of effects of price differentials as applied to markets in which business enterprises are buyers, it is therefore difficult to form any sound judgment as to whether a given broad class of such price differentials is or is not in the public interest. Good effects and bad effects are likely to be inextricably mingled. However, when price differentials are so applied as to have effects primarily upon purchases by ultimate consumers, it is much easier to isolate the socially desirable effects from the socially undesirable effects.

The Stamp Plan of the Department of Agriculture may be considered as illustrating a situation in which social effects primarily of a desirable character can be isolated from undesirable effects. In general, for the commodities so far selected the Stamp Plan may well be argued to be an instance of our Minimum Standard of Life Case.[2] Thus, it makes available various essential foodstuffs at prices low enough to be within the reach of needy persons who would otherwise largely be compelled to do without these foodstuffs. Somewhat less clearly it may be argued to illustrate the Fuller Use of Resources Case. It may under certain conditions have the effect of increasing output beyond the point that would otherwise be reached and of inducing consumers as a whole to pay an added dollar amount to cover the added identifiable costs of the added production and distribution. However, the added buyers do not pay for the added product under the Stamp Plan. Moreover, as we have noted above, the distinction between the Fuller Use of Resources Case and the Charging What the Traffic Will Bear Case is a shadowy one. Whether we regard the Stamp Plan as applied to a particular commodity at a particular time as an instance of the Fuller Use of Resources Case or as an instance of the Charging What the Traffic Will Bear Case depends upon the accidental relationship between two quantities. One of these two quantities is the average actual realization by farmers. The other may be designated as the normal price, that is, the price below which cut-throat competition may be said to prevail and above which there may be said to be a monopoly return. If the average realization is less than what one considers to be the normal price, one will presumably hold that the Stamp Plan

---

[2] Strictly speaking the Stamp Plan involves a conditional sales feature which should exclude it from consideration as an enumerated price differential in the sense of that term defined above. However, this feature is not essential to our present argument. Hence the Stamp Plan may reasonably be discussed here.

illustrates the Case of Fuller Use, and is in the public interest. If the average realization is above what one considers to be the normal price, one will presumably hold contrariwise.

One special feature distinguishes the situation exemplified by the Stamp Plan from the situations contemplated by our nine cases. In the situation usually contemplated by the Charging What the Traffic Will Bear Case, the seller is a single enterprise exercising monopoly control. Under the Stamp Plan we have a large number of different sellers receiving varying returns for the employment of their labor and their property. An improved price for a farm product, by virtue of its inclusion in the Stamp Plan means in general an improvement in all of these returns. The existence of varying returns complicates the problem of deciding whether a given application of the Stamp Plan represents the Fuller Use Case or Charging What the Traffic Will Bear. If the mere presence of excess returns be taken to establish that there is Charging What the Traffic Will Bear, the Fuller Use argument will be largely inapplicable, for even with a very low price there may be some excess returns.

The proponents of the Stamp Plan have called attention to the advantages of a device which gives special treatment to the lower income classes on the buyer side of the market. The question may fairly be asked whether there is not equal need for differential treatment as between different income levels on the seller side of the market. Specifically, it is suggested that there is need for seeking an analogue to the minimum wage device which will be applicable to the agricultural field.

Our consideration of enumerated price differentials from the point of view of economic theory has called attention to the great variety of social effects of such differentials in instances where buyers are businesses, and to the consequent difficulties of broad statutory rules in this field. Our consideration of enumerated price differentials has also emphasized the prevalence of shadowy lines between instances of enumerated differentials which are in the public interest and instances which are against the public interest. Further, it has revealed the lack of objectivity and the lack of stability in determinations of cost differences as guides to public policy in price differentials. The clearest broad uses of price differentials as in the public interest are those affecting ultimate consumers. The Stamp Plan as a form of differential treatment for different income levels of consumers appears as an instance of the Minimum Standard of Life Case, of an enumerated differential which is in the public interest. Consideration of the Stamp Plan suggests the need for exploring the possibility of differential treatment for different income levels among producing farmers as well as for differential treatment for different income levels among consumers.

· XVII ·

Full Employment and Economic Stability

(1944)

A

How Achieve Full and Stable Employment *

IF we attempt to look into the postwar future of our economy, there are many uncertainties. There are some certainties, too, and one of these is general unemployment.

It is not intended to suggest that general unemployment is a malady of our system of private competitive enterprise which is incurable. It is suggested that we can be sure this malady has not been cured by accumulating the makings of a postwar business boom through deferment of civilian demand. There will be an era of relatively buoyant business while the deferred civilian demand is being met, an era in which business recessions will be short; after that there will be an era of relatively stagnant business in which the average volume of unemployment will be substantially larger than during the period of buoyant business. Either of these two eras may be longer or shorter than a decade. And in either era the volume of unemployment may be more or less than it was in the corresponding era after World War I.

---

* Substantially condensed.

Factors other than the employment level from which we start, the volume of war labor to be reabsorbed, and the volume of deferred civilian demand will affect the pattern of the total employment curve for the postwar period ahead. Among these are factors suggested by the "secular stagnation hypothesis." One need not accept that hypothesis in its entirety to recognize and accept two of its corollaries: first, that on balance the development of our economic system in recent years has probably been such as to aggravate the problem of unemployment; and, second, that business fluctuations over a period of a decade or more may take place on a level such that even peak employment is considerably below full employment.

When we ask how we can remedy unemployment within our system of private competitive enterprise and what are its causes, we find agreement among economists on the first step in causal analysis. Seasonal unemployment and between-job unemployment, on the one hand, and cyclical and peak-business unemployment on the other can be treated separately. What follows is concerned exclusively with the latter phases of the problem.

Beyond this first step in the analysis of causes the situation presents a paradox. On the one hand, there is wide disagreement as to the basic causes both of business fluctuation and of the failure to reach full utilization of our resources even during prosperity. Writers have sought the causes variously in the maldistribution of income and the failure of corporations to distribute all their earnings, in the movements of interest rates, in changes in price margins, in monopoly, in the acceleration aspect of the derived demand for capital goods, in the short-term labor contract, in miscalculations by businessmen, in financial chicanery, in monetary and fiscal mismanagement, in technological change, in the relation between population and natural resources, in the opening up of new territories, and even in sun spots.

On the other hand, in spite of the diversity of views on ultimate causes of cyclical and peak-business unemployment, there is some measure of agreement on major proximate causes of business fluctuation. There is some measure of agreement, too, as to several important forms of public action available to deal with business fluctuation and stagnation, and as to the effects that may be expected of these measures. Fortunately these matters on the whole rather than ultimate causes are pertinent to the question of remedies.

Four proximate causes, on which there is a fair measure of agreement, may be noted:

First, year-to-year fluctuations in the orders for durable goods and construction work contribute to business fluctuations. (a) During a depression much of the demand for capital goods is deferred, thus diminishing the volume of business during depression. (b) At the turning point the swelling of demand for capital goods when deferment stops may contribute to recovery. (c) During prosperity the demand for capital goods may be swollen not only by deferment but also *by anticipation.* (d) At the turning point exhaustion of the source of swollen demand for capital goods may help to bring prosperity to an end. (e) During depression again the more there has previously been of forward buying of capital goods, the greater and more prolonged the subsequent decline in demand for them.

Second, inventory variations contribute to business fluctuations. (a) During recession liquidation of inventories decreases demand for the goods in the inventories. (b) At the turning point stopping inventory liquidation tends to increase demand. (c) During business expansion inventory accumulation increases demand. (d) At the turning point stopping inventory accumulation tends to decrease demand.

Third, business expansion is a favorable environment for the development of unsound financial structures, narrow residual equity structures and operations that with even small market changes may involve financial distress—bankruptcy or receivership. Such financial distress in turn may cause unemployment and thus contribute to a recession or to its inauguration.

Fourth, the informational bases on which businessmen make commitments and the diagnoses of business prospects on which public officials base policy are inadequate, particularly in the areas of durable goods production, construction work, and inventory variation. This inadequacy contributes to the amplitude of business fluctuations.

It may be urged that to these four proximate causes we should add a fifth major proximate cause of business fluctuations and business trends—variations in external trade balances. No question is raised here as to the reality or the importance of this fifth factor. However, for our present purpose it will be passed by on the ground that so large a country as the United States cannot manipulate its external balances to stabilize business or to support a high level of business activity without unfortunate international repercussions.

So much for proximate causes; next as to forms of remedial action. Some of these, when taken, are of a continuing nature: improvements in business information, modifications in our tax structure and our financial structure, etc. Except for improvements in information it can hardly be said that there is much agreement on these more general forms of action and on the effects to be expected from them. No discussion of them will be attempted here. Other forms of remedial action require to be taken (or aimed) at an appropriate juncture in the development of the business situation. In general, these latter forms may be used in either of two ways: as checks and as stimulants. Three of such forms of remedial action may be considered: (1) credit controls, (2) tax and subsidy policy, and (3) public expenditure programs.

1. Hitherto the chief usefulness of credit controls has been in checking an overexpansion of business. For this purpose they need to be promptly resorted to. Except as credit has been a means of financing public expenditure programs, credit policy has not proven very effective in stimulating business expansion during recession, or in stimulating a rise in the level of business volume when there is peak-business unemployment as well as cyclical unemployment.

2. In theory, adjustment of the tax level is possible both as a means to discourage business overexpansion and as a means to encourage expansion when encouragement is needed. However, if any such adjustments are to be useful they must be promptly made; some way must be developed to make the necessary adjustments through administrative action rather than by legislative process. Such adjustments today are painfully slow.

But there are other uses of tax policy that for the most part avoid the problem of administrative adjustment. Specific tax differentials can be enacted, designed to check specific forms of business overexpansion or to penalize formation of specific unsound financial structures. Specific incentives to business expansion during depression and specific incentives to improved business information may be provided through tax differentials, through tax rebates, or through subsidies.

3. Public works and other public expenditure programs are chiefly useful for the present purpose as a business stimulant. They can be used as a check on overexpansion, also, when the occasion requires a check, to the extent that the volume of programs in operation can be cut back.

At present the use of public action as a check on business expansion is in disfavor. A boom of vast proportions is in prospect—in housing construction in spite of the original plan of the FHA, in commercial structures, in automobiles and many other durable goods, in goods for relief and rehabilitation, even in public works.

Applying checks to business expansion is never popular. Today its unpopularity receives theoretical backing from two opposing trends of economic thought. Many of those optimists who have as a postwar objective "less government in business than we had in 1939" will be likely to oppose the use of checks on business expansion as a form of unneeded government interference. There are also opponents of the use of checks among the pessimists and planners. They are concerned about the possible extent of unemployment during reconversion and are opposed to vigorous use of checks on the ground that peacetime booms have never yet achieved full employment. But at the worst, unemployment during the reconversion period is likely to be a short-lived interruption to the boom.

In spite of this strange agreement between advocates of laissez faire and advocates of economic planning it is submitted that there is serious danger that too big a boom during the postwar period of buoyant business will lead to another 1929. The employment of checks during the peacetime boom ahead is urgently needed. But there is reason to oppose checks, as checks have too often been conceived in the past. Heretofore some have held that we should seek to identify some instant in the boom period at which business expansion becomes over-expansion, and then, having identified it, proceed simultaneously to tighten credit, to raise the tax level, and curtail public expenditure programs. But general business expansion can never be overexpansion so long as we fall short of full employment. Checks should not be applied to the total volume of business to remedy specific trouble spots. We need not burn down the house to roast the pig. The need is for a selective employment of checks. The selection of checks and areas of application should be made in terms of the proximate causes of business fluctuation, and the checks should be tailored to the factors on which they are to operate.

Checks are needed for two main purposes: (1) to prevent the development of unsound financial structures and operations, and (2) to prevent the forward buying and overaccumulation of durable goods and to prevent overconstruction during a boom.

The first of these purposes requires early identification of unsound financial structures, early identification of business that is trading on too thin an equity. Because of the variety and continual change of financial organization, early identification of unsound structures when only a few have developed is by no means easy. Each major boom is likely to bring forth new forms of unsound financial structure. The remedy must vary with the varying form of unsound structure with which it has to deal. There may be need for public regulation of the terms on which specific types of credit are extended as well as of their rates. Specific financial and sales practices may need to be prohibited. And besides preventing the organization of additional structures that are unsound, there will be need to reorganize those already formed. Immediate stopgap action is likely to be required, pending the time when specific statutes can provide more lasting measures.

The second major application of checks is to restrain overconstruction and overaccumulation of durable goods. Before considering this application certain broader aspects of our problem should be noted. Consistent with our system of private enterprise there are two main approaches to the problem of eliminating the cyclical fluctuations of business. (1) Unsound financial developments may be prevented and we can seek to stabilize the production or sale of those goods that fluctuate most by offering incentives when business is slack and applying checks when the volume is too large. (2) A sufficient volume of public construction and other public programs [1] may be scheduled as compensatory expenditure programs. The second approach commends itself as involving the lesser modification of our free enterprise system. But if the compensatory expenditure approach is to be relied on alone, the volume of projects must be adequate. At the very least it would be necessary to be able to expand or contract the annual rate of compensatory expenditure by as much as 10 or 15 billion dollars and to accomplish an expansion of this magnitude within a period of a year on a time schedule determined in the light of the business situation, if we were to rely on this approach alone.

Let us consider what is involved in the checks and stimulants approach as applied to any type of private construction or to the production of any durable good; e.g., public utility construction. The general plan of a system of checks and incentives is clear. Checks should be applied to decrease the volume of utility construction (to give an illustration) during the peak period, possibly some form of peak-volume tax, possibly some method of tightening up on the extension of credit, possibly other devices. And incentives should be provided to increase the volume of utility construction during the low period—special advantages in obtaining credit, tax rebates, or even outright subsidy. The aim of these policies should be to influence the timing of utility construction. No over-all encouragement or discouragement to utility construction over a period of years need be involved to iron out the fluctuation.

As a basis for the system of checks and incentives there is need for a clear public determination on a current basis as to what volume of utility construction can be supported by existing and expected demand with year-to-year stability. This would involve forecasting the trend of demand. Such a current

[1] Such expenditure programs include census-taking, theater projects, unemployment insurance benefits, agricultural benefits, relief, etc.

determination alone would make an important contribution to general business stability.

As applied to the problem of inventory liquidation and accumulation the system is primarily one of incentives rather than of checks. If liquidation during recession can be prevented most of the disturbing effects of subsequent accumulation will be avoided. Preventing general inventory liquidation during recessions is a problem of providing an adequate inducement to hold onto inventories, without giving incentives to over-accumulation and without restraining desirable inventory liquidation in individual cases.

It has been urged that it is important to distinguish between the problem of business stabilization and the problem of full employment. For the latter objective there is little need for checks. The mechanisms of incentives to induce additional private business and of public expenditure programs are the chief recourse. But there is a difference in the projects and in the forms of incentive that can be used. Works projects can be added to the compensatory expenditure program by transferring them from an area which augments cyclical fluctuations, provided only that arrangements can be made for their proper timing. State and local projects illustrate the point. It is not so clear that projects can be retimed to raise the trend of the level of business activity. For this purpose it may be necessary to plan projects that will constitute a net addition to the total volume of business, projects that would otherwise not have been planned at all. Similarly with incentives. A change in our tax structure that encourages one type of private business rather than another needs be distinguished from one that raises the trend of the level of business activity by inducing private business that otherwise would not have taken place at all. Again, for works projects designed to compensate cyclical fluctuations the case for recourse to deficit financing is fairly strong. But when it comes to projects designed to raise the trend of the level of business, the case for deficit financing is anything but clear.

These distinctions are easier to draw in theory than in present practice. So long as we have business cycle fluctuations of substantial amplitude, there is likely to be danger of confusion between business stimulants that augment business expansion in a cyclical sense and business stimulants that help to raise the level of the trend of business activity. It is often difficult to tell when an addition to business today is a net addition to total business, and when it is gained by borrowing business from the future and so by borrowing trouble.

To indicate more clearly the distinction between these two types of business stimulants, let us assume that measures have been taken to prevent development of unsound financial structures and that we have a system of checks and incentives designed to iron out much of the fluctuation in durable goods production, private construction, and inventories. Let us consider the problem of managing public expenditure projects under these conditions.

Public expenditure projects will be needed (1) to stabilize the total volume of business activity and of employment by compensatory expenditure, and (2) to promote a high level of employment and business activity. Both purposes require that the volume of public projects to be started in any period be controlled centrally and with reference to the business situation. Fortunately this means determining centrally how many projects are to be carried out in a given period. For state and local projects at least it does not mean determining in detail what projects are to be carried out, or in what order they are to be undertaken.

Thus far we have considered only three of the four factors we have listed as proximate causes of business fluctuations. It remains to consider the fourth proximate cause—the inadequacies of present business information—and to consider what improvements in information are most needed. Much progress has been made in the past twenty-five years in providing current business information. Indeed most of what we have today on a semiannual or more frequent basis has come into being in that period. There are important gaps and defects in that information still, but our major need is not for additional current data, but for better business forecasts, especially for better forecasts of free production. Much progress has been made, too, in the art of business forecasting, but much more remains to be accomplished, particularly in the area of durable goods production, private construction, and inventory variation. The types of development needed are clearly indicated. They are types of development in which there is need for private enterprises and individuals and public agencies to participate and to co-operate. There is need that each separately should do more and better forward-planning, and planning farther into the future. There is need, too, for firming up these plans, so that we can be assured, by and large, that when adopted, they will be carried out. Again there is need that each should make his plans available to some central agency so that these separate plans may be combined into a total forecast. In a word, what we need is a consolidated national production schedule for a year or more into the future for our whole economy.

B

Business Stabilization by Agreement

It is the purpose of this paper to outline a plan for stabilizing business activity at a level of full employment. The plan is designed to eliminate that type of unemployment (other than seasonal and between-job unemployment) which persists even when business is at a peak. It aims also to eliminate cyclical unemployment.

The plan will be referred to as business stabilization by agreement.

It has been pointed out that while there is a wide diversity of opinion among economists as to the ultimate causes of cyclical and peak-business unemployment, there is a good deal of agreement as to the measures that can contribute most to a solution of the problem of unemployment.[1] Six measures merit special consideration:

1. Credit controls should be devised to prevent the development of unsound financial structures and practices—too narrow equity arrangements—during periods of business expansion.

2. The volume of taxation should be promptly expanded

[1] See "How Achieve Full and Stable Employment" [part A, above].

during good business and contracted during slack business. If such expansion and contraction are to be adequate and properly timed, it will probably be necessary to provide for administrative changes in tax rates, local as well as federal.

3. Better business information should be developed—especially better business forecasts, and especially forecasts of construction and of durable goods production.

4. Capital formation both by private parties and by state and local government needs to be encouraged in periods of slack business and restrained in periods of prosperity. The bunching of orders for durable goods and for construction work in periods of prosperity should be replaced so far as is compatible with our private enterprise system by an even flow of orders. Maintenance of business inventories during business recession should as far as possible be encouraged.

5. Public expenditure programs should be made to fluctuate so as to compensate fully any remaining business fluctuations.

6. Public expenditure programs should be large enough, if there is unemployment when business is stabilized, to stimulate a controlled and even expansion of business, continuing without recession set-backs until full employment is reached.

The first two of these measures are of relatively minor importance. Many of the former defects in our credit system have been eliminated. What remains to be done, on a national basis and so far as business stabilization is concerned, is not a major operation. Again there are difficulties, due in part to our governmental structure, in pushing tax flexibility as a compensatory device as far as purely economic considerations might seem to make desirable. Business stabilization by agreement is not directly concerned with these first two measures, though it would greatly facilitate tax level adjustments by the business forecasts it provides. It is concerned with all of the last four measures.[2]

Business stabilization by agreement will be outlined here as

---

[2] The public expenditure programs with which the plan deals are construction and other works projects. It is recognized that other expenditure programs (*e.g.*, improved and extended unemployment insurance) offer important possibilities for business stabilization.

a national plan, although theoretically it might be operated on a wider basis.

To the four last measures, listed above, business stabilization by agreement adds two main ingredients, ingredients which are familiar features of our private enterprise system. These ingredients are free contract and sales effort. The plan is based on voluntary forward agreements with and government bonuses to persons who coöperate by forward-planning their orders. The federal government will "sell" these forward agreements or policies to individuals, private enterprises and state and local governments. The agreements will provide a continuous dependable business forecast, publicly available to all.

Persons will be free to enter or not to enter these agreements. Reliance will be placed on the government's offer of bonuses (or tax credits) and on sales effort rather than on compulsion. Individuals, private enterprises, and state and local governments (hereinafter called subscribers) will enter into these agreements with a federal officer (hereinafter called the forward agreement agent or simply agent).

The forward agreement agent will offer three main types of agreement: (1) In the *definite period agreement* a purchaser (or subscriber) undertakes to place an order for an article to be delivered or job to be done during a definite future period and the agent undertakes to pay him a small amount when he carries out his agreement. (2) In the *stable inventory agreement,* the agent guarantees inventory losses and carrying charges so as to give businesses an incentive to maintain stable inventories during business recessions. (3) In the *slack period reserve agreement* the subscriber undertakes, in return for a bonus, to have a construction or other project ready for prompt activation on, say, three months' notice from the agent. These agreements give the plan a wide flexibility in its details. This flexibility is illustrated in the comment on detailed terms of agreements below. The principles on which the plan operates are as follows:

Definite period agreements. In definite period agreements covering commodity purchases subscribers will agree some three months in advance to place orders for goods for delivery in a definite period, say a calendar quarter. Each subscriber will buy from a seller of his own choosing as usual, except that his agreement will govern the timing of his order. The subscriber will receive a small tax credit or a small bonus from the agent for such advance planning and for carrying the plan out, say 2 to 5 per cent of cost. A somewhat smaller penalty might apply in case of defaults.

The agent will offer these agreements to prospective ultimate purchasers of major durable goods—autos, ships, planes, industrial equipment. Items costing less than, say, about $500 would not be covered. Similar agreements will be offered, governing the time of starting and finishing construction projects—houses, factories, commercial structures, public works, and so on.

The agent will maintain an index of the physical volume of production of goods of types covered by definite period arrangements. Using outstanding agreements he will project this index into the future.

Some six months in advance of a quarter, the agent will announce a quota-level for the index. Assume the quota-level for some quarter is 120 index points. The agent will seek enough subscriptions to definite period agreements for that quarter to bring the projected index up to 120 points. When the quota-level is reached, he will close subscriptions for that quarter. To obtain bonuses, additional customers (subscribers) will have to sign agreements for succeeding quarters.

The agent will fix quarterly quota-levels with a view to eliminating business-cycle fluctuations in orders for major durable goods. In general, the agent will estimate the long-term trend of demand for such goods and set quotas at the maximum levels at which he finds demand and hence production can be sustained.

Similar procedures will be followed for construction projects (except for a modified method of fixing quotas for public projects to be considered later).

Sales techniques will be used to reach quota-levels and will be the agent's first reliance in discouraging excess orders not covered by agreements.

If, despite such discouragement, a quarterly overage were to continue to grow, credit restraints would be invoked first through the stricter credit analyses by lenders which would result from announcing such an overage and then as a matter of public policy.

The agent will offer to register intentions to order not covered by agreements, until the index shows an excess over quota of, say, 15 per cent (138 index points in the case supposed). Unregistered orders for delivery before the end of the over-quota quarter will be subject to a small tax, not more than 2 per cent ad valorem. Prospective buyers will thus be induced to register.

Since both purchaser and seller will know definitely when the purchaser is responsible for over-quota buying, mild restraints should in general suffice. With quotas reasonably well administered and campaigning for subscriptions and after-quota publicity reasonably well conducted, a close approach to demand stability in the lines of business covered should be achieved, especially after the plan gains momentum. Covered business including state and local government projects might amount to 30 billion dollars a year.

Stable inventory agreements. In order to maintain inventories in periods of potential inventory liquidation, the agent will undertake in stable inventory agreements with business concerns of appropriate types to reimburse them during "guarantee periods" for paper losses and carrying charges on a portion of their inventories designated as "inactive inventories." Subscribers will agree not to liquidate "inactive inventories" without, say, 30 days' notice. "Inactive inventory" will be so defined that it will pay the subscriber to maintain his inventory throughout the guarantee period in spite of any decline in price or in his operating requirements.

Guarantee periods will begin at the agent's declaration. He will select a time when he finds that inventory accumulation is approaching the danger stage. (The mere declaration will be notice to the business community that the agent views the inventory situation with concern.) The guarantee period would continue until the agent finds that danger of serious inventory liquidation is past. He would then declare the guarantee period ended, and reimbursements for losses on inactive inventories would cease and reimbursements for carrying charges would be tapered off.

In general, stable inventory agreements will apply only where goods do not depreciate or go out of style rapidly, and where good current inventory records and good *market* price quotations are available.

Slack period reserve agreements. The damping down of business-cycle fluctuations in durable goods and construction through definite period agreements and in inventories through stable inventory agreements will tend to damp fluctuations in other lines. But a substantial task of providing a "counter-cycle" through compensatory public expenditure programs will remain.

If public works and other public expenditure programs are to offset business fluctuation and stagnation without resort to made-work, we must plan enough projects for this purpose and plan them far enough in advance—and it often takes two years or more to plan and get approval for a substantial project. We must also hold some projects in reserve until needed and we must be able to mobilize such projects promptly when they are needed.

Slack period reserve agreements provide a mechanism for mobilizing and for reserving projects. State and local agencies will be offered these agreements. They will run for, say, two,- three,- and five-year terms. Each subscriber will undertake to begin his project (or make his purchase) within the term of his agreement, on three months' notice from the agent. He will be offered an attractive credit proposition and a bonus, say, 6 per cent of cost under a 2-year agreement to 15 per cent under a 5-year agreement. Agreements will fix the terms on which credit will be extended when projects are activated. For federal projects funds will be appropriated in advance, with a special proviso making them available for obligation during a period to be fixed by the agent.

Both federal and local projects can thus be mobilized promptly; and until activated, they will be held in reserve. But Congressional appropriating power will not be delegated to the agent. Nor will states' rights be infringed, for he will not pass judgment on the merits of state and local government projects.

Through slack period reserve agreements, the agent can increase the reserve file of expenditure programs. Private concerns and individuals will be eligible to subscribe. Thus a railroad may make a reserve agreement for a new passenger terminal. The agent will analyze his "market" for reserve agreements. He will adapt the terms of agreements to subscribers' convenience. He will stage a publicity campaign, seek out prospects, and solicit subscriptions. The fact that he offers something definite, an agreement carrying a bonus clause, should facilitate the promotion of adequate forward-planning of reservable expenditure programs.

Sponsors of public projects not attracted by reserve agreements will be solicited for definite period agreements. Six months in advance of a quarter, the agent will make preliminary diagnoses of business prospects and will fix the quarterly quota-level for public construction under definite period agreements so that the volume of such work will contribute to the *counter-cycle* of compensatory expenditure programs instead of aggravating the cycle at present.

Some three months before the beginning of a quarter, the agent will close subscriptions for all types of definite period agreements and will revise his diagnosis of the quarter's business prospects. He will use this revised diagnosis to determine the additional volume of countercycle business needed, and will activate reserve agreement projects accordingly. An overdose of reserve projects applied to one quarter will be counteracted by an underdose the next and vice versa.

The dose of compensatory projects will be applied, not after symptoms of business recession develop to a stage so advanced that the malady is unmistakable (this is our present procedure), but on the basis of a forecasting schedule three months before each quarter begins. The dose, being applied so much earlier, will accomplish so much the more. A stitch in time saves nine.

Full employment. The agent will consult with various federal and local government officials as to projects they might undertake during the next five to ten years; he will also suggest proposals on his own initiative. His file of prospective proposals and of signed agreements will in effect become a master plan for construction and other public works projects for the United States.

The agent will deal with public projects under both definite period and reserve agreements regionally, so as to even out regional disparities in business activity—a boom in the Middle West, a slack period in the East, and vice versa.

When business is stabilized, there may still be a substantial volume of secular unemployment. If the stable level of unemployment were slightly below full employment, if what may be called the "depressionary gap" were small, the entire gap between stable and full employment could be filled by setting high enough quotas under definite period agreements for public projects and by activating enough projects from the reserve file.

If the depressionary gap is large, it may not be feasible to fill it immediately even if bonus rates on definite period and reserve agreements are raised. To activate enough reserve projects to fill it would too soon exhaust the reserve file, and it may not be possible to obtain enough subscriptions to definite period agreements. Instead the agent will schedule each quarter a stimulus sufficient for a gradual, sustained expansion of business, avoiding the setback of any substantial business recession and maintaining expansion until full employment is achieved.

Terms of agreement. The forward agreement agent will need to have sufficient discretion to modify the terms of agreements and the rules of subscriber eligibility from time to time. Those projects and purchases should be included first in the area covered by agreements which because of their size and nature will involve the smallest administrative problems (and political obstacles) in relation to results. The agent should be authorized to exclude all projects and purchases from eligibility which amount to less than some appropriate minimum cost limit, *e.g.,* $500.[3]

---

[3] A flat limit probably should not be applied. Thus where two models of a good compete closely, both should be included or both excluded.

The agent should have no responsibility for excluding a project from coverage by an agreement on the ground that it is contrary to or not in accord with the public interest. Of course no project would be eligible for coverage by an agreement with the agent, if otherwise unlawful.

The agent will need to establish broad classifications of subscribers, with special terms in the agreements offered to each classification. And in the case of slack period reserve agreements further classification by locality and possibly by industry may be desirable for purposes of determining activation. In general the agent should be required to deal with all agreements of the same classification and termination date equally and without discrimination. Presumably, however, reserve agreements of the same classification and same termination date would be activated in the order in which they were entered into.

The subscriber should have a right to amend project plans, and to shift from one type of agreement to another. However, restrictions should be imposed on this right through appropriate adjustments in consideration so as to prevent the subscriber from gaining an undue advantage, *e.g.,* by so great a modification of a project as to warrant its reclassification by the agent. Most public construction projects should be brought under either definite period agreements or reserve agreements, but reserve projects would be clearly identified as such. One difficulty with works programs today is that there is no such identification of reserve projects.

It would probably not be desirable to permit the transfer of any type of agreement by processes other than bequest or corporate succession.

The subscriber should have an opportunity to make a blanket definite period agreement or reserve agreement, *e.g.,* for all contracts and purchases connected with one construction project. Similarly he should be able to make a blanket stable inventory agreement covering all of his eligible inventories.

Several varieties of definite period agreement would be needed to accommodate different classes of subscribers. By way of illustration it will be assumed that all the following varieties are on a quarterly basis:

1. In the case of purchases of stock or shelf items, the sub-scriber would undertake, three months or more in advance of a calendar quarter, to make a purchase during that quarter. The consideration offered to the subscriber to induce him to enter into a definite period agreement might be a specific sum. Where the item he agrees to purchase is subject to a sales tax, the consideration might be a tax credit. Otherwise a cash bonus would be made available at the time of payment for the purchase.

Special further tax concessions might be offered in periods of slack business to facilitate reaching quotas.

2. In the case of a construction project agreement the sub-scriber would agree to start his project during a definite quarter and would agree to a definite completion period. The bonus might be based on a percentage of cost, actual cost or esti-mated cost, whichever proved lower. Failure to complete the construction project in the stipulated period, plus possibly three months of grace, would be construed as a partial failure to carry out the agreement. That is, only the cost of that part of the work done during the agreed interval would be counted in computing the consideration. The bonus might be made available on an installment basis.

3. Special administrative problems are raised by force ac-count construction, *i.e.,* construction carried on by the sub-scriber with his own force of employees. For railroads and other large private enterprises and for some types of governmental unit, it should be possible to provide a form of agreement in which the total normal force account construction (and main-tenance) scheduled for any quarter by the organization would be treated as a single project eligible to a definite period agree-ment, all additional force account construction being treated as a separate project eligible to a reserve agreement. Since the subscriber in this case would be his own contractor, the con-tractor's certification would not provide a check on the sub-scriber's statement in claiming a bonus. The subscriber would, therefore, have to maintain special records and give the agent access to them as evidence of the carrying out of an agree-ment.

4. It would be possible to include exports in definite period

agreements. However, it would presumably be necessary in general to make the exporter rather than the foreign customer responsible for forward planning unless two countries adopted business stabilization by agreement on a reciprocity basis. Definite period agreements might be made available to large foreign customers, subject to approval by their governments.

5. The use of definite period agreements covering public projects to schedule countercycle business would make it desirable to accompany such agreements with arrangements for extending credit to subscribers.

Particularly in the case of these definite period agreements there would be occasion for a higher rate of bonus during periods of business recession and depression than during periods of prosperity, before the plan has brought about stability. But to announce an increased rate while a recession is under way might lead subscribers to wait for a still higher rate. It would be better to establish and announce in advance two rates, a prosperity rate and a recession rate, and to make no upward adjustment during a recession beyond this announced differential. When recession stops and there is stability at a depression or stagnation level, the schedule of prosperity and depression bonus rates can be raised to encourage additional projects so as to help fill the depressionary gap, provided the new schedule is to be kept in force for, say, five or more years.

While quotas for private subscribers to definite period agreements, except for seasonal variation, would in general hug the trend-line of demand, quotas for public subscribers and possibly for public utility subscribers would be set above the trend in slack periods and below it when business is prosperous.

Various administrative arrangements might be advantageous from the point of view of subcribers' convenience and so help in getting subscriptions. Thus the agent might arrange with local authorities to make the agreement form covering construction projects serve also as an application for a building permit.

The tax proposed on orders in excess of, say, 115 per cent of the quota should be a nominal one. Otherwise it might have the effect of imposing a ceiling on purchases. A larger tax in conjunction with the competition of buyers who have signed agreements, when the plan gains momentum, would force others to sign agreements or go without, and would involve serious restraints on individual freedom. No ceiling should be imposed.

The purposes of the nominal tax are (1) to provide a warning against business overexpansion, and (2) to induce registration of orders in excess of the quota.

So much for definite period agreements. There would be need also for several varieties of slack period reserve agreement. Thus it has been noted that, in lieu of the bonus feature in arrangements with other federal agencies, there should be a special form of appropriation, under which funds would be made available for obligation during a period to be specified by the agent. The appropriation act would fix the term, two to five years, within which the agent would have to activate the project.

Special forms of reserve agreement might be needed to provide for the extension of credit to the local government or private subscriber upon activation of his project, the details depending on what credit agency is most appropriately to be made a participant.

A special form of reserve agreement might apply to deferred force account maintenance, *e.g.*, by a railroad. The agent should have broad authority to develop and provide additional features to make such reserve agreements attractive to subscribers. Two types of device may be suggested by way of illustration: (1) some form of guarantee to the subscriber against price changes affecting the cost or worthwhileness of a potential project and (2) means of transforming the "time-shape" of a subscriber's expenditure pattern so that the main burden of expenditures could be met by the subscriber in the period of his greatest ability to pay and yet have the maximum expenditure rate come in a quarter determined by the agent.

It might be possible to get a substantial number of individuals to subscribe to reserve agreements for home improvement.

All stable inventory agreements would bind the subscriber

to make current (probably monthly) reports and to give the agent access to records and to the place of storage on request. They might all require notice (for example, thirty days) before any liquidation of "inactive inventory."

All stable inventory agreements would have to define (1) "inactive inventory," and (2) "carrying charges" and (3) "paper loss" thereon. In general, "carrying charges" could be specified in dollars per unit per month. The special problems raised by (1) and (3) may be considered briefly.

An illustrative, oversimplified formula for merchandise may serve to indicate possible methods of defining "inactive inventory" in terms of a base turnover ratio (average inventory during, say, the three years preceding the date of the beginning of the guarantee period ÷ average monthly sales during the three years) and a base month (the month preceding the date of the beginning of the guarantee period). It will be convenient to define "base inventory" and "active inventory" first, thus:

Base inventory ÷ sales in base month = base turnover ratio.

Active inventory as of current date ÷ sales in the preceding month = base turnover ratio.

Inactive inventory could then be defined as follows:

Current inactive inventory = current inventory or base inventory, whichever is less, minus active inventory as of the current date.

Under this definition, reimbursements for losses and carrying charges would not cover any current inventory in excess of the base inventory. A more complicated formula would be needed, if there were a marked seasonal variation in inventory.

In the case of materials and supplies inventories, the quantity used during the month might be substituted for sales in the formulas defining "inactive inventory." Work in process might be handled by expressing it either in finished item equivalents or in some raw material equivalent.

Computation of the loss during the month on the inactive inventory held would require a determination of price per unit in the inventory as of the end of each month. Where several producers turn out the same item and there is a market price no problem arises. But the subscriber's list-price changes clearly would not provide a satisfactory basis for computing inventory losses. It might be possible to handle such a case by a special price index based on material and labor costs, the index being used to measure the finished item inventory loss.

ESTIMATE OF FUNDS NEEDED FOR OPERATION DURING ONE YEAR SHORTLY AFTER THE PLAN IS INAUGURATED

Type of Agreement	Average Cost Per Year (in billions)	
	From	*To*
Definite Period Agreements:	$1.0	$1.5
Business covered $25 to $30 billion. Average tax rebate or bonus rate 4% to 5%.		
Stable Inventory Agreements:	.2	.5
Average annual loss $1 to $1.5 billion, 10% to 15% of this on "inactive inventories" under agreements. An equal cost for carrying charges.		
Slack Period Reserve Agreements:	.2	.4
$3 to $6 billion of projects per year, a third of them federal. Average rate on nonfederals, 10%.		
Other Expenses—Handling Charges:		
General administration, publicity, reserve agreement credit costs, etc.	.1	.3
TOTAL	$1.5	$2.7

These considerations suggest that, if sufficient coverage can be obtained in that way, application of stable inventory agreements should be limited to cases where an objective determination of "inactive inventory" and of inventory valuations is a relatively simple matter. In general, those lines should be covered first where the terms of agreements are the simplest and where the inventory liquidation problem has been most acute.

Cost of the program. The federal appropriations that would be required to operate *business stabilization by agreement* can be estimated only very roughly. If the plan is undertaken with the help of a back-log of deferred civilian demand, or if it has wide popular support, the cost to the Treasury will be much less than it would be if launched without such a back-log or with somewhat hesitant popular support. It would be especially difficult to launch the plan during a period of business depression.

The cost of the plan, particularly of definite period agreements, would vary inversely with the strength of the restraints imposed to prevent orders in excess of the quota-level for durable goods and construction. Theoretically the forward-planning of orders under definite period agreements can be induced either (1) by offering a financial consideration or (2) by creating a situation through restraints on excess orders such that failure to forward-plan means going without. Actually there are various intermediate possibilities, which rely more or less on the financial consideration and less or more on the restraints. The spirit of business stabilization by agreement calls for one of these in which the emphasis is chiefly on the financial inducement and the restraint is mild. With stronger restraints, the cost of providing effective financial inducements would be less than in the following estimates. Even with mild restraints, the cost of effective financial inducement will decrease, after customers in the lines covered by definite period agreements come to understand the plan and become accustomed to the forward-planning of their orders.

After the plan gets well under way it will also be possible to operate with a relatively smaller proportion of reserve agreements and a relatively larger proportion of definite period agreements. As forecasts of the total volume of business improve in accuracy the need for indefinite-date reserve agreements diminishes.

Business stabilization by agreement will be worth far more than its cost to the Treasury, measured in added national income. The above considerations indicate that the plan will take 2 to 3 billion dollars a year to operate while it is getting established, and 1 to 2 billions a year, or even less, afterward. These sums are certainly modest compared to the losses in national income which cyclical and secular unemployment entails.

Congress should define full employment. Within the limits of his appropriations, the agent will exercise discretion as to terms of agreements and rules for subscriber eligibility, so as to expand or contract the area of business covered by agreements as may be necessary in order to provide full and stable employment. But his exercise of discretion should be confined to the purpose of full employment. Except for its effect on the timing and volume of business, business stabilization by agreement should leave private enterprise as free to pursue its own course as it would be without the plan.

In justifying his estimates for appropriations, the agent will indicate the employment level which, in view of current practices regarding working hours and working ages, he regards as the level of full employment. His estimates will aim to provide for bonus rates and a volume of agreements sufficient to achieve stability and reach this level. Thus Congress will face squarely the question, "At what level is our economy to operate?"

· XVIII ·

The Keynesian Reformation*
(1952)

SOME enthusiastic disciples of J. M. Keynes have claimed that he brought about a revolution in economic thought. And some have compared his contribution to that of Adam Smith. On the other hand there are Keynesian critics, members of the older school, who regard the *General Theory of Employment, Interest, and Money* as purely static and who characterize the explanation of the business cycle it offers as purely tautological.

The title of these lectures is intended to indicate that the truth lies somewhere between these two extremes. But my purpose is not primarily an appraisal of Keynes. Rather I wish in this and the two following lectures to make at least a start toward appraising the present status of economic theory. Now that some of the emotions aroused by the first appearance of Keynes's great work have died down—there was a good deal of emotion both pro and con for a time—it seems appropriate to ask, where are we in economic theory? And where do we go from here?

Since a comparison to Adam Smith has been suggested, a comparison in which I do not concur, it seems appropriate to begin with a brief contrast. Adam Smith, as I see it, did two main things. He crystallized economic thinking in terms of the national income and product account, i.e. in terms of a two sector economic circuit: one sector selling the final product

---

* The first of three lectures.

326

of all productive efforts and distributing the proceeds (wages, etc.); the other sector receiving the proceeds and spending them to purchase the final product. And he used this conception to explore the impact of what we call industrialization on per capita levels of product and proceeds in various nations.

He concluded that those industrial processes which were more efficiently productive on the whole brought higher per capita national proceeds, and that a fair measure of laissez faire was conducive to more efficient industrial processes. His analysis exhibited a broad perspective both historically and in regard to the cultural differences prevailing in his day. No doubt he failed adequately to recognize that the nation that leads the procession in developing industrialism has an advantage not only by virtue of its more efficient industrial processes but also because it leads the procession. Probably we can see this point more easily today than Smith could.

Keynes, in his *General Theory*—and it is chiefly that work that concerns us here—operated on a much narrower front. He knew India at first hand. But his *General Theory* is not particularly applicable to India or to any of the less industrialized countries. I have been surprised to find how many students concerned especially with the problems of these countries look to the *General Theory* for help. It cannot help them much because it is largely irrelevant to their problem; it concentrates on the major ailment of highly industrialized free private enterprise countries, viz: cyclical or cyclical plus secular unemployment. Its contribution is a contribution to the handling of this industrial ailment.

Some of Keynes's critics have alleged that there is nothing in the *General Theory* on this subject that is both new and true. This kind of criticism has been made of many great thinkers, but it is a criticism that often misses the point. The component parts of a system of thought may all be borrowed, but they may be put together into a new whole, a whole that brings out new relationships and has new meaning. I think Keynes did something like this, as had Smith and many others before him. The Keynesian aggregative economic model was a new whole.

My quarrel with this model is not that Keynes borrowed the parts, though no doubt he did. My quarrel is that his *General Theory* was so highly selective. Because it was selective it could be neat and schematic and couched in the language of the neo-classical tradition, and the fact that it was a neat, schematic formulation in neoclassical terms helped to make converts for it. But it was too selective; it omitted points that ought not to have been omitted. I have elsewhere characterized the Keynesian statement of the business cycle as an expurgated edition Wesley C. Mitchell.

Let me indicate first some of the points in Mitchell's period analysis theory that Keynes omitted. Mitchell attempted to show how each phase of the cycle grew out of the preceding phase and how both business expansion and business recession gained momentum by tracing the impacts of the sectors of the economy on one other. He regarded profit changes as the main motivating force in changes in the level of business activity. He indicated the rapid improvement in profits during much of the expansion phase of the cycle as idle plant capacity is brought into use; and the narrowing of profit margins as plant capacity is approached. Noting that the farther the market from the ultimate consumer the wider the cyclical amplitudes of its price fluctuations, he stressed the effects on profits, during both expansion and contraction, of the differing amplitudes of price change. He recognized the importance of capital gains for both businesses and households when security prices improve, and conversely of capital losses when such prices go down. He emphasized the roles of calling loans and cancelling orders, of shaky credit structures and of business failures during a crisis. He considered consumers durables (e.g. autos) as well as business plant and equipment to be significant prime contributors to the instability of aggregate demand. On all these points the *General Theory* says very little.

This does not purport to be a complete list of the points slighted by Keynes, still less a rounded summary of Mitchell's theory. But perhaps I should add one point that does not come from Mitchell: To purchasers of final products the cost of purchase is a direct cost. It is a cost that can be dodged by not

making the purchase. To the seller a part of the cost is overhead
that he cannot dodge. And while he can dodge another part
(e.g. by not buying raw materials), most of what he can dodge
is overhead for someone else. From a social viewpoint nearly
all the cost of a final product is overhead cost. The private individual reckoning of cost is one thing; the reckoning from the
point of view of the economy as a whole quite another; and
this is one of the reasons why we have business cycles.[1]

Mitchell was concerned to understand how business cycles
operate. But this was not all. He also investigated the historical
origin of business cycles. He traced the growth of the conditions responsible for them—the development of the money
economy, of production for a market and for profit, of the
private enterprise system, of various forms of credit and of
financial institutions. The *General Theory* does not really tell
us much of anything about the historical origin of business
cycles.

Perhaps there are some of you who are not very orthodox
neoclassicists; some who will wish to ask at the juncture: If
Mitchell did a systematic, objective study of business depressions, and if the Keynesian aggregative model failed to take
full account of Mitchell's findings, why speak of Keynes as having made a major contribution in this field of inquiry?

To answer this question I think we must be quite candid
about the kind of intellectual discipline economics has been,
and in particular about the role of what may be called the neo-
classical apparatus in that discipline. By the neoclassical apparatus I mean equations that are designed to express or explain supply and demand relationships, equations that are designed so as conjointly to explain values in exchange as an
equilibrium adjustment. Economists of the neoclassical tradition have often claimed that economics was a science and have
rested that claim on their use of the value in exchange equilibrium apparatus.

The history of economics since Ricardo has been partly a

[1] See J. M. Clark's *Studies in the Economics of Overhead Costs*, University of
Chicago Press, 1923, especially pp. 379 et seq. See also my contribution to the
Trend of Economics, edited by R. G. Tugwell, A. A. Knopf, 1924.

history of the development of that apparatus. The word 'partly' should be underscored. All along there have been students of economics who questioned whether progress in economic enquiry consisted exclusively or even mainly in the development of the value in exchange equilibrium apparatus. I will mention by way of illustration the German historical school, Karl Marx, and more recently the institutionalists. Mitchell was an institutionalist.

No doubt it should be added that I share the questioning attitude of these dissidents. I think there is a great deal to be said for the neoclassical apparatus, provided its limitations are clearly recognized. Up to a point it makes for precision of economic concepts and for accuracy of reasoning, but it can take us only part way along the path of economic inquiry.

The neoclassicists claim this apparatus has made economics scientific. It would seem better to say that this apparatus has given economics some of the attributes of a science. It has made economists seekers after new truths. And it has given them a common standard by which to judge the validity of new ideas. Economics has been a growing body of accepted propositions. Nor has growth been merely a matter of accretion. Old propositions have been revised over and over again.

In these respects economics has been like a science. But note that I spoke of a growing body of propositions, not of a growing body of knowledge. The neoclassical apparatus is what today is called a model, or rather a set of closely similar models, for different economic theorists have postulated slightly different ones. A neoclassical model is a set of simultaneous equations which together are assumed approximately to describe the more significant relationships of the real economic world. To the extent that the model resembles the real world one can investigate causal economic relationships by manipulating some of the variables in the model while holding other variables constant. This is what is meant by the pound of ceteris paribus. But we should never forget that an economic model is an hypothesis. It may not accurately describe the particular economy we wish to use it to investigate.

I have avoided calling the progressive development of a better and better economic model for highly industrialized private enterprise economies the growth of a body of knowledge. I had two reasons. First, what we know about business depressions can be presented without the use of a mathematical model. Mitchell's presentation did not use one. Second, even an elaborate model such as the one postulated by J. R. Hicks in his *Value and Capital* gives us no knowledge of actual business depressions taken by itself. To give us such knowledge it would in the first place need to be adequately documented to show both the pertinent resemblances to and the pertinent differences from some economy such as that of the United Kingdom in the 20th century. And in the second the pertinent resemblances would have to be shown to preponderate. There is grave doubt that they would. For these two reasons I prefer to speak of the growth of a body of economic doctrines.

If the neoclassical value in exchange equilibrium apparatus —or model analysis—has made economics develop like a science in several respects, there are others in which it has been more like a religion. It has not been intolerant of new ideas, to be sure, but it has been intolerant of ideas not couched in the language of the neoclassical apparatus. Economic heterodoxy has consisted mainly in refusal to conform to the ritualistic requirement of model analysis terminology. While those who do not conform are not excommunicated, their contributions are likely to be ignored and forgotten. Marx is perhaps an exception to this rule. But he developed a variant of the neoclassical apparatus of his own, a variant that has proven to be extremely viable.

Bearing in mind these comments on the kind of intellectual discipline economics has been, let us return to the question. What did Keynes contribute to our understanding of business depressions? At least a part of the answer to this question should be clear. He helped us to understand them in model analysis terms. His *General Theory* was very nicely calculated, and incidentally very nicely timed, to make a major impression. It was nicely calculated, because it was just orthodox enough to have a wide appeal among economists. Keynes's contribution was essentially the contribution of a new model. It was nicely timed because it appeared in the mid-1930's.

But if all Keynes had done, was to provide a slightly different, somewhat better model than his neoclassical predecessors, it is doubtful whether one would be justified in talking about the Keynesian reformation. His model had several new features, and because of these new features it had, and is continuing to have, far-reaching repercussions.

First as to the new features. I propose to consider the following: (i) It is an aggregative model. (ii) As such it does not deal with the individual entrepreneur, the individual consumer, or the individual final product. (iii) All the variables in the model save one are quantities capable of statistical measurement and the model is so devised that it lends itself to statistical investigation. These three features are easy to specify. Two others to which I would direct your attention are not. Let me simply say here that (iv) relates to his handling of time and (v) relates to his concept of equilibrium.

I shall not attempt to consider all five of these features this evening because I want to say something about the repercussions of the Keynesian model. But (ii) can be quite briefly dismissed. The fact that this model does not deal with the individual consumer, entrepreneur, or final product makes it appear somewhat neutral so far as· many neoclassical doctrinal issues are concerned. This gives it a kind of entering wedge quality. Much of the traditional neoclassical doctrine appears to go unchallenged. No obvious question is raised about the marginal utility theory—or if you prefer indifference analysis. Nor does the model appear to require any revision of the customary forms of market analysis or of the theory of price and cost relationships. Of course there are other doctrines that do not fare so well. A principal prop is knocked out from under the uniqueness of the marginal productivity determination of factorial distribution, and the applicability of the quantity theory is restricted to full employment conditions. Nonetheless the first general impression created by the Keynesian aggregative model is that the bulk of neoclassical doctrine is left intact. My title implies that this first impression is incorrect, that the indirect implications of the model are by no means so narrowly restricted.

Let me take up next what has just been referred to as feature (iv), Keynes's handling of time. One of the virtues of the neoclassical model analysis tradition is that it pushes in the direction of an explicit, somewhat precise statement of time reference for the variables. The distinction between past, present, and future is a common-sense one, and it would seem an easy thing to handle time reference correctly in a model. But in point of fact it has proven to be a major hazard; many a model has foundered on this difficulty. Also it is only fair to say that what is correct here is currently a matter of dispute. I urge the merit of the handling of time reference in Keynes's *General Theory,* and of the similar handling in Hicks's *Value and Capital.* But the similarity is perhaps not entirely obvious, and Keynes's handling has been criticised by some of those who accept the Stockholm distinction between ex post and ex ante.

Let me digress to propose amendments to this distinction. These two Latin phrases are widely used both as adjectives and as adverbs. As adverbs they are presumably to be taken literally to refer to past and future. But this terminology was introduced to distinguish between expected income and actual income, between planned and actual savings. The use of ex post to mean actual raises no special problem; the use of ex ante to mean planned or expected does. We need to be able to talk about the planned savings, the ex ante savings, of last year and of this year. As an adjective ex ante can refer to the past or to the present as well as to the future. Moreover any one who works with a statistical statement of a plan or program needs to identify the date of the plan as well as the period for which it is made. Plans get revised. A nation's ex ante production of military airplanes for 1950 as of the first of the year may be larger or smaller than it is by the end of June. Further an economist who is concerned with forecasts and projections into the future has need to distinguish his own expectations regarding consumers' incomes from the expectations of the consumers.

In part my objection to the ex post ex ante distinction is that ex ante means one thing as an adverb and several other things as an adjective. So far as the adjectival use is concerned I think we would do well to follow Alfred Marshall's advice. If ex ante is just a Latin translation of planned or expected, let's drop the esoteric terminology. Let's just say planned or expected.

But my objection goes further. There is ambiguity in the adverbial use of ex ante. Hicks in his *Value and Capital* takes what he calls a week as his fiscal period. In common-sense fashion he distinguishes past weeks, the current week, and future weeks. We need this threefold distinction in model analysis. The Stockholm terminology avoids the ambiguity of our English adverb 'then' (which may mean 'yesterday' or 'tomorrow'), but it provides only a twofold distinction. Since ex post has been construed narrowly to mean the past, ex ante has been stretched to cover the current fiscal period as well as the future. But we ought to have two terms for the two meanings. I propose that we say ex nunc when we mean present, ex ante only when we mean future.

It is commonly said that savings need not be equal to investment ex ante. This statement is valid only if we exclude the current fiscal period. Present plans and expectations express themselves in present decisions regarding savings and investment. Keynes speaks of short term expectations in this connection. In the Keynesian model short term expectation of savings and investment must be equal, i.e. S and I must be equal ex nunc. A corresponding but more complicated statement applies to Hicks's current week.

One merit of Keynes's handling of time in the *General Theory*—not in the *Treatise on Money*—is that the present expectations and intentions—i.e. the short term expectation and intentions—of the various parties in a national economy must work out to a balance of the current national savings and investment account.

Another merit relates to the long term expectations he selected for special emphasis. Some economists in trying to take account of the way expected future wants influence present economic adjustments have felt impelled to assign to each individual an impossibly elaborate and in some sense a complete set of anticipations of future economic adjustments. Irving Fisher was a case in point. But Keynes simply confined his model to the expectations he thought important for changes in the level of employment, to the expectations of the investor regarding the future course of investment income and the expectations of the lender regarding possible defaults by his debtors. This is one respect in which his model was explicitly selective, a mere rough approximation, an oversimplification that made no pretense of covering the minor details. A part of Keynes's greatness lay in his ability to identify minor details as minor and in his ruthless way of ignoring them.[2] I shall return in another connection to the explicit approximateness of his model. My present point is, most men picture the future very incompletely. Keynes recognized this [3] and confined his model to two kinds of expectations, investment prospects and lender confidence. The former finds expression in his marginal efficiency of capital, the latter in liquidity preference.

So much for Keynes's handling of time. Next as to his handling of the equilibrium concept. The neoclassical concept derives from, or rather is an extension of, the so-called law of supply and demand. This 'law' presupposes a supply schedule expressing the quantity of a good as one function of its price and a demand schedule expressing the quantity as a second function of the price. The two functions are treated as two simultaneous equations which together determine the two variables, market price and amount marketed. Thus far we are on very familiar territory. Surely you have all been over this simple two equation model many times.

With the next four steps some of you may not be so well acquainted. They give the technical conditions this model must conform to:

(1) The independence condition. There must be two independent equations. This condition requires that neither equation shall be deducible from the other.

[2] As I have indicated above he was sometimes too ruthless.
[3] So did Hicks in his *Value and Capital*.

(2) The existence condition. The two equations must be consistent, i.e. they must have a common solution. They must not contradict each other.

(3) The stability condition. The solution must be unique and stable. It will be if the amount by which demand exceeds supply always decreases as price increases.

(4) The significance condition. The solution must be real and positive. As we have stated the case, imaginary values and negative values of the two variables are lacking in economic significance. A minus quantity price or amount marketed would have no economic significance, nor would a $\sqrt{-x}$ price or quantity marketed.

The independence condition needs no elaboration. Two separate equations are essential to the model.

The stability condition implies the prevailing neoclassical equilibrium concept for the simple two equation model of the law of supply and demand. The price at which supply and demand are equal is the equilibrium price. A higher price would attract additional sellers. Some of them would find no buyers and would force the price downward. Similarly with a price below the equilibrium price; buyer competition would force it upward. The neoclassical equilibrium concept includes a self-righting mechanism.

That an economic model ought to meet both the existence condition and the significance condition needs no argument. There must be a solution, and one that is meaningful. I suggested above that model analysis does something to encourage careful reasoning. It does something, but not necessarily enough. A good deal of attention has been devoted to the stability condition and to the independence condition. But it would be difficult to find any neoclassical statement of general equilibrium theory that deals adequately with the two essential conditions of existence and significance. Doubtless a model builder can build a model that satisfies both these conditions without his giving much thought to either. Such an accomplishment is by no means unlikely. In fact mathematicians have a special term for reaching a plausible conclusion without taking all the necessary logical steps; they speak of mathematical intuition. Mathematical intuition often works, but it is not in-fallible.

I have introduced these four conditions partly as a back-ground for considering Keynes's handling of the equilibrium concept. Partly too I wished to indicate that the present logical foundations of neoclassical model analysis are not very secure. The existence condition and the significance condition have been sadly neglected. And even the stability condition is today a rather controversial matter.

But we need to indicate what is meant by a general equilib-rium as distinguished from an equilibrium in a single market. The economy may be conceived as a set of related markets. Say we have N markets for N commodities. We are concerned with N prices and N quantities. Since the markets are related let us assume that the demand for each commodity is a function of all the prices, similarly for supply. This gives us $2N$ equations. We still have just as many equations as we have variables. How-ever, when we deal with the economy as a whole, there are dif-ficulties not present in the supply and demand model for a single market. There are strong reasons for imposing the condi-tion that any one of the $2N$ equations shall be deducible from the other $2N$-1. The reasons are somewhat technical. I shall simply ask you to accept the conclusion. It leaves us with $2N$ unknowns and $2N$-1 equations; this is an awkward situation. There are two classical ways out of it, two ways provided by monetary theory. The quantity theorist adds an equation—the equation of exchange. The commodity theorist gets rid of one of the variables; he treats money as one of the N commodities and takes its price to be given as unity.

We need not here attempt to choose between these two ways out. When we progress from the model for a single market to a model for an economy consisting of N markets, we go from a system of two simultaneous equations in 2 unknowns to a sys-tem of $2N$ or $2N$-1 simultaneous equations in an equal number of unknowns. And we still expect our four conditions to apply. We expect the equations to be independent. We expect them to be consistent. We expect the solution to be unique and stable. And we expect it to be real and positive.

All four of these conditions are easy to handle at the two equation level. At the level of $2N$ or $2N\text{-}1$ equations only the first condition—independence—has proven easy to handle. I am no mathematician. But my mathematical friends tell me that the other three taken collectively involve equation problems no mathematician has yet worked out.

However, let us assume these equation problems solved. The neoclassicist would like to have a model in a large number of independent, consistent equations and an equal number of unknowns. And he would like to have their solution determinate and significant. But no matter whether he accepts the quantity theory postulate or the commodity theory postulate, he will still find it difficult to steer between the Scylla of too many unknowns and the Charybdis of too many equations. I think the neoclassical hope of escaping both these obstacles is a forlorn one.

It was suggested earlier in this lecture that the Keynesian aggregative model had far reaching repercussions. A part of what I had in mind is that Keynes makes model analysis bump against Scylla and Charybdis. He finds too many equations; and he finds too many unknowns.

Let us take first the problem of what to do with an excessive number of unknowns, because Keynes deals with this problem explicitly. To use the current jargon, he distinguishes in his model between endogenous variables and exogenous variables. Given a model in which we have V independent consistent equations and $U + V$ variables, we must classify U of the variables as somehow predetermined by factors outside the system of equations, so that the other V variables can be handled by the model.

Let me put this a bit differently. The model analyst proposes to explain the behavior of an economy by offering us a model that is alleged to behave like it. Assuming for the sake of argument that the resemblance between model and reality is significantly complete, what the model analyst can explain is the behavior of the endogenous variables. The exogenous variables by hypothesis lie entirely outside the scope of the analysis of his model.

Exogenous variables have been implicitly present in economic theory for a long time. But with one exception neoclassicists have tended to minimize their importance. There has been some disposition, too, to regard the study of the behavior of such variables as outside the field of economics. The one exception was monetary policy. Both the quantity theory postulate and the commodity theory postulate require one monetary exogenous variable.

Keynes did not introduce exogenous variables into economic theory. He merely compelled theorists to realize they could not draw the line at one. He did this directly by dramatizing the importance of public investment as an exogenous variable and by overtly discussing the problem an excessive number of variables poses for the model analyst. Indirectly he forced things somewhat farther. Neoclassicists had long been struggling to find a satisfactory way to handle private investment as endogenous. One of the many great merits of Hicks's *Value and Capital* is the particularly effective handling his neoclassical model gives this part of the gross national product. But—to anticipate consideration of the empirical aspect of the Keynesian reformation —we must note that handling private investment in a neoclassical model is one thing, handling it statistically is quite another, and Keynes stimulated a great deal of statistical investigation of economic models. In particular for our immediate purpose, he stimulated extensive and intensive efforts to account statistically for both components of private investment, new capital assets and the inventory increment—efforts to treat them statistically as endogenous variables. So far these efforts have not been marked by much success. And until the builders of statistical models discover a way to tame these variables, they have no recourse but to treat them as exogenous.

Thus all told Keynes has given a considerable push toward the wide recognition of exogenous variables. And with this recognition I think must come an admission. Economists must admit they have other ways of understanding the behavior of economic variables in addition to model analysis. Economists must admit that model analysis instead of being the whole of economic analysis is only a part. They could not leave the study of their exogenous variables to sociologists and historians without abdicating a major fraction of their field.

So much for Scylla. What of Charybdis? What if the economic model has too many equations? Strictly speaking Keynes did not have too many equations in his model. But that was because—as we have already noted—he was selective about it. He discarded the extra equation. A model cannot have one too many equations, if they are all independent, and have them all consistent, except perhaps by accident. In general the extra equation will contradict the others. So it did in Keynes's case, as he was at pains to point out. The extra equation was the supply schedule for labor. His model did not satisfy this equation, except at full employment. At other employment levels the labor market was not cleared, i.e. there was involuntary unemployment. Supply exceeded demand.

Perhaps this is quite obvious. But Hicks did not see it when he wrote *Value and Capital*. A model analyst, even an extraordinarily able one like Hicks, is apt not to see the things that conflict with his model. In *Value and Capital* Hicks presents us with a model that is remarkably like a highly industrialized private enterprise economy in many ways, a model that exhibits something of a business cycle. But a crucial feature is missing. He has set supply equal to demand in each market including the labor market, and focussed his attention on prices. Involuntary unemployment is in contradiction to his assumptions. In effect Hicks has postulated something very like Say's Law. And this is the more surprising when we recall that he started out to provide a supporting supplement or complement to Keynes.

Before the *General Theory* it was widely assumed that for a general equilibrium the clearing of all markets was a necessary condition. (Even in a monopolized market all the supply the monopolist chooses to sell is sold.) On this assumption model analysis was not competent to deal with actual business depressions. Thus this assumption helped to foster the growth of a group of economists—the institutionalists to whom I have referred above—who sought to replace model analysis with a more realistic and factual approach to economics. For a time the place of model analysis in economic inquiry seemed in jeopardy.

Keynes's model is a general equilibrium model, but it does not make this assumption. On the contrary it assumes the labor market is seldom cleared. Yet he reaches equilibrium in the sense described above. His equilibrium level of employment is determined by the solution of a set of simultaneous equations; and his model includes a self-righting mechanism. A higher level of employment would be reduced by inventory accumulation, a lower level raised through the depletion of inventories.

If Keynes's handling of the extra variables has tended to give model analysis a more modest role than many have claimed for it, his discarding of the supply schedule for labor as an extra equation has been a conservatizing influence. The institutionalists have been very silent during the past 15 years. Model analysis has gained a new vigor and vitality.

But model analysis is not what it used to be. Model analysis has been undergoing a metamorphosis.

Bibliography of the Writings of Morris A. Copeland

The following abbreviations have been used:

AER   American Economic Review
JASA Journal of the American Statistical Association
JPE   Journal of Political Economy
NBER National Bureau of Economic Research
QJE   Quarterly Journal of Economics

BOOKS AND MONOGRAPHS

Concerning a New Federal Financial Statement. (NBER, Technical Paper, No. 5.) New York, 1947. Pp. 58.

A Study of Moneyflows in the United States. (NBER, No. 54.) New York, 1952. Pp. 338 and 241.

The Keynesian Reformation: Three Lectures. (Delhi School of Economics, Occasional Papers, No. 4.) Delhi, 1952. Pp. 62.

Trends in Government Financing. (NBER, Studies in Capital Formation and Financing.) Princeton, N.J., to be published in 1959–1960.

ARTICLES AND OTHER SHORT ITEMS
(Arranged chronologically)

"Seasonal Problems in Financial Administration," *JPE*, December 1920.

"Some Phases of Institutional Value Theory." In *University of Chicago Abstracts of Theses*, Humanistic Series, vol. II, 1921.

"Communities of Economic Interest and the Price System." In *Trend of Economics*, ed. by R. G. Tugwell. New York, 1924.

"The Economics of Advertising," *AER*, Suppl., March 1925.

"Studies in the Economics of Overhead Costs," review of J. M. Clark, *Political Science Quarterly*, June 1925.

"Professor Knight on Psychology," *QJE*, November 1925.

"Desire, Choice, and Purpose from a Natural-evolutionary Standpoint," *Psychological Review*, July 1926.

"An Instrumental View of the Part-Whole Relation," *Journal of Philosophy*, February 17, 1927.

"An Estimate of Total Volume of Debits to Individual Accounts in the United States," *JASA*, September 1928.

"An Index of the Dollar Volume of Retail Trade 1924–1927," *Harvard Business Review*, January 1929.

"Two Hypotheses concerning the Equation of Exchange," *JASA*, Suppl., March 1929.

"Special Purpose Indexes for the Equation of Exchange for the United States, 1919–1927," *JASA*, June 1929.

"Money, Trade, and Prices—A Test of Causal Primacy," *QJE*, August 1929.

"Recent Changes in the Wholesale Price Level of the United States," *Federal Reserve Bulletin*, December 1929.

"The National Income and Its Distribution." In *Recent Economic Changes in the U.S.*, vol. II. (NBER, No. 13.) New York, 1929.

"Recent Changes in Our Wholesale Price Level," *JASA*, Suppl., March 1930.

"Psychology and the Natural-Science Point of View," *Psychological Review*, November 1930.

"Economic Theory and the Natural Science Point of View," *AER*, March 1931.

"Some Suggestions for Improving Our Information on Wholesale Commodity Prices," *JASA*, Suppl., March 1931.

"Herbert Joseph Davenport, 1861–1931—An Obituary," *Economic Journal*, September 1931.

"The Future of the General Price Level," *Journal of Farm Economics*, January 1932.

"Some Problems in the Theory of National Income," *JPE*, February 1932.

"How Large Is Our National Income?," *JPE*, December 1932.

"The Theory of Monopolistic Competition," review of Chamberlin, *JPE*, August 1934.

"National Wealth and Income—An Interpretation," *JASA*, June 1935.

"Current Business Statistics and Economic Stabilization" (with Richard L. Funkhouser), *Bulletin of the Taylor Society and of the Society of Industrial Engineers,* November 1935.

"Commons's Institutionalism in Relation to Problems of Social Evolution and Economic Planning," *QJE,* February 1936.

"The Significance of Archives to the Economist and Sociologist." In Society of American Archivists, *Proceedings.* 1936–1937 (mimeo.).

"Concepts of National Income." In NBER, *Studies in Income and Wealth,* vol. I. New York, 1937.

Comments on papers by S. Kuznets and by R. Blough and W. Hewett. In NBER, *Studies in Income and Wealth,* vol. II. New York, 1938.

"The Correction of Wealth and Income Estimates for Price Changes" (with Edwin M. Martin). In NBER, *Studies in Income and Wealth,* vol. II. New York, 1938.

"The Distribution of Wealth and Income," an address before the Academy of Political Science at its semiannual meeting, March 25, 1938 (published by the Academy, New York, 1938).

"Public Investment in the United States," *AER,* March 1939.

"National Income and Capital Formation" (with Edwin M. Martin), review of Kuznets, *JPE,* June 1939.

"Aims and Purposes of United States Central Statistical Board," *The Controller,* July 1939.

"Professional Personnel in the Federal Service," *Personnel Administration,* January 1940.

"Competing Products and Monopolistic Competition," *QJE,* November 1940.

"Economic Research in the Federal Government," *AER,* September 1941.

"Government Procurement Methods and Prices." In *Price Problems in a Defense Economy.* (NBER Conference on Price Research.) New York, 1941 (mimeo.).

"National Income and Wealth." In Inter-American Statistical Institute, *Statistical Activities of the American Nations.* Washington, 1941.

"Production Planning for a War Economy," *Annals of the American Academy of Political and Social Science,* March 1942.

"A Social Appraisal of Differential Pricing," *Journal of Marketing,* April 1942.

"The Defense Effort and the National Income Response Pattern," *JPE,* June 1942.

"The Capital Budget and the War Effort," *AER,* March 1943.

"How Achieve Full and Stable Employment," *AER,* Suppl., March 1944.

"Business Stabilization by Agreement," *AER,* June 1944.

"The WPB Index of War Production" (with Jerome Jacobson and Herman Lasken), *JASA,* June 1945.

"Problems of International Comparisons of Income and Wealth" (with Jerome Jacobsen and Bernard Clyman). In NBER, *Studies in Income and Wealth,* vol. X. New York, 1947.

"The Social and Economic Determinants of the Distribution of Income in the United States," *The American Statistician,* June 1948.

"Suitable Accounting Conventions to Determine Business Income," *Journal of Accountancy,* February 1949.

"Social Accounting for Moneyflows," *Accounting Review,* July 1949.

"Introduction." In NBER, *Studies in Income and Wealth,* vol. XII. New York, 1950.

"A Note on Negotiable Claims: Who Owns and Who Owes What." In NBER, *Studies in Income and Wealth,* vol. XII. New York, 1950.

"Institutional Economics and Model Analysis," *AER,* Papers and Proceedings, May 1951.

"The Income and Product Circuit and the Money Circuit in India and the United States," *Bulletin of the International Statistical Institute,* vol. XXXIII, pt. 3 (1951 Proceedings).

Comment on paper by A. Smithies. In NBER, *Long-Range Economic Projections.* (Studies in Income and Wealth, vol. XVI.) Princeton, N.J., 1954.

"Statistics and Objective Economics," *JASA,* September 1955.

Comments on papers by S. Sigel, W. Leontief, C. Christ, and H. Liebling. In *Input-Output Analysis.* (NBER, Studies in Income and Wealth, vol. XVIII.) Princeton, N.J., 1955.

"The Feasibility of a Standard Comprehensive System of Social Accounts." In *Problems in the International Comparison of Economic Accounts.* (NBER, Studies in Income and Wealth, vol. XX.) Princeton, N.J., 1957.

"Proposal for a Revised Set of Summary Accounts and Supporting Financial Details." In NBER, *A Critique of the United States Income and Product Accounts.* (Studies in Income and Wealth, vol. XXII.) Princeton, N.J., 1958.

"On the Scope and Method of Economics." In *Thorstein Veblen: A Critical Reappraisal,* ed. by D. F. Dowd. Ithaca, N.Y., 1958.

DOCUMENTS EDITED OR PARTLY WRITTEN
BY MORRIS A. COPELAND

"A Constructive Program for Price Statistics," recommendations of a technical conference held under the joint auspices of the Social Science Research Council and the American Statistical Association, *JASA*, March 1932.

"Annual Reports of the Central Statistical Board," Washington, 1934–1938.

"Report of the Central Statistical Board on the Returns Made by the Public to the Federal Government, January 10, 1939." Washington, 1939.

"Government Purchasing—An Economic Commentary" (with Clem C. Linnenberg, Jr., and Dana M. Barbour), a study made for the Temporary National Economic Committee. (Monograph No. 19.) Washington, 1941.

"The Impact of the War on Civilian Consumption in the United Kingdom, the United States, and Canada," report of a Special Combined Committee set up by the Combined Production and Resources Board, September 1945. London and Washington, 1945.

"Report of Subcommittee on Economists in the Public Service," *AEA*, May 1946.